KOREA AT THE
TURNING POINT

KOREA AT THE TURNING POINT

Innovation-Based Strategies for Development

Edited by
Lewis M. Branscomb
and Young-Hwan Choi

PRAEGER

Westport, Connecticut
London

Library of Congress Cataloging-in-Publication Data

Korea at the turning point : innovation-based strategies for
  development / edited by Lewis M. Branscomb and Young-Hwan Choi.
    p.   cm.
  Includes bibliographical references and index.
  ISBN 0–275–95147–2 (alk. paper)
    1. Technological innovations—Economic aspects—Korea (South)
  2. Korea (South)—Economic policy—1960–   I. Branscomb, Lewis M.,
  1926– II. Choi, Young-Hwan.
  HC470.T4K67 1996
  338'.064'095195—dc20   96–24360

British Library Cataloguing in Publication Data is available.

Library of Congress Catalog Card Number: 96–24360
ISBN: 0–275–95147–2

First published in 1996

Praeger Publishers, 88 Post Road West, Westport, CT 06881
An imprint of Greenwood Publishing Group, Inc.

Printed in the United States of America

The paper used in this book complies with the
Permanent Paper Standard issued by the National
Information Standards Organization (Z39.48–1984).

10 9 8 7 6 5 4 3 2 1

CONTENTS

TABLES AND FIGURES

TABLES

FIGURES

PREFACE

In 1993, shortly before his one-hundredth day in office, President Kim Young-Sam addressed a group of business leaders, stating that "the Korean economy is poised at a crucial turning point." This book addresses the importance of Korean innovation and its roots in scientific and technological capacities, which must be nourished to realize the vision of growth and sociopolitical development to which Korean society is dedicated.

This book is the product of a cooperative agreement between the Science and Technology Policy Institute (STEPI) of the Korean Institute of Science and Technology (KIST) and the Center for Science and International Affairs (CSIA) of Harvard University's John F. Kennedy School of Government. This agreement enabled Mr. Young-Hwan Choi, former vice minister for Science and Technology of the Republic of Korea and first president of STEPI, to spend two years at Harvard's CSIA and collaborate with Professor Lewis M. Branscomb, director of CSIA's Science, Technology, and Public Policy program.

The expert authors of the chapters in this book made important contributions to our understanding of Korean science and technology policy. Sadly, Dr. Hyung-Ki Kim, chief of the Economic Development Institute at the World Bank and senior author of Chapter 3, passed away on September 20, 1995. We dedicate the chapter, completed posthumously, to his memory.

We also want to thank other experts who made important contributions to this project. Dr. Il-Young Maing made a study of the current status of Korean science, technology, and innovation. Dr. Dong-Joon Hwang of the Korea Institute for Defense Analysis examined the role of the defense industry in innovation and the development of dual-use technology. Dr. Won-Hoon Park, director of the Environment Research Center and now president of KIST, addressed Korea's environmental security and the economy. Dean Gill-Chin Lim of Michigan State University and Professor Anh-Jae Kim of Seoul National University conducted a study of science and technology complexes for the promotion of nationwide innovation. These studies further confirm the basic thesis of the book: that Korea's future requires a substantial enhancement of its indigenous innovation and scientific and technological development.

A number of other experts on Korean science and technology affairs made helpful contributions to the book. Dr. Denis Fred Simon of the Fletcher School of Law and Diplomacy at Tufts University was particularly helpful in portraying the changing international contexts for Korean markets and how they influence the acquisition to technology. Professor Soung-Soo Chun read the manuscript, making substantive and constructive suggestions. Dr. Donald Hornig, who was science advisor to President Johnson and personally assisted Korea in establishing KIST, provided much useful background for the book. We especially wish to thank all the Korean scientists, businesspersons, and government officials who generously gave their time to help us with our study. Special thanks are owed to the Honorable Dr. Shang-Hee Rhee, chairman of the National Council of Science and Technology, and to three Ministers of Science and Technology: the Honorable Jin-Hyun Kim, Si-Joong Kim, and Kun-Mo Chung, who encouraged this project at various stages.

We are also thankful to the officials at STEPI, headed by the late Young-Woo Kim, who greatly facilitated our fieldwork in Korea in 1993. In addition, one of us (Lewis M. Branscomb) benefited substantially from the privilege of serving as an expert advisor to the Organization for Economic Cooperation and Development (OECD). The OECD, in response to a request from the Korean government, prepared a report on the Korean science and technology system in December 1995. STEPI served as host to these OECD examiners, providing great opportunities to inquire and learn.

The book project has enjoyed the expert services of consulting editor Christopher Edwards and the support of Veronica McClure and Marie Allitto at Harvard University and of Sung-Chul Chung and others at STEPI.

In this book, we have adopted a number of conventions for the convenience of the reader. We have written Korean names in the western order, with family name last, as in "Young-Hwan Choi." We make an exception, however, in the special case of heads of state and certain historical figures. Here we follow the press, which commonly uses the Korean form of listing the family name first, as in Kim Young-Sam. We have used "chaebol" as a singular noun and denoted the plural by using "chaebols." The Korean currency, the won, is sometimes used in the book, while at other times money is expressed in U.S. dollars. In each case, we used the currency that more clearly expressed our point. In the fall of 1995, there were approximately 770 won to the U.S. dollar. Throughout this book, "Korea" refers to the Republic of Korea, that is, South Korea.

We and our co-authors have tried to be forthright about the challenges facing Korea, which has reached an important turning point in Korean history. We are convinced that if Korea earnestly pursues innovation-based strategies for development, the nation and its people shall overcome all obstacles and realize its long-cherished dream of parity with the industrialized nations in the next millennium.

Lewis M. Branscomb and Young-Hwan Choi
November 26, 1995

Part One

CHALLENGES AT THE TURNING POINT
A History and Overview

Chapter One

A FRAMEWORK FOR DISCUSSING KOREA'S TECHNO-ECONOMIC FUTURE

Lewis M. Branscomb and Young-Hwan Choi

Looking to the new millennium, Korea faces challenges requiring it to transform its policies, institutions, and talents to realize the aspirations of its leaders and its people. A new techno-economic order has been forming in the aftermath of the Cold War, with the emergence of technology-based innovation as the primary source of economic and social development in the more advanced industrialized nations. Korea is committed to this path.

The nation's ambition, as expressed by government leaders, is to bring the nation's economic and social development to the level of the most highly industrialized nations—the members of the G-7 group—early in the twenty-first century. The level of the government's fiscal commitment to research and development (R&D) is nothing less than astonishing. The fiscal year (FY) 1995 budget for R&D was 36 percent higher than the prior year; in FY 1996, it is slated to rise another 28 percent. The stated policy of the government is to continue this rate of growth, at levels from 25 to 30 percent annually, through the beginning of the twenty-first century.[1]

Is it reasonable for Korea to envision displacing Britain as the seventh-largest economy in the world? Does this goal lie beyond Korea's reach? It will certainly be a stretch. As of 1992, Korea was the second-largest producer of ships, the sixth-largest producer of electronics products, and eleventh in trade volume, where it now stands in GDP.[2] However, a study by the Korea Institute for Industrial Economics and Trade (KIET) in mid-1994 placed Korea fifteenth out of eighteen industrial economies ranked for their competitiveness.[3] By the Ministry of Science and Technology's (MOST) assessment in 1993, Korea ranked thirteenth out of fourteen market economies with science and technology capabilities. In another MOST study, Korea ranked only twenty-fourth or twenty-fifth in basic science, according to publications cited in *Science Citation Index* and other information.[4]

In contrast, the pace of Korea's development since 1960 has been a source of admiration, even astonishment, around the world.[5] With a dedicated, literate, and relatively inexpensive workforce, a high savings rate, and a national strategy devoted to building economic strength as the best path to security, Korea was able to lift its per-capita annual income from less than $300 in 1955 to more than $10,000 in 1995.[6]

Will the successful policies of the past enable Korea to continue its growth unabated? It seems clear that they will not. The very basis of Korea's winning strategy—cheap, disciplined labor; nationally managed allocation of capital; imported technology and tools; and imported higher education in science and engineering—compels a change in strategy. Thus, with President Kim Young-Sam, we conclude that Korea is at a turning point in its history. This book is an assessment of the assets, institutions, and policies that Korea will need to master an innovation-based development strategy.

At present, Korean corporations have established leading roles in international markets in a number of high-technology products. Korean students have demonstrated excellent performance in the best graduate schools of science and engineering in the West. The emergence of a more mature, democratic political system creates conditions that favor creativity and entrepreneurship. Competition in the domestic market, resulting from a more open economic system, will spur improvements in efficiency.

Korea also faces some serious difficulties, which will be explored in the following chapters. The country is too dependent on foreign institutions for education of its scientific and technical leadership. The economy is too heavily skewed toward large corporations, which are still too dependent on foreign sources for new technologies and the tools to implement them. The sum paid by Korean firms for imported technology equals 20 percent of what they spend on R&D. This ratio seems independent of the magnitude of their R&D spending, which has been growing rapidly. Licenses for imported technology in 1991 still consumed about 12 percent of sales in the electronics industry, up from 3 percent in the 1970s.[7]

The small- and medium-size entrepreneurial business sector is weak, both technologically and economically, compared to competitors like Taiwan (see Chapter 10). This weakness deprives Korea of a critical element of the high-technology infrastructure required for the next stage of technological development (see Table 1.1).[8]

Table 1.1
Number of Establishments in the Manufacturing Sector

Year	1980	1985	1990	1992
Small	24,362 (79.0%)	35,676 (81.0%)	58,859 (85.5%)	65,413 (87.6%)
Medium	5,417 (17.6%)	7,274 (16.5%)	8,820 (12.8%)	8,244 (11.0%)
Large	1,044 (3.4%)	1,087 (2.5%)	1,193 (1.7%)	1,022 (1.4%)
Total	30,823	44,037	68,872	74,679 (100%)

Source: Organization for Economic Cooperation and Development (OECD), *Reviews of National Science and Technology Policy: Republic of Korea,* Appendix Table 9 (Paris: OECD, 1995).

Despite policy declarations about economic liberalization, Korea's government still plays too heavy a hand in guiding the economy. In fact, economic growth depends on how firms and banks enact entrepreneurial policies and on how new sources of innovation can be created from public and private laboratories and universities. Bureaucracy continues to exact high transaction costs in almost every facet of Korean society.

Korea is not alone in facing such challenges. The United States, Europe, and Japan and the other Asian "tigers" have all focused on building their economic growth by accelerating investments in innovation and the science on which it rests. Other nations are searching for more effective cooperation between government and the private sector, making substantial investments in knowledge and information infrastructures, continuing strong investments in basic science and in generic technology while providing greater focus, and creating new roles for the nation's premier laboratories to boost economic performance.

Japan, as described in Chapter 9, is emerging in 1995 from a period of recession triggered by the collapse of the balloon economy and the renewal of U.S. industry. Recognizing that labor costs are high, Japanese firms are relocating much of their cost-sensitive production overseas, often moving to Asian countries where costs are lower than in Korea. The Japanese government is investing heavily in basic science to increase the rate of indigenous scientific discovery, while changing the education system to stimulate more creativity in students. International cooperation in science and technology is also high on the national agenda.

U.S. firms have sustained their global leadership in industries such as chemicals, pharmaceuticals, aircraft, and software. They have reversed the market share losses to Asia in electronic components and automobiles by paying much more attention to manufacturing processes, with reductions in cost, quality, and time to introduce new products. In addition, the U.S. government has become much more assertive in defending its commercial interests, especially in opening foreign markets and protecting intellectual property.

Europe is integrating its markets, removing political and economic barriers to create an economic entity whose scale, in population and gross product, exceeds that of the United States. The European Community is providing substantial financial incentives to collaborate transnationally among corporations and between sectors such as firms, universities, and research institutions. In summary, nations around the world are seeking a new source for adding value and are finding it in technology.[9] Scholars now focus on "national systems of innovation," composed of economic policies, institutional capacities, human resources, and their fruitful interactions.[10]

Thus, as Korea competes with other nations, it is chasing a moving target. While Korean policy turns more to science and technology, other nations will have done the same. Korean progress toward this rather elusive goal of a creative, entrepreneurial, self-confident, and risk-prone society must continue to be more rapid than that of a number of impressive competitors.

INNOVATION-BASED STRATEGIES FOR DEVELOPMENT

Why has science-based innovation become the path that so many nations now seek? The reasons are not hard to find. First, the pace of competitive progress sets a very high standard. This accelerated rate of innovation results from the extraordinary progress that science has made in the past forty years, especially in the United States, and the discovery that science can and does contribute directly to production process quality and efficiency as well as to product conception and design.

Second, innovation, still dependent on creative people sensitive to society's needs, has become a more managed process. Modeling of applications and markets, as well as simulation of products and processes, all shorten product cycle times and reduce the risk of investment in production. Firms have become more sophisticated about selecting innovation strategies and identifying core competencies.[11] For example, they use alliances and joint ventures with suppliers to access the innovation capability of small- and medium-size firms. In short, the most advanced high-technology firms have learned to apply science and computer technology quickly and effectively to the innovation process.

Nations also seek science-based innovation because science has been proven to lead to major new products and entirely new industries. Science continues to drive this "linear model" of the innovation process. Today, the most impressive newcomer to the list of science-created new industries is biotechnology, arising from the sciences of microbiology and biochemistry. Similar expectations surround "designer materials" and other areas of forefront science.

Science has played an even more important role with well-established technologies, reducing the risk of making mistakes about technological opportunities—a rising source of corporate costs. Science used in this way has immediate payback.

The international race toward science-based innovation also results from acknowledging the environmental consequences of economic decisions. These consequences have grown in importance and complexity. If a balanced environmental and economic strategy is not adopted, countries will suffer from deferred expenses as well as a degraded social environment. A new field of study called "industrial ecology" examines how production processes can minimize waste and how to make by-products that can be used as inputs by other industries.[12]

Governments and corporations are also embracing science-based innovation because the tools of modern industrial economies are growing more complex. Integrated production systems receive design and process instructions from automated design and production divisions, which also monitor manufacturing to produce high-quality output. Internationally competitive firms must be able to develop their own processes and analytical and production tooling.

Customer satisfaction, the ultimate test of competitive advantage, increasingly requires a well-integrated offering of hardware, software, and service. Thus, skills in systems analysis and systems engineering have emerged as primary requirements for success for end-product vendors. If Korean products are to establish brand-name identification to compete against Sony or Honda, Korean firms must master this integration capability while gaining access to the relevant markets. This is a major technological challenge.

Finally, all the key characteristics we have mentioned, which are found in the economies of Japan and the United States, depend on a level of technical and information infrastructure whose development is expensive, complex, and time consuming. The United States, Japan, and Korea are all embarked on major national efforts to create the switched, broad-band digital networks through which their economies—indeed, their societies—are tied together into a functioning whole. The most difficult and expensive parts of the infrastructure are not the optical fiber networks but the software and institutional structures for applications in the fields of enterprise integration, public education, worker training, health care delivery, and the national network of libraries and information services.[13]

REQUIREMENTS FOR NATIONAL S&T CAPABILITY

What are the components of national capability necessary to sustain an innovation-based growth economy in this kind of world? It takes more than the capacity to engage in research and the resources to do so with adequate vigor. Following is a list of some of them:

Intellectual and Human Capital

This includes a well-supported group of research-based universities as the primary source of fundamental science and technology (S&T) capability. It also demands participation in the world's S&T and the ability to diffuse technology to small and medium industry. Finally, full participation must be available for women in creative and managerial roles in an innovation-based society.

Economic and Business Capital

A strong transportation, financial, and information infrastructure must exist to provide a competitive cost structure. A market-oriented national industrial policy must be in place, based on a managerial culture that celebrates entrepreneurship and new firm creation. Finally, alliances must be made with overseas firms, providing market and technology access based on technological parity.

Innovation-Friendly Culture

Despite the extraordinary success large Korean firms have had in the importation and absorption of western technology, Korean scientists are almost universally persuaded that their society does not respect technicians—high school graduates who are adept at managing the sophisticated tools of a modern, high-technology economy. Even at the level of technical professionals with advanced degrees in science or technology, university teaching carries much higher social prestige than does industrial research and development. These cultural factors place Korea at a significant disadvantage when compared to the United States, where innovation is highly—perhaps even excessively—admired.

Social Capital

Nations must possess strong capabilities for S&T policy analysis and design, providing objective assessments of S&T and innovation performance. Also, there must be institutional and political maturity based on trust and a shared value system. Finally, the political leadership must be sufficient to mobilize the society and all ministries behind a national, public–private, innovation-based strategy.

S&T policies in Korea are too heavily contingent on politicians and the higher levels of government officials. Economists have much more influence than technical professionals, even in making S&T policy. The transition from authoritarian government to democracy is still in process. Korea needs a long period of political stability in S&T policy, one in which private-sector and academic views are influential. This is the prerequisite for productive social capital.

No nation, including the United States and Japan, can lay claim to sufficiency in all these categories, or perhaps in any of them. In all four of these categories, Korea will find challenge enough, but the basis for progress in each is present. This list is useful, however, as a standard against which self-evaluation should be made.

STRUCTURE OF THIS BOOK

In summary, the conception of Korea's new innovation-based strategy must rest on four kinds of analysis:

1. Anticipated trends in leading innovation practices and the state of world science and engineering, as well as monitoring changes in the global economic environment
2. Reflecting on Korea's past experience with S&T policy and institutional development
3. Reassessing Korea's current capacity, structure, and policy for S&T and their applications
4. Analyzing the successes and failures of other nations that seek to base their development on science, technology, and innovation

Given these premises, the rest of this volume is organized as follows.

Part I examines Korea's environment and its implications for science, technology, and innovation policy. It traces the post–World War II history of Korean technical and economic development, a legacy of policy and practice that both constrains and supports the next stage of development. The decades from 1960 through the 1980s are summarized, and the authors trace the evolving relationships between public and private technical institutions and policies. The chapters discuss why Korea must achieve increased added value from indigenous innovation and from international business alliances, given the rising wages that accompany Korea's hard-earned affluence. The primary conclusion is that Korea is poised to compete on equal terms with the industrialized nations in a more open and competitive global economy. However, to be successful it must pursue an innovation-driven strategy based on a strong national scientific and technological capability and flexible, creative entrepreneurship.

Part II evaluates Korean scientific and technological resources for innovation. Korea's history, going back to ancient times, is rooted in important scientific accomplishments. But the long periods of influence by much larger Chinese and Mongolian neighbors, followed by a period of colonial occupation by Japan, weakened Korea's institutional and political development. Its dominant Confucian culture proved a strong asset in its emphasis on the importance of education and in subordinating the individual to the common purposes of society. However, it failed to confer prestige upon those with the practical scientific and engineering skills that drove the technological revolutions of western societies. Chapters 7 and 8 explore the strengths and limitations of Korea's primary institutions for developing the personnel and the basic technical knowledge that serve as the foundations for industrial innovation: the universities and the government-funded research institutions. Both are in need of revitalization.

Part III looks for other national models from which Korea might draw lessons for charting its own future. Japan serves as Korea's primary model for forced-draft economic development under a government-led strategy. Japan has served as both a mentor and, more recently, a strong competitor. Taiwan faced historical circumstances that were, in some respects, much like Korea. It thus offers the best comparison for testing the effects of different innovation strategies in these two competing Asian "tigers." The model of Taiwan shows great strength in an area of conspicuous Korean weakness: the vitality of its small- and medium-size enterprises. Brazil offers a contrast to Korea, having at one time enjoyed rapid growth not unlike Korea's. But Brazil pursued (for too long) protectionist and interventionist economic policies that maximized the rate of acquisition of new technology. The effects can be seen as a warning for Korean policy.

The smaller but industrially sophisticated European nations of Switzerland, Sweden, and the Netherlands suggest this question: Given that they, like Korea, are small and lean on resources, what accounts for the superior standard of living they offer their citizens? Can Korea emulate their success, albeit in a much shorter time? The answer lies in the superior social capital that the smaller European nations have developed. These assets contrast with the inefficiencies of Korean bureaucracy, the immature state of Korean democratic political institutions, and the absence of the constructive relationships that Europe has developed between large and small firms and a supportive but nondirective government.

Part IV builds an innovation-based model for Korean development, based on two elements: strong international linkages and a more mature infrastructure that relies upon information technology and communications networks. This part traces the complementary roles to be played by the laboratories of Korean firms, the government-funded research institutes, and the universities. It suggests that Korea can continue to acquire technology from firms abroad, but it can no longer rely on the purchase of licenses or on foreign direct investment for its success. Korea must build innovation alliances with firms abroad, based on the exchange of technology of comparable value. This will spur internal investment in scientific and technological development. Finally, this part of the book shows that Korea's trade relationships will shift from its narrow dependence on Japan and the United States to a broader set of choices that entail a strong focus on China and other Asian economies. This trend will make Korea a technology exporter as well as importer.

Part V recapitulates the preceding arguments and presents the editors' conclusions. We advocate a comprehensive, integrated, technology-based innovation strategy, suggesting appropriate organizational arrangements for the government and investment policies for both public and private sectors. Finally, we present a basic philosophy and paradigm for a new national Korean system of innovation that is based on S&T.

Can Korea make the changes in policy and institutional development needed for an innovation-based economy? Despite Korea's limitations—relatively small size, paucity of natural resources, and geopolitical situation—the goal of parity with the G-7 would not seem such a stretch if it could continue into the twenty-first century with its past policies. These policies generated double-digit annual growth in the 1970s and through the 1980s. In the judgment of the authors, however, the old policies will not be sufficient without intensively promoting science, technology, and the capacity to innovate. This effort requires much more than investing in the needed resources; it calls for a fundamental change in strategy and attitude, for new and reinvigorated institutions and national policymaking, and for heightened expectations by the people of their own creative capabilities.

NOTES

1. The Honorable Kyong-Shik Kang, *Third U.S.–Korea Science and Technology Forum*, Washington, D.C., December 12–13, 1995 (proceedings to be published by George Mason University), confirmed by the Honorable Bohn-Young Koo, vice minister of Science and Technology.

2. Organization for Economic Cooperation and Development (OECD), *OECD Reviews of National Science and Technology Policy: Republic of Korea* (Paris: OECD, 1995), Table 8, p. 177.

3. Denis Fred Simon and Changrok Soh, "U.S.–Korean Industrial and Technological Cooperation in the Context of Globalization and Regionalization," October 15, 1995, unpublished paper for the sixth U.S.–Korea Academic Symposium on Economic and Regional Cooperation in Northeast Asia, Chicago, September 6–8, 1995.

4. Ministry of Science and Technology, "Uri Naraui Gwahak Kisul Sujun" (The Scientific and Technological Level of Korea), unpublished internal document, Seoul, 1993. The ranking was measured on the basis of such statistics as R&D expenditures, number of scientists and engineers, number of patents registered, citation index references to Korean publications, and the number of those publications.

5. See Chapters 3, 4, and 5 for a brief history of this development from 1960 to the current time, as well as *The Korean Miracle* and other general references on Korean development.

6. OECD, *OECD Reviews of National Science*, 135.

7. Dieter Ernst, *What Are the Limits to the Korean Model? The Korean Electronics Industry under Pressure* (Berkeley, Calif.: Berkeley Roundtable on International Economics, June 1994), 60, quoting Jin-Joo Lee, "The Status and Issue of Management Dynamism and Four Case Studies in the Republic of Korea," in *Management Dynamism: A Study of Selected Companies in Asia* (Tokyo: Asian Productivity Organization [APO] 1991), 132, 139.

8. OECD, *OECD Reviews of National Science*, 178–179.

9. Henry Ergas, "Does Technology Policy Matter?" in *Technology and Global Industry: Companies and Nations in the World Economy*, ed. Bruce Guile and Harvey Brooks (Washington, D.C.: National Academy Press, 1987), 191–245.

10. Richard R. Nelson, ed., *National Systems of Innovation: A Comparative Analysis* (New York: Oxford University Press, 1993).

11. Lewis M. Branscomb and Fumio Kodama, *Japanese Innovation Strategies: Technology Support for Business Visions* (Lanham, Md.: University Press of America, 1993).

12. Robert A. Frosch, "Industrial Ecology: A Philosophical Introduction," in *Proceedings of the National Academy of Science* (February 1992), 800–803; John S. Hoffman, "Pollution Prevention as a Market-Enhancing Strategy," in *Proceedings of the National Academy of Science* (February 1992), 832–834; Jesse Ausubel, "Industrial Ecology: Reflection on a Colloquium," in *Proceedings of the National Academy of Science* (February 1992), 879–884.

13. Information Infrastructure Task Force, *The National Information Infrastructure: Agenda for Action* (Washington, D.C.: U.S. Department of Commerce, September 15, 1993). For Japan, see report of the Telecommunications Technology Council, advisors to the Ministry of Posts and Telecommunications, Government of Japan, in "TTC Issues Report on Next Generation Infrastructure," *New Breeze* (summer 1994): 14–18.

Chapter Two

THE PATH TO MODERNIZATION
1962–1992

Young-Hwan Choi

For all appearances, Korea's economic accomplishments in the three decades between the 1960s and 1980s have been truly remarkable. Having failed to ride the wave of the first Industrial Revolution, Korea has undergone a condensed industrial revolution in the latter half of the twentieth century. The gross national product (GNP) increased an average of 9 percent per year since 1962, from $2 billion in 1962 to $276.8 billion in 1992, which ranked Korea, according to the International Monetary Fund (IMF) statistics, as the fourteenth nation in size of its GNP. The GNP per capita also grew from $87 to $6,749 in the same period.

The volume of export trade has increased from $40 million in 1962 to $66.5 billion in 1992. Moreover, the percentage of manufactured goods in exports took a gigantic leap from 14.3 percent to 96 percent. Korea has become one of the leading members of the so-called Newly Industrialized Economies (NIEs), having successfully transformed itself from an agrarian economy to an industrial nation.

This chapter explores the policies on science and technology (S&T) pursued by successive Korean governments during the period of rapid economic growth and industrialization, based on the analysis of each government's understanding of internal and external situations and specific industrial objectives. The segmentation into periods follows the terms of the presidents. Thus, the three decades of economic growth are divided into the Park Chung-Hee era (1962–1979), the Chun Doo-Hwan era (1980–1987), and the Roh Tae-Woo era (1988–1992). The policies and developmental strategies can best be illustrated by contrasting the strategies and policies of these presidents.

THE PARK CHUNG-HEE ERA (1962–1979)

The First Half of the Park Chung-Hee Era ("The Third Republic" Period): 1962–1972

The military regime of General Park Chung-Hee, born out of a *coup d'état*, seized upon economic development as the first priority in the name of "Modernizing the Fatherland" and establishing the legitimacy of the new regime. The people desperately desired national economic recovery from the previous stagnation and chaos.

Only one year after the coup, General Park initiated the First Five-Year Plan for Economic Development (1962–1966), setting the objective of "rectifying all forms of vicious circles endemic in society at large and constructing the basis for an autonomous national economy." However, the plan lacked a clear developmental strategy and suffered from numerous trials and errors, until the "export-oriented strategy" was established as the foundation principle of economic policy. This strategy, which continued throughout the Second Five-Year Plan (1967–1971) as well, sought import substitution and promotion of export industries, relying on import of foreign capital, technologies, and raw materials and on the use of low-wage labor. Lacking both capital and advanced technology, this strategy turned out to be most appropriate at a time when international trade was continuously expanding. Emphasis was placed on light industries—such as textiles and plywood—and cultivation of key industries—such as cement, fertilizer, petroleum, and electricity, along with some intermediary industries.

Unfortunately, the Korean industry of that time had no technological capacity to follow through these ambitious plans and was forced to depend on the imported technology. The foreign technologies imported in this period were very limited; examples were processing, assembly, and product specifications in the area of light industries and technologies embodied in manufacturing equipment. One scholar refers to them as "pseudotechnologies."

Korean companies could export their products—assembled or processed from imported parts and raw materials, making use of foreign capital and technology—fairly easily in that period of expanding international trade. As a consequence, they did not feel a strong need for developing their own technologies; the level of technological investment was extremely low: only 0.3 percent of the GNP through 1960s.

To aid firms in absorbing and adapting foreign technology and to build a base structure for S&T in the long term, the government established several government-funded research institutes and formulated the mid- and long-term S&T promotion plans. The Korean government established the Ministry of Science and Technology (MOST) in 1969 as an independent central administrative organization, spun off from the existing Bureau of Technological Management of the Economic Planning Board (EPB). This may be regarded as recognition by the Korean government of the significance of S&T for national socioeconomic development.

MOST was empowered by the law to make comprehensive plans for the development of S&T, including research and development (R&D) and human resources development, through which MOST could coordinate policies and programs on S&T planned and executed by other ministries and agencies. Unfortunately, there was a considerable gap between the ideal of the coordination system and the reality it encountered. Not only were other ministries reluctant to adjust their policies to the new guidelines and directions provided by MOST, but MOST itself lacked institutional mechanisms or administrative power to respond to the situation in a flexible manner.

Nevertheless, MOST made great efforts to fulfill its mission. It promulgated the basic "S&T Promotion Law." It established technical human resource development plans. It presented the basic direction for S&T development through the Long-Term Comprehensive Plans for S&T (1967–1986) and the Long-Term Prospect for Supply and Demand of Manpower (1967–1986).

Second, the Korean government, one year prior to the establishment of MOST, had established the Korea Institute of Science and Technology (KIST) as a result of the technological cooperation projects between Korea and the United States. There were a few government-supported research institutes attached to universities in Korea at that time, but KIST was the first comprehensive and interdisciplinary research institute, funded by the government yet maintaining an independent identity as a legal body.

KIST has since become a model for all the government-funded research institutes established later in Korea. In the beginning, it concentrated on providing technological support for the private industries in adopting, digesting, and modifying imported foreign technologies. It provided technical troubleshooting services for the private sector. Although it had to tackle many obstacles in the process, KIST has been performing the leading role in scientific and technological development in Korea. (KIST is dealt with more extensively in Chapter 8.)

Third, in the last year of the Second Five-Year Plan for Economic Development, the Korea Advanced Institute of Science (KAIS), Korea's first special graduate school in the field of science and engineering, was established. Placed under the jurisdiction of MOST rather than the Ministry of Education (MOE), KAIS was created to cultivate high-grade personnel in the field of science and engineering and to induce improvement in the graduate programs of the existing universities. In order to recruit top students, the government provided many privileges, such as exemption from military services, scholarships, tuition, and room and board. The same extraordinary level of financial support was guaranteed to faculty members as well.

When the plan for building KAIS first became public knowledge, many professors from Seoul National University and other institutions strenuously objected to it. They argued that it would be ultimately more efficient to channel such an extraordinary level of support to the existing universities. However, it would have broken the "principle of equity" for the government to ask the MOE to support one specific university from among the many under its jurisdiction. Even if this were possible, it would not be able to maintain autonomy and stability as a research-oriented graduate school for science and technology because of the requirements for uniform treatment written into the Education Law. This problem continues to this day (see Chapter 8).

In the end, KAIS—established along with KIST under MOST—managed to create momentum for enticing many Korean scientists and engineers abroad back into Korea. And as the graduates of KAIS have gradually become more prominent in both private industries and academia, the contribution of KAIS in improving the quality of higher education in the fields of science and engineering has accelerated. Its importance to technology was recognized by changing the name to KAIST.

Some scholars point out that a triangular system of promoting S&T in Korea was constructed, with MOST as the pinnacle and KIST and KAIS as two pillars. In sum, the first half of the Park Chung-Hee regime may be characterized as a period of total reliance on imported foreign technologies in the short term and a period of government-led construction of the basis for development of S&T for the mid-to-long term.

The Second Half of the Park Chung-Hee Era ("The Fourth Republic"): 1972–1979

In 1972, Park's declaration of the so-called "Yusin Constitution" replaced the fledgling democracy in Korea by a dictatorship, which ensured his own personal reign for an unlimited duration. Confident from the largely successful implementation of the plans for economic development in the 1960s, President Park started to implement even more activist industrial policies. In his New Year interview with the press in January 1973, Park issued the Declaration for Heavy and Chemical Industries, the objective of which was to intensively promote heavy and chemical industries. The government's goal was to make these products 50 percent of total exports by 1980. For that purpose, the six industries of steel, petroleum, shipbuilding, machinery, mining, and electronics were designated as strategic industries.

The emphasis on heavy and chemical industries was to upgrade the industrial structure of Korea, as well as to strengthen domestic national defense capacity.

President Jimmy Carter of the United States had warned President Park that the U.S. government would withdraw its military forces from Korea if the latter's human rights violations continued. This warning only made Park more determined to accelerate the promotion of heavy and chemical industries.

The industries targeted by the government were provided with tax exemptions, financial aid and various subsidies, permission to use foreign capital, technological assistance, restrictions imposed on competing foreign goods, and privileges for industrial sites. These aggressive industrial policies required greater expanding imports of sophisticated levels of industrial technologies, which could not be met by the technological capacity of Korea itself at that time.

The criteria for approving importation of foreign technologies by the domestic heavy industries were substantially relaxed. At the same time, foreign direct investment (FDI) and joint ventures with foreign companies were also encouraged. Heavy industries were now exempted from prior restrictions such as obligations to export and limitations on shares held by foreign owners.

Access to foreign exchange was improving, thanks to the success of construction companies in the Middle East and the favorable turn in balance of payments due to export growth. Under these circumstances, the demand for foreign technologies continued to increase. The government adopted the First-Step Liberalization Measure on the Importation of Foreign Technology in 1978. This measure allowed certain industries such as machinery, shipbuilding, metal, electronics, chemicals, and textiles to receive permission automatically for importing foreign technologies.[1] In 1979, the object of such automatic permission was expanded from selected industries to the entire industrial sector, with the exception of atomic and defense technologies; after the "Third Republic," even these exceptions were removed.

This liberalization of technology importation contributed to a huge growth in imported foreign technology. However, the Korean Industrial Technology Association revealed that close to 63 percent of foreign technologies imported in the 1970s were in declining stages or in the maturing stages of the technological life cycle. The technological capacity of Korean industries was still low, and their ability to choose among foreign technologies and negotiate the terms and conditions for technology imports was weak.

Korean industry was now faced with the necessity of improving its capacity for indigenous R&D. To satisfy these needs, the Technology Development Promotion Law was promulgated in 1972. One example of tax incentives based on this law was the Reserve Fund System for Technological Development. This system allowed companies to set aside a certain proportion of their net income or profit for reserve funds and to utilize these funds as expenses for technological and human resources development within the next four years. Then these companies could receive a tax incentive by reporting these expenses as "savings" when calculating balance sheets. Firms thereby were indirectly induced to invest in technological development.

The Technology Development Loan System, initiated by the Korean Development Bank (KDB), allowed the KDB to lend capital for technological development under unusually favorable conditions, such as a three-year grace period, twenty-year repayment, and 5 percent interest rate. In addition, to encourage cooperation among firms, the Industrial Technology R&D Consortium System was adopted, for which tax exemptions and preferential financing were granted. However, these incentive systems for indigenous technologies did not turn out to be as efficient as expected. The technology development loan from the KDB was seriously underused; few firms had joined the Industrial Technology R&D Consortium by the early 1980s.

The Korean government established numerous government-funded research institutes in such fields as machinery, shipbuilding, electronics, electric parts, communications, chemistry, resources, and energy. These government-funded research institutes have helped firms develop technology and accumulate the ability to perform R&D by actively recruiting Korean scientists and engineers from abroad. (These specialized government-funded research institutes are discussed in detail in Chapter 8.)

During this period, the government also made a blueprint for a "Science Town" in Daeduk, located in the middle of Korea. Construction of the town, which would physically accommodate many government-funded research institutes as well as private research institutes and educational facilities, was begun. The objective was to create an intellectual community in which researchers and professors could exchange knowledge and information. It has taken nearly twenty years to complete the construction of the Daeduk Science Town.

One of the noteworthy achievements by the government was the "specialization of science- and engineering-related universities." Universities were induced to specialize in the fields of science and engineering that were most appropriate to the condition of the region where each was located. Incentive support was given in the form of research grants, scholarships, equipment, and facilities. (For instance, the engineering college of Pusan University was induced to specialize in machinery, since the Chang-Won Industrial Site near Pusan City was strong in the machine industry.) The specialization policy resulted in relative strengthening of selected science and engineering departments in certain universities but has not met with as much success as expected because of the lack of general support from academic communities (see Chapter 7).

The 1974 Special Law for Vocational Training compelled firms to train a certain number of skilled workers, proportionate to the number of regular employees; if they failed to carry out this duty, then they were obligated to pay contributions to commit the public vocational training programs. (France has a similar program, requiring investments in employee training at a minimum level of 1.25 percent of payroll, with the alternative of remitting this sum to the government to pay for worker training.)

Moreover, if a skilled worker passed a national skill test, then he or she would be certified as having technological qualifications. This national skill test system was designed to cultivate high-caliber skilled workers and to improve their social status against the traditional prejudice against those with practical skills. This system has contributed to skill development of Korea. Nevertheless, it has not been able to break down the subconscious contempt for manual skills inherent from the traditional Confucianism.

While Park Chung-Hee's policies brought a number of negative consequences, such as overconcentration of economic power in a handful of conglomerates (chaebols), chronic inflation, and decline of small- to medium-size firms, it undeniably contributed to the upgrading of industrial structure and to eventually elevating Korea to the rank of the NIEs. In terms of S&T, the activities in industrial technology development were more meager than expected. Technological investment only increased from 0.3 percent to 0.7 percent of the GNP. The reasons for such lukewarm responses by the industry were (1) the lack of industrial capacity to independently carry out R&D activities, (2) lower risk of importation and utilization of foreign technologies, and (3) the lack of economic incentives to invest in mid- and long-term technological development. Korean firms could profit with much less risk and greater proficiency from real estate speculation, which resulted from continuing inflation, the rate of which averaged higher than 20 percent annually, as well as from the influx of foreign currency that followed the construction boom in the Middle East.

According to an analysis conducted by the Korea Development Institute (KDI), one of the most authoritative think tanks in Korea, the rate of contribution from technology to the growth of the GNP was 7.6 percent between 1966 and 1976, and 7.3 percent between 1972 and 1983. The contribution of labor, in contrast, was 49.5 percent and 39 percent, respectively. We can infer from these data that the major factor for the growth of the Korean economy in the 1960s and 1970s had been a low-cost but skilled workforce rather than technology.

The Chun Doo-Hwan Era ("The Fifth Republic"): 1980–1987

In October 1979, the assassination of President Park Chung-Hee created political chaos and a power vacuum. The leadership was soon seized by General Chun Doo-Hwan and other members of the military. General Chun established the Committee for National Security Planning and initiated a wide range of political and social reforms in the name of eliminating corruption and inefficiency. S&T areas proved no exception to his drive to consolidate resources and reorganize bureaucratic administration. Nineteen government-funded research institutes were collapsed into nine, citing the lack of efficiency in management as a reason.

Having thus impacted the S&T community with a chilling atmosphere of massive integration and consolidation, General Chun was soon elected as the legitimate president of Korea through a collegial election system. And yet, his violence against procedural democracy in his early reign continued to provide the fodder for Korean citizens to undermine his political legitimacy. This, in turn, further exacerbated the needs of the "Fifth Republic" to demonstrate its differences from previous governments to the Korean people.

Certainly the regime was not helped by changing circumstances. Domestically, the national economy was plagued by the aftereffects of heavy industry–oriented policies of the 1970s, such as inflation, overconcentration of economic power, and aggravation of sectoral imbalance and trade deficit. Internationally, the second oil shock and the resultant jump in petroleum prices, the rise in the exchange rate, the pressure from the advanced countries to open Korea's domestic market, and the protectionism trends among the developed countries were some of the main factors adversely affecting the Korean economy.

In order to respond to these problems, the Fifth Republic government focused on the competitiveness of Korean firms in international markets. The first measure regarding S&T taken by Chun Doo-Hwan was to hold a Technology Promotion Conference. The intent behind the conference was similar to that of the Export Promotion Conference conducted by President Park Chung-Hee during the 1970s: to encourage exports and technological development. The conference was presided over by the president himself, and its 220 participants included all ministers and representatives from industry, academia, and research institutes. The conference proceedings consisted of the presentation of reports on worldwide S&T trends, technology policy directions, and success cases of technology development. Awards recognizing contributors to technology development were given by the president; and finally, presidential instructions were issued to the participants and ministries concerned.

As the conference proceedings were authoritative, many participants felt dissatisfied that they could not express their sentiments because of the political and social atmosphere at that time. Nevertheless, the conference contributed to societal awareness of technological development. The mass media, largely under the control of the government, extensively covered the conference proceedings.

In order to support the conference at a working level, a Working Committee for Technology Promotion was established in the presidential office, consisting of vice ministers concerned in the government as well as civilian specialists. The chairman of the committee was directly appointed by the president, concurrently assumed the post of MOST, and presided over the meetings of the committee held inside the "Blue House" (presidential office). A large number of policies for technology development were developed through these two mechanisms, despite some criticisms against the conference for its top-down authoritarian management style. These policies included the following:

1. Tax incentives, such as tax exemptions for technological and personnel development–related expenses, and tariff exemptions for research facilities and equipment

2. Preferential financing (e.g., low-interest, long-term capital loans through various endowments for machinery, electricity, textile, and other industries)

3. Expansion of exemptions for researchers from military services

4. Providing venture capital—for example, through the newly established Korean Technology Development Corporation (KTDC)

5. Adoption of the technology credit guarantee system

6. Concentrated support for promising small- and medium-size firms

7. Support for the formation of a R&D consortia for industrial technology development

These policies encouraged the establishment of private research institutes and R&D consortia, resulting in a great expansion of the civilian investment in technological development.

With the increasing reluctance of firms in advanced countries to license advanced technologies to Korea, the Chun government took additional steps to liberalize foreign technology imports. In 1982, review of individual items of technology imports were delegated to each ministry concerned. In 1984, the requirement for reviewing individual items of technology import was eliminated altogether, replacing the appraisal system with a declaration system. However, the government left room for itself to control the technology imports by putting in place a clause empowering the ministries concerned to nullify declarations for exceptional cases.[2] Even though the intent behind this clause was understandable, it has been criticized for being an instrument for unnecessary interventions by the government.

On the other hand, the liberalization policy was extended to FDI. In 1983, the existing Positive Listing System, which allowed FDI only for the industries listed by the government, was converted to the Negative Listing System, which granted FDI in all industries unless they are listed by the government. At the same time, restrictions put on the foreign ownership of company equity and the remittance of the profits to the foreign investors were also reduced.

The government launched the Special National R&D Program in 1982 to make efficient use of the limited resources for R&D under a system of collaborations among industry, academia, and research institutes. In the early phase (1982–1983), this program was focused on the five strategic core technologies. By 1987, as the scale of funding for R&D increased and the national and social demands for technology changed, the areas of specialization were expanded to ten core areas:

1. Machine parts and localization of materials

2. Development of new materials

3. Ultra-highly integrated semiconductors

4. Computers for national computer network
5. Energy-saving technology
6. Fuel for nuclear plants
7. Development of new antibiotic and germicidal agents
8. Bioengineering technology
9. Localization of the experimental equipments in engineering college
10. Basic research for universities

Thus, for five years between 1982 and 1987, the government invested 194 billion won and the private sector 140 billion won respectively into these projects, for a total of 334 billion won. Some 1,053 firms participated, among which 729 were small- to medium-size firms, and 22,140 researchers also participated in these projects.

It is difficult to measure accurately the economic effects of these R&D projects. Some critics pointed out that the rate of commercialization of these projects was very low and that effectiveness was lagging. However, it is undeniable that these special projects initiated substantial collaborative activities among industry, academia, and research institutes and also generated momentum for R&D in the so-called "cutting-edge" technologies and acted as a catalyst for R&D activities in the private sector.

Entering the 1980s, the basis of government industrial policies was deemed in the need of a major re-evaluation. The government consolidated seven individual laws providing selective assistance of specific industries into one Industry Development Law.[3] This signaled a change of direction from the existing policy of targeting specific industries to a neutral industrial policy that emphasizes the general development of technology and personnel. Such a switch of direction was significant in the sense that the government adopted a neutral industrial policy based upon the principle of market-oriented competition, even though the industrial targeting was not completely removed from the government policies.

Based on the new Industry Development Law, the Industrial Base Technology (IBT) Project was launched under the jurisdiction of the Ministry of Commerce and Industry. Implemented in 1987, this project was designed to help out industries and to enhance their technological abilities by providing some or all of the funding for technological development to be directed at certain technological areas requiring immediate attention. While the Special National R&D Projects by MOST were geared toward mid- to long-term objectives, this IBT Project dealt with more short-term, pragmatic problems. As both projects gradually expanded, the problem of overlaps emerged, thus making coordination and definition of boundaries a problem.

Because of massive increases in science and engineering college enrollments following the high industrial growth of the 1970s, the supply of scientific and technological personnel was not perceived as a serious problem. The size of the student enrollment in science and engineering colleges was thus maintained at the same level. (However, see concerns about the quality of the training, expressed in Chapter 7.) Some efforts were made to increase the quality of these colleges by such means as the upgrading of experimental equipment and the increase of the ratio of faculty to students. Unfortunately, the supply and quality of scientists, engineers, and skilled workers came to be insufficient to meet the quantitative and qualitative demands in the 1980s.

Entering the 1980s, as R&D activities of industry became more vigorous, the need for venture capital, which could generate and diffuse the technological innovations by assisting commercialization of the results of such activities, was heightened. In 1981, the government, working closely with the private sector, established the KTDC with financial investment and loans from the International Bank for Reconstruction and Development. Investment companies for supporting the to-be-inaugurated, technology-intensive, small- and medium-size firms were established one after another, until the total reached fifteen in the mid-1980s.

It was remarkable, considering Korean technological and financial conditions, that such a number of venture capital companies were established. However, in reality, the operation of these companies was reliant on collateral-based loans, and real venture capital as investment or conditional loans was very meager in supply (only 12% of total capital). Newly established venture capital companies were reluctant to take risks, the amount of available finance was too small or was borrowed from foreign resources, and technological foundations were very poor. The very concept of venture capital—sharing of risks and profits arising from commercialization of R&D results—has never become truly rooted.

Despite the Fifth Republic's lack of legitimacy and authoritarian rule by President Chun Doo-Hwan, its technological achievements went beyond initial expectations. Investments in S&T showed an annual average increase of 16 percent from 0.7 percent of the GNP in 1980 to 1.87 percent of the GNP in 1987. Most significant, the pattern of investment in S&T has changed from 63.7 percent from government and 36.3 percent from the private sector to the government 24.7 percent and the private sector 75.3 percent.

One tremendous opportunity was lost, however, by the government's failure to lay the foundations for technological innovation and workforce development by properly managing the first trade surplus in Korean history. This surplus was all too briefly obtained in the mid-1980s, thanks to the so-called "three lows" (low oil price, low interest rate, and low exchange rate). In the short term, the adaptation of foreign technologies and the development of indigenous technologies were beginning to be harmonized, and in the mid- to long term, national R&D projects were promoted and activated through the collaboration among industry, academia, and research institutes.

The Roh Tae-Woo Era ("The Sixth Republic"): 1988–1992

In one of his campaign promises, then-presidential candidate Roh Tae-Woo stated: "If I were elected as the president, I would make the Republic of Korea one of the ten most technologically advanced countries in the world, and for that purpose, I would increase the investment in science and technology to 3 percent of the GNP by 1991, and 5 percent of the GNP by 2000." Unlike Chun Doo-Hwan, whose entry into national politics brought a chill to the S&T community, the election of Roh Tae-Woo gave a rosy picture of hope to the S&T community.

The year 1988, when Roh was elected, was marked by a trade surplus of more than $10 billion. The country was in a festive mood with the Seoul Olympics. But the rosy prospect did not last long. The Korean people, long oppressed by military dictatorships, now vented their desire for democracy and more equitable economic development among the classes and regions. Labor disputes, wage increases, deterioration of the favorable conditions created by the three lows and the resulting diminution of capital investment, and rampant real estate speculation resulted in declines in the competitiveness of manufacturing industries. This, in turn, weakened the drive for export; and to make things worse, international pressures to open domestic markets and concurrent protectionism of the developed countries all signaled the end of the good times for the Korean economy.

In a January 1990 press conference, President Roh announced a new direction for S&T policies as follows:[4]

We will develop the level of science and technology in our country to that of the seven advanced countries within the next ten years. We will actively support industrial technology development and high-technology R&D activities to be conducted by universities and research institutes, and we will expand the S&T complexes. We will also invest more in the cultivation of scientific and technological manpower, and participate in internationally joint R&D projects.

We will make with our own hands state-of-the-art semiconductors, supercomputers, communications satellites, and develop the state-of-the-art industries such as new materials and genetic engineering.

Although hopeful in outlook, these pronouncements provoked considerable skepticism among not a few scientists and engineers, not to mention those industrialists whose immediate concern was to boost technological capacity in the declining manufacturing sector. Nonetheless, various policies and programs were planned and executed in line with President Roh's declarations as follows.

First, the Korean government decided that it needed a symbolic project for national R&D which could actualize the goals expressed in the President's announcement of the G-7 (Group of Seven) objectives. MOST, engaged since 1991 in planning and selecting appropriate areas of technology, initiated the so-called "G-7 Project" in 1992 (later renamed HAN [i.e., Highly Advanced National] Project due to the persistent controversies associated with the label "G-7"), modifying the core areas of the existing Special National R&D Projects.

The G-7 Project could be said to be a goal-oriented and strategic national R&D project, which focused on essential technologies deemed necessary for Korea to advance to the technological level of the G-7 countries and, in particular, core technologies in which Korea has great potential, concentrating limited amounts of capital and personnel on these technologies (see Chapter 13).

Even though it is questionable whether this Project would really ensure Korea's entry into the rank of technologically advanced G-7 countries, it set a precedent for involving ministries other than MOST in actively encouraging industry participation in the early stages of innovative R&D and in reaching out to foreign sources for experts and specialized knowledge.

Specialized R&D projects under the responsibilities of related ministries grew in number and diversity—among them, the (Industrial Base Technologies) IBT Project (1987) spearheaded by the Ministry of Commerce and Industry; the Alternative Energy Technology Development Project (1988) by the Ministry of Energy and Resources; and the Information and Communications Technology Development Project (1992) by the Ministry of Communications.

These projects, which emphasized fusion between S&T and building Korean capabilities for innovation, heightened the significance of basic research. Through a new Basic Science Research Promotion Law, government increased basic science research funding from 9.7 billion won in 1987 to 112.9 billion won in 1992, while the budgets for academic science (from MOST and MOE) increased from 10 billion won to 70.4 billion won (the former, based on the "principle of excellence," and the latter, based on the "principle of universality"). In addition, basic science research in universities was allowed to receive financial support from the IBT Project, the defense budget, and technology-development expenditures of public corporations.

However, such increases in basic science research could not satisfactorily meet the demand for basic science research in all 114 universities and colleges. MOST opted to deal with this sobering reality by adopting the principle of competition, selecting as the targets for concentrated financial support a small number of outstanding research centers in universities. MOST contributed 400 billion to 900 billion won every year for basic research activities for nine consecutive years to sixteen science research centers and fourteen engineering research centers. It also constructed a common utilization system by which the research facilities and equipment that were large, sophisticated, and expensive could be used jointly by the universities on a regional basis.

The significance of basic science research had, of course, been emphasized time and again prior to the Sixth Republic, but it was from the early 1990s that substantial support for basic science research was put in place.

Daeduk Science Town was finally completed in 1992, near the end of President Roh Tae-Woo's term, almost twenty years since the initiation of the project under President Park Chung-Hee in 1973. In 1995, the town accommodated twenty-two government-funded research institutes, eight private research institutes, and three educational institutions of higher learning. However, despite the presence of R&D and academia, there is little representation from industry, which constitutes an obstacle to the generation and diffusion of technological innovation. Also, with growing demands for S&T the need for technical infrastructure could no longer be met by the Daeduk Science Town alone. The government thus made plans for constructing additional S&T complexes according to regional characteristics in the five regions: Pusan, Taegu, Chonju, Kangneung, and Kwangju. In particular, Kwangju in the southwest region was designated as a site for the second incarnation of KAIST. If these S&T complexes retain the four critical elements of R&D, academia, industry, and housing and fulfill their functions of scientific research and technological innovation in the next ten to twenty years, then the Sixth Republic could claim a historic achievement.

President Roh created the National Science and Technology Advisory Committee to advise the president directly on matters relating to S&T. Through this mechanism and a much more open Technology Development Conference, he permitted more input to policy from outside the government.

The Sixth Republic government pushed technology development from a short- and mid-term perspective to strengthen the competitiveness of the manufacturing industry and to rectify the trade imbalance with Japan. From a long-term perspective, President Roh's government sought to achieve the G-7 objective in specific fields of S&T, endeavored to increase S&T investment, promoted basic science research for creative technological development, and supported the construction of S&T complexes.

In spite of these efforts, which seemed to produce some visible results, a closer inspection reveals a paucity in concrete achievements on the part of the Sixth Republic, in part, because of labor disputes following the relaxed social atmosphere and democratization process; an economic environment chronically predisposed against technological innovation but favoring land speculation; and the skepticism rampant in the industries and the general public concerning the consistency and credibility of the government policies.

A COMPREHENSIVE EVALUATION
OF THE PAST THIRTY YEARS

In spite of the radical growth of the economy in the past thirty years, Korea is faced by a legacy of challenges. The export-oriented growth strategy is partly responsible for the fattening of the chaebol conglomerates, due to the focus on capital-intensive and certain high-technology–intensive industries, which contributed to the weakening of small- to medium-size industries and their eventual technological fragility. Korea faces an excessive structural dependence on Japanese intermediate and capital materials, to be assembled and exported to the United States and other countries. The national-level investment in human resources has been, proportionally speaking, rather scanty and has serious quality problems (see Chapters 7 and 8). Korea is a latecomer in realizing the importance of information infrastructure as a key to stimulating innovation and enhancing productivity, although the new Ministry of Information and Communications is dedicated to this task now (see Chapter 14).

Some scholars cite the example of Japan as a justification for the claim that the 80-percent ratio of the private-sector share in investment for S&T is a positive indication. However, they tend to overlook the historical fact that since the Meiji Restoration the Japanese government consistently built upon its S&T infrastructure and let its investment accumulate. Considering that Korea has poor infrastructure and little accumulation of government investment compared to Japan, the Korean government should strive to increase its investment in S&T more substantially.

A rational decision should be made concerning the desirable level of national investment in S&T. Although a target has been set up during the Sixth Republic to increase the ratio of the investment in S&T up to 5 percent of the GNP, and especially the government's share in the investment up to 35 percent, it is doubtful that this goal will be retained, much less achieved by the year 2000.

The consistency, coherency, and credibility of science, technology, and innovation policies are other important problems that the Korean government must solve as soon as possible. Unlike the Park Chung-Hee regime, which allowed not only the Minister of Science and Technology but also other economic ministers to perform their tasks usually without the fear of high turnover, the latter half of the Chun Doo-Hwan and Roh Tae-Woo presidencies saw overly frequent replacements of ministers related to science, technology, and innovation.

The cabinet reshuffling almost became an annual event at the end of each year, as exemplified by the average term of the Minister of Science and Technology, which was about one year. Such high turnover rates in key posts inevitably resulted in the lack of consistency in government policies and, in turn, the decline in the credibility of government policies.

During the past three decades, the Korean economy and society have grown in scale and complexity; and the capacities of industry, universities, and research institutes have improved while the international environment has changed dramatically. Under these circumstances, many scholars argue that the role of the Korean government in developing the economy and promoting science, technology, and innovation should be more decentralized, more indirect, and more demand-side oriented. These directions are the right ones for

Korean development. But more in-depth study should be conducted about the most appropriate role which the Korean government should assume, in the light of the rapidly changing global environment and the specific circumstances facing Korea in the present and in the future.

NOTES

1. Conditions included the following: if the contract duration was less than three years, if royalties were less than 3 percent of net sales, and if the entire amount of royalties paid was less than $100,000 with the advance payment less than $30,000.

2. These could involve (1) the utilization of trademarks or franchise only, (2) sales of raw materials and machine parts only, (3) technology import under unfair conditions of export limitation, and (4) low-grade or declining-stage foreign technologies.

3. These laws included the Machine Industry Promotion Law, Shipbuilding Industry Promotion Law, Electronic Industry Promotion Law, Petrochemical Industry Promotion Law, and others.

4. The seven countries are popularly known as the "G-7" countries, modified from "the ten most technologically advanced countries" in the presidential campaign promise.

Chapter Three

KOREA'S INTERNATIONAL ENVIRONMENT
Maintaining Competitive Advantage

*Byoung-Joo Kim, in collaboration
with the late Hyung-Ki Kim*

THE NEW INTERNATIONAL
ENVIRONMENT: AN OVERVIEW

A new era of global adjustments, regional and international competition, and collaboration has begun. This time, the past is not necessarily an indicator of the future. This is especially true in East Asia and for Korea in particular. With an expected Organization for Economic Cooperation and Development (OECD) membership in 1996, Korea has become a *de facto* and *de jure* entrant into the league of advanced industrial countries. The astonishing success that the Korean economy has enjoyed during its "followership" strategy is now being put to the test. Some segments of the economy, such as semiconductors, need to create and implement a leadership strategy—a role that Korean firms have not previously played. This chapter examines the new international environment within which Korea must operate and how Korea should deal with these changes.

Five categories of global changes stand out, among others, as elements of the changing international environment that Korea faces today: (1) the demise

of centrally planned economies and the economic liberalization of many developing economies; (2) the resurgence of government activism in support of
national technological capabilities; (3) a shift in international trade regimes
from open multilateralism to regionalism and bilateralism; (4) an increasing
need for regulatory harmonization between countries as the global economy
is further integrated; and (5) increasing political uncertainties in the Northeast Asian region, where Korea is located.

The fall of communism has left the world with one military superpower and
a few economic superpowers, including the United States, Japan, and Europe.
In East Asia, China has successfully engineered the shift from a centrally
planned economic system to a quasi-market-based system, while maintaining
virtually intact the political system and some presence of the state in productive sectors. The government has played an important role in agenda setting
in this balancing act. More recently, Vietnam and Laos are following suit in
transforming their economies. Within this transformation process, the composition of the market players has begun to change as well. Private enterprises, rather than the state, are becoming the moving force for industrial
production and trade. Some of those enterprises include new forms that are
under transition from state ownership to private ownership (as we often see
in defense conversion processes), like the enterprise in China led by the North
China Corporation.

Stemming largely from this trend toward a market-based economy in developing countries, the foundations and roles of government and corporations
are evolving. These trends affect property rights, legal and regulatory structures, and how both competition and cooperation are managed. The reshap-
ing of the rules of the game in political and economic transactions has led to
the "hardening" of soft budget constraints on enterprises in those economies in
transition, as well as the restructuring (and/or recapitalization) of state banks.

In contrast to the formerly centrally planned economies of developing
countries, government activism in industrial and trade policies has begun to
emerge in western economies and in the United States in particular. Despite a
decade of conservative movements in key western industrial economies, this
resurgence of government activism puts the triad of the three advanced economies—the European Union, Japan, and the United States—into a fiercely
competitive mode. This trend has serious implications for Korea. It will affect how the country manages its economy and how it copes with the ever
more formidable competitive strengths of the United States and other western countries as they pressure for changes in Korea's institutional and policy
frameworks.

Another trend that should concern Korea is the transformation of world
trade. The recent birth of the World Trade Organization (WTO) has raised
hopes for the return to a multilateral free trade order. However, world trade
policies are shifting from open multilateralism and "benign" regionalism to

an "aggressive unilateralism" and inward-looking—hence exclusionary—regionalism.[1] At this point, it is doubtful whether the birth of the WTO will end this trend. Rather than eliminating the regional free trade arrangements, the new WTO system is expected to coexist with more of them. The spread of regionalism by big players like the European Union (EU) and the United States has recently created precarious relations between industrialized and developing countries. Major industrial powers have begun to substitute Most Favored Nation (MFN)–based Generalized System of Preferences (GSP) treatment with negotiations to grant coverage and duration of preferential treatment only on a reciprocal basis.[2] (Industrialized countries often use their regional integration arrangements as the mechanism for these negotiations.) The "Europe Agreements" between the European Community (EC) and the East European countries are an example of this trend.

Aggressive regionalism tactics pose a significant challenge to Korea, since it needs to retain its foothold in those trading blocs located outside of East Asia. At the same time, within the Asia-Pacific Economic Cooperation forum (APEC), Korea has an interest in seeing that regionalism somehow serves as a building block instead of a stumbling block for open multilateralism. Korea must determine how to balance its regional stance with its international trading position.[3]

Korea faces additional challenges in opening trade during the beginning of the WTO era, including promoting more open trade in agriculture and textiles and reducing the remaining tariffs and quantitative restrictions. New WTO-based rules, such as trade-related investment measures (TRIMs) and the agreement on trade-related aspects of intellectual property rights (TRIPs), call for significant reforms in regulatory regimes for trade, investment, and production. The rules apply to the flow of capital and financial transactions across and within national political boundaries.

At the same time, Korea faces hurdles in introducing new regulatory regimes that must protect the welfare of the country while complying with the demands of other nations. Environment and health are especially sensitive areas, since new regulations inevitably require the screening and testing of goods imported into Korea from advanced countries. One such problem was resolved by the Ministry of Environment in Korea in April 1993, when a compromise was struck on the enforcement of Korea's Toxic Substance Control Law after reviewing recommendations from the U.S. Environmental Protection Agency and the Chemical Manufacturers Association in the United States.

Korea must also update its technology-related regulatory frameworks such as those in telecommunications, taking into account the new technological advances. Building its relationships with the United States is most important in these areas.

In addition to world trade trends that we have already mentioned, Korea needs to address the opportunities and problems posed by changes in the political climate of East Asia, where there should be growth in intraregional trade and investment. This opportunity blossomed when Korea and Russia normalized diplomatic relations in 1991 and diplomatic relations between China and Korea commenced in 1992.

A number of factors could potentially bring future instability in this area. China's steady military buildup, in tandem with deterioration of Sino–U.S. relations and friction over the status of Taiwan, may prompt China to become an aggressive superpower. The Chinese military buildup is already frightening all its neighbors, including Vietnam, Taiwan, Japan, and the Association of Southeast Asian Nations (ASEAN) countries.

North Korea poses another set of problems. The long dispute and tension over North Korea's nuclear program reminded the world of the instability of the Korean peninsula. The uncertainty over North Korea's future behavior has been heightened by the death of Kim Il-Sung, the North Korean leader of nearly half a century.

There is a hope, however, for stabilization between the two Koreas. North and South Korea recently resumed talks about South Korea providing aid in the form of food to the North, and there are reports that South-to-North investment projects are under discussion. Increased interaction between the two Koreas, if continued, would increase the stability of the peninsula and the Northeast Asian region as a whole.

Stabilization in the region may also be brought about by North Korea's willingness to improve relationships with other countries. Chances that the United States might open up a trade relationship with North Korea have improved because of recent interactions over resolving the nuclear issue and the building of light-water reactors, possibly with aid from the United States. If these relationships improve, Japan is likely to follow suit. This could, in turn, open North Korea to additional western economies and regional and international institutions, including the Asian Development Bank, the World Bank, and the International Monetary Fund. The opening of all these markets to North Korea should benefit South Korea in many ways; thus, South Korea should proactively support any relevant discussions and policies.

THE EMERGENCE OF MULTILATERALISM AND REGIONALISM IN TRADE AND INVESTMENT

The birth of WTO will further help Korea continue its export growth in several ways: by lowering trade barriers in the major market countries and by ensuring that trade retaliation measures are implemented according to recognized and accepted rules. The guarantee of open access to the major markets of the world is also likely to boost FDI. East Asia is expected to receive the lion's share of FDI, as in the recent past. The continuing strength of intraregional trade in East Asia and greater regulatory liberalization of world trade will favor

Korea's continuing success. How Korea benefits from increased FDI, however, will depend critically on two factors: (1) the degree to which it liberalizes regulations and (2) Korea's ability to develop its own high technology using the knowledge and experience from the incoming FDI.

Korea should expect different types of gains from the trends toward increased trade. Apart from the static gains related to re-deployment and more efficient allocation of resources, Korea could enjoy the more important dynamic gains resulting from increased competition and economies of scale.

The largest gains will accrue to exporters of manufactured goods. The magnitude of the gains will depend on (1) Korea's ability to compete in the global market; (2) the soundness of Korea's domestic policies; and (3) the degree to which Korea liberalizes its own trade regime and carries out the market-access provisions of the various bilateral, regional, and multilateral agreements. In order for Korea to benefit from global change, it must build a more open, agile, and technologically independent economy that can adjust quickly and take advantage of new market opportunities.

The chemical and petrochemical industries provide examples of how this new economy can operate. These industries, whose products are extensively used as intermediate inputs by a wide range of manufacturing industries, have enjoyed substantial gains based on these forward linkage characteristics. Furthermore, the increase in exports has helped domestic chemical and petrochemical firms cut their imports by U.S.$400 million per year. As the exports further increase, these industries will be able to improve the efficiency of their plant operations based on economies of scale, further boosting their competitive strength.

Another industry that should benefit from the free trade agreement is the semiconductor field, which is currently enjoying robust business. The lowering of tariffs in its overseas markets will be a major factor in helping this industry.

Prospects for the automobile industry are promising as well, since high tariffs and import restrictions imposed against Korean automobiles will be reduced. But imports of foreign automobiles will also increase, since Korea will be asked to further open its automobile market. In response, domestic automobile manufacturers must improve their technological capabilities to survive this future competition. They must leverage their existing relationships with foreign automobile companies. In the past, such alliances included Hyundai–Mitsubishi, Daewoo–Isuzu–GM, Kia–Mazda–Ford, and Ssangyong–Mercedes. Samsung's efforts to link up with Nissan further illuminates the need for alliances. The challenge for the Korean automakers will be to build autonomous domestic technology capability based on strengthened foreign ties.

The need for building an independent domestic technology base also applies to the Korean electronics industry. This industry has relied on exports to the United States, the EC, and Japan, from which it has imported technology in the past. The electronics industry is now seeking to diversify its markets to eastern Europe, Russia, China, and other developing countries. While new markets offer the potential for growth, the ability to capitalize on such opportunities will depend upon the industry's progress in innovation and its independent development of cutting-edge technology.

All of the industries we have mentioned will be affected by calls from the WTO system for strengthened protection for intellectual property rights (IPRs), a source of increasing friction between developed and developing countries. The agreement includes new international guidelines to protect IPRs by curtailing copyright violations of films and videos (including "bootlegged" copies) as well as other published and recorded materials.

Under the WTO agreement, Korea has agreed to protect the IPR of 221 products of EC origin—193 medical items and 28 agricultural chemicals, retroactive to July 1987. In terms of publishing copyrights, Korea has been complying with the guidelines of the Universal Copyright Convention since becoming a member in 1987. Following the Uruguay Round accord, Korea may be required to join the Berne Convention, which is being spearheaded by the advanced countries. Under the Berne Convention, copyright protection would extend for fifty years after the death of the author of a creative work.

The strengthening of IPR protection will require higher royalty payments to the advanced countries, which could potentially reduce levels of technology transfers and increase the struggle to fill a widening technology gap. However, Korea has a strong interest in enforcing strengthened IPR rules as its technological edge increases in a growing number of industries.

ENVIRONMENT AND LABOR ISSUES FOR TRADE REGIMES

Two items failed to get incorporated in the Uruguay Round stipulations: the establishment of linkages between trade and environmental considerations and those between trade and "acceptable" labor standards. International politics on this issue was played out between the industrialized economies and developing economies; the lack of support on the part of the latter put these issues on the future agenda for deliberation. These linkages will remain a lively and highly contentious item of discussion in bilateral trade negotiations.

In general, the developed countries have pro-labor and pro-environment groups that are politically stronger (because, in part, of their stages of their economic development) than their domestic opponents, while the developing countries may experience the opposite. These domestic political balances play out in the international arena of trade liberalization negotiations in the form of a general division between developed and developing countries.

The pro-labor and pro-environment groups and many businesses in developed countries worry that their domestic markets are flooded with goods from developing countries that are underpriced, since developing countries do not bear the costs of rigorously protecting the environment and providing good conditions for labor. They worry that this price-driven competition from the developing countries will either wipe out their domestic producers, force them to export jobs by moving production overseas, or pressure them to lower their own labor and environmental standards.

In contrast, the developing countries see these concerns of the developed countries as protectionist motives in the guise of humanitarian notions. Most of the developing countries accept the long-term necessity for raising labor and environmental standards, but they resist the necessary short-term adjustment. They argue that production with lower labor and environmental standards is an inevitable stage of development that the developed countries have already passed through.

As long as the disagreement over labor and environmental issues persists, these issues will come back to the negotiating table in future WTO talks and will eventually result in compromises. Korea suffers from great international division between pro-labor/pro-environment groups (developed countries) on one side and free traders (developing countries) on the other. Its stance internationally on these points is perhaps closer to that of developing countries, but this may soon have to change. Korea will not be able to argue both ways for long, if indeed it anticipates an economy at the G-7 level in less than a decade.

PATTERNS OF INTERNATIONAL AND
EAST ASIAN REGIONAL TRADE

Korea must accommodate to two major developments in the international trade environment: the robust export growth from the East Asian region as a whole and the rise of regionalism. (See Chapter 13 for additional discussion of changing patterns of opportunity for Korean trade.)

Most of the estimates of the gains from the WTO order suggest that East Asia, including Korea, will continue to fare better than other regions, increasing its share of world trade. Despite talk of rising trade barriers in the United States and the EC, manufactured exports to those regions have been growing rapidly during the 1980s and 1990s. East Asian Newly Industrialized Economies (NIEs) were the main drivers of this surge. In fact, East Asia dominates the world in manufacturing production: Eight East Asian economies produce nearly three-fourths of all developing-country exports of manufactures. Their collective shares now exceed those of the EC or Japan in the U.S. market, and those of the United States or Japan in the EC market. East Asian NIEs have managed to capture increasing shares of the markets in both the United States and the EC, despite their weak power and often defensive styles of bargaining. This trend indicates that multilateral rules and norms, rather than bilateral power politics, still drive the international trading system.

Korea must squarely face the challenges of trading globally. To do so, the country must address its lingering lack of integration with world capital markets. It will become increasingly difficult for Korea to attract resources and simultaneously increase the share of world trade in a more competitive world. To succeed, Korea must maintain sound macroeconomic management, and it must develop exchange-rate and capital-control regimes that build strong links with the global market.

Regional integration arrangements have become very popular in world trade, influencing more than 40 percent of international trade flows in 1992.[4] This figure has probably surpassed the 50 percent mark by now, with the implementation of the North American Free Trade Agreement (NAFTA), as well as the "widening" of the European community through preferential trade arrangements between western Europe and the former socialist economies. Many non-NAFTA and non-EU countries, including Korea, may be adversely affected by these developments in the long run. These new regional arrangements may cause diversion of trade and capital, which will then result in shrinking market share and higher capital cost for those developing countries that are left out of the arrangements.

Under NAFTA, U.S. firms hope to turn Mexico into the same kind of export platform that Southeast Asia provides for Japan. If successful, this will potentially create much stronger competition against Asia in the world trade arena. U.S. producers of labor-intensive goods located in Asia may be tempted to relocate to Mexico.

Not all regionalization trends are worrisome to Korea, as we see in the increasing consolidation of investment and trade within Asia. In 1991, Asia surpassed the United States as Japan's largest export destination. By 1993, Japan's trade surplus with the region had swelled to outstrip its surplus with the United States. Records should show that in 1994, for the first time, the level of new Japanese FDI in Asia was greater than its new FDI in the United States. In 1993, Asia overtook Europe as the second most important destination of Japanese bank loans. Although Japan may be indifferent about the issue of "hard" regionalization of Asia, it is actively creating "soft" regionalization based on expansion of its financial power and production bases throughout East Asia.[5]

All of the aforementioned trends will transform Korea's technology relationship from one of importing from Japan, the United States, and Europe to one of exporting its own technology to less developed trading partners in the Asia Pacific region; this will eventually put Korea in competition with the United States, Japan, and Europe.

PATTERNS OF FOREIGN DIRECT INVESTMENT

The shift in Korea's technology relationships with the industrial powers are closely related to changing patterns of FDI. Among the changes that Korea faces, four patterns stand out: (1) an increase of FDI to developing countries, in general, and those to Korea, in particular; (2) a growing trend in intra-East

Asian FDI flows; (3) the increasing importance of overseas Chinese as a source of intra-East Asian FDI flow; and (4) the importance of China as the main destination of such capital flow.

The inflows of FDI to developing countries are quite highly concentrated. According to data from the 1980s, more than half of all FDI flows to developing countries went to just ten countries.[6] In 1993, East Asia and Latin America received U.S.$66 billion, more than 80 percent of all FDI sent to developing economies. China, Malaysia, Indonesia, and Thailand were the major recipients in East Asia.

FDI often yields benefits above and beyond providing capital. When well negotiated, it can facilitate technology transfer and improve acquisition of management know-how.[7] For instance, Endogenous Growth theorists, arguing that ideas are as important as capital and labor inputs, have tried to demonstrate how developing human capital can accelerate the growth rate.[8] A new idea introduced in one industry by FDI projects may spill over to other industries nationwide. Once the mechanisms for disseminating these foreign-originated ideas are firmly established in a nation, well-negotiated FDIs could significantly improve national economic development and growth (see Chapter 13).

The large volume of incoming FDIs is matched by the outward investments by Korea and the other East Asian NIEs, which have been growing at a remarkable rate in the past few years. In 1986, Japan had accounted for 38 percent of total FDI in Southeast Asia, compared to 23 percent from the NIEs. In 1990, the East Asian NIEs as a group surpassed Japan as the largest investor in Southeast Asia. The shares of Japan and the NIEs in total FDI in Southeast Asia were 22 percent and 27 percent, respectively. This trend of faster growth in NIEs-originated FDI should continue.

Korea's outward FDI nearly doubled between 1993 and 1994, from U.S.$1.25 billion to U.S.$2.3 billion. China and Vietnam became the hottest destinations for Korea's future FDI. Korean investment in China, which Korea started only in 1989, already amounted to U.S.$309 million by 1993. Several different factors contributed to this growth. First, the Korean government had eliminated the rules limiting the number of companies in any industry that can invest in a particular country. Second and more important, the strong won and rising wages in Korea have made production in those other countries more profitable. Therefore, small, low-end, light industrial firms engaged in the garment, toy, and footwear industries have started relocating overseas in search of cheap labor. (In 1993, 81% of South Korean overseas investment was made by small- and medium-size companies, up from 78.8% in 1992. They accounted for less than 3% of total outward investment before 1985 and about 12% as of June 1990.) Third, major changes in international market access spurred the FDI outflow. With rising protectionism in Europe and North America, investing in Southeast Asia has helped Korea bypass trade restrictions and retain GSP benefits. Asia accounted for 46 percent of the total

Korean outward investment in 1994, compared to 24.5 percent toward North America. Finally, Korea has directed some of its FDI toward the United States to gain access to the newest, most promising technologies.

Korea must use its FDI strategically to continue to build its technology base, especially in light of China's development of its economic zone, broadly known as the "Golden Triangle." With the gradual opening of the Chinese mainland, the economies of Taiwan, Hong Kong, and China's Guangdong and Fujian provinces have been integrated into a de facto regional economy. Together the triangle is home to more than 130 million people, commanding a gross domestic product of U.S.$320 billion. Economic activities in the triangle are more dynamic and rapid than in any other area in Asia, changing the basic profiles of the three economies. Investment from Taiwan and Hong Kong has provided the capital, manufacturing experience, technology, market access, and much needed foreign exchange necessary to spur China's development. At the same time, Taiwan has shifted away from low-cost, labor-intensive production, and toward the manufacturing of advanced-technology products with a focus on electronics and other high-technology engineering. Finally, impressive growth in China's eastern provinces and cities is being propelled by private entrepreneurs from Hong Kong, Singapore, and Taiwan who use their connections in China.

Chinese businesspeople living outside the mainland have mobilized world-class talent to assist in S&T development efforts in other parts of Asia. The Industrial Technology Research Institute in Hsinchu, Taiwan, and its affiliated entities in electronics (which employ many overseas Chinese engineers and managers) act as the engine for the promotion of the electronics industry in Taiwan (see Chapter 10). A major molecular biology laboratory in Singapore, again staffed mostly with and advised by overseas Chinese scientists, illustrates Singapore's strategic move toward establishing a foothold in the biotechnology industry. Korea must be prepared to link up with these developing Chinese capabilities, based on its own internal scientific and technical achievements.

INTERNATIONAL PROTECTION OF INTELLECTUAL PROPERTY RIGHTS

The growing importance of technological innovation demands that Korea provide better protection of its IPRs. Korea needs to foster indigenous technology development and abide by the increasingly strict international rules, while assuring that increased IPR protection does not limit the spillover of foreign technology.

International IPRs have a firm base in WTO agreements, which cover both TRIPs and TRIMs. These TRIPs and TRIMs agreements will significantly affect both global and domestic investment and technology flows and the promotion of economic development in Korea and elsewhere. Current WTO efforts include the adoption of the national treatment and the MFN treatment principles, together with the extended coverage of IPRs to patents, trademarks, industrial designs, computer software, databases, computer chip design, broadcasting materials, music, and other forms of art. In addition, WTO's work strengthens the international regulations for various forms of patents, royalty agreements, trademarks, specification of place of origin for IPRs, and other important details for protecting property.

These types of increased protection for intellectual property should lead to more innovations and increased economic activity, including greater trade, FDI, and flows of technology. Legal protection of intellectual property should provide a necessary incentive for Korea to invest resources in technological innovation and offer the security needed for new technology development and trade. Conversely, inadequate levels of IPR protection would discourage investment and technology flows. Investment in and diffusion of high-technology activities crucially depend on effective IPRs.

Many developing countries have very weak protection for intellectual property or are lax in enforcing the protection that does exist. Under the WTO system, such practices can weaken their access to foreign technologies. An inadequate intellectual property protection system may deter local innovation as the process of industrialization deepens. This point has been supported by several empirical studies, including that of Edwin Mansfield in 1994.[9] Over the long term, Korea will benefit greatly from more stringent enforcement of universally accepted IPRs regulation. Doing so will guarantee that they will be well protected. Such incentives and guarantees are what Korea needs now.

ASSESSING THE POLITICAL CLIMATE FOR SETTING INDUSTRIAL AND ENVIRONMENTAL STANDARDS

Industry standards can play a critical role in shaping market structure and determining who gets to exercise market power, to limit market entry, and to extract rents.[10] Industrial standards matter when different brands have to share common parts or common inputs, when government regulations are necessary to prevent market failures, or under both conditions. Thus, industrial standards matter in virtually all markets. They have recently gained more importance for four reasons: (1) the increasingly integrated world market, which seems to be threatening national control; (2) an increased awareness among nations about how their competitive strength compares to other countries; (3) the growth of fierce competition within information industries; and (4) the increase in environmental concern.

Sometimes a country's government can set specific industrial standards that keep overseas players out of its domestic market. This policy can backfire in industries where the pace of worldwide technological innovation is rapid. Japan has often been accused of practicing this in the form of Nontariff Barriers (NTBs). Since governments do exercise the power to set standards, either autonomously or under political pressure from their constituents, it is important to harmonize their standards both regionally and globally.

Because of its fierce competition in global high-technology markets, Korea does not possess the market scope or power to set global standards. Thus, the best standard-setting strategy for Korean innovators should entail setting up strategic alliances with the global leaders in related markets. In the long term, the technical superiority of Korean firms will eventually enable them to set standards that protect their lead.

With regard to environmental standards, Korea needs to acquire flexibility in manufacturing to meet fluctuating standards in different parts of the world market. Regional arrangements in Europe, North America, and other parts of the world can create competitive barriers by either raising or lowering standards, depending on the individual situation. For example, in the industries where it is difficult to relocate production and only a small number of producers exist, they are likely to team up to raise the standards and thus limit additional market entries. In contrast, for industries where producers are plentiful and can easily relocate, governments may try to compete with each other for more FDI inflow by encouraging lower standards.[11]

In order to compete under all of these conditions in different regions of the world, Korean producers need flexibility in manufacturing. Korean firms have already shown such capacity to innovate quickly in response to changing standards. For example, Korean companies were able to develop refrigerants and solvents that did not contain chlorofluorocarbons (CFCs) after their production was curtailed by the Montreal protocols.

R&D CONSORTIA AND STRATEGIC ALLIANCES

R&D consortia among firms have been used widely in European countries since the turn of the century. They have been proven to reduce risks and costs involved with developing technology and expediting its use. More recently, they have been most useful in Japan with the Very-Large-Scale Integration consortium and the fifth-generation computer consortium. Bolstered by Japan's successful entry into the world chip markets, the United States also enacted the Cooperative Research Act in 1984.

Unlike those in the United States and Europe, the Japanese R&D consortia have taken up competitive technologies, not science, and leveraged competition among the participating firms by assigning separate parallel tasks to develop slightly different prototypes. The proactive role of the Ministry of International Trade and Industry (MITI) has been most important (see Chapter 9). MITI has long acted as the facilitator of R&D consortia, providing funding and technical support using government laboratories, as well as choosing and creating harmony between corporate members of the consortia.[12]

Korea applied the lessons from other countries' experiences with consortia, especially in its telecommunications industry development. The Korean government has suffered from coordination problems and conflicts in this industry. However, consortia of small and medium enterprises should be encouraged, since they may be helpful for balancing the power of the chaebols and giving smaller firms a less costly source of technical assistance.

Besides R&D consortia, Korea must develop strategic interfirm alliances, which enable companies to quickly gain access to skills, technology, markets, supplies, and other resources. Unlike cross-border acquisitions, cross-border alliances can work well for moving into new or related businesses. In strategic alliances, flexibility, trust, and complementary assets are the three keys to success.

The collaboration between Japan's NEC Corporation and Korea's Samsung Electronics entailed a fundamental restructuring of the global semiconductor business, uniting the most powerful forces in this sector. In other alliances, Daewoo Electronics entered into an agreement with Sony for technical cooperation in broadcasting equipment, while Hyundai and Samsung have teamed up with Nintendo and Sega, respectively, in multimedia software. In automobiles, Kia Motors agreed with Mazda to jointly develop deluxe cars, complementing their existing equity and other relations.

In July 1992, Korea's two electronics giants, Samsung and LG (formerly known as Lucky Goldstar), joined hands for the first time to share their patented technology. Such technological alliances, although common in other countries, particularly in Japan, had never been formed before in Korea. This pattern of sharing local technology through industrial collaboration among companies in common fields can strengthen Korea's domestic technological capabilities in the future. Alliances with foreign firms—when Korea has technology to trade and the conditions of trust prevail—will provide a way to continue to gain access to foreign technology, even from competitors.

DOMESTIC IMPERATIVES FOR INNOVATION

At the micro-level of S&T development, Korea needs to address a few basic internal issues that will play critical roles in the country's capacity to innovate. First, it must broaden its domestic basic science research while reaching out to new international partners who can teach and share their pathbreaking discoveries.

Second, Korea must ensure ways to encourage technological development in areas that are not covered by national projects. Although innovators tend to do well under concentrated government support, this type of development is no longer viable. The range of crucial technologies is too broad, while the government is losing its capacity to provide concentrated support because of the growing power of the Korean private sector and increasing pressure to harmonize with new international standards.

Third, the government must do what it can to encourage innovations by the numerous small- and medium-size firms. The new pattern of international competition requires flexibility and rapid response. Small and medium firms are inherently well suited for such flexibility and responsiveness, yet they comprise one of the weakest sectors of the Korean economy. New, small firms are not being created at an adequate rate, and too few have advanced technical capabilities (see Chapter 4).

Fourth, Korea has to find ways to prevent its chaebols from exercising their predatory market power to strangle the potential of small firms. Furthermore, it needs to ensure that chaebols direct their enormous economic and human resources toward technological and marketing innovations.

Fifth, chaebols must decentralize their internal structure and operations in order to encourage autonomous and spontaneous innovation from below.

CONCLUSION

As it develops its ambitious plans for gaining a level of economic performance comparable to the industrial societies that comprise the G-7, Korea is chasing a moving target. The international environment in which Korea must now compete is itself changing rapidly, even as Korea struggles to take the final steps of its transition from a government-led economy based on low costs, hard work, and imported technology. Some of these changes, such as the growing importance of the international trading system, are "good news, bad news" stories for Korea. As an emerging economy, Korea senses the need to cling to tools that it has used in the past to regulate the path to development: the ability to regulate FDI and market access, continued government influence over financial institutions, and flexibility on the environmental and labor regulations that the industrialized nations expect Korea to respect. On the other hand, Korea stands to benefit greatly from falling tariffs and more open markets, the ability to invest in China and Vietnam, and industrial alliances that it can negotiate with Japanese and North American firms.

The most dramatic and important change in the international scene for Korea is probably the opening up of China and other Asian states to Korean investment. This has provided a market for Korean technology in nations other than those from which the core technologies were originally imported. This trend should make it easier for Korea to continue its access to advanced technology, enabling it to develop alliances with and direct investments in U.S. and Japanese firms, while Korea exports products based on its own technology to the rest of Asia.

The problem with Korea's transitional status is one of timing and the inevitable fact that some sectors of the Korean economy will advance more rapidly than others. Korea cannot be said to be either a developed or a developing economy; it is both. But its policy position must be grounded on the future, not the past. This involves taking some risks, including betting on the continuation of its exceptional growth rate, which continues to outpace Japan, the United States, and Europe. This places even more emphasis, then, on the importance of building a strong technology base for indigenous economic development, on creating the conditions for a high innovation rate, and on the liberation of Korean business and technical organizations from outdated bureaucratic controls.

NOTES

1. Benign regionalism refers mainly to the European Community (EC) Common Market before it became too introverted. In the place of benign regionalism, a new concept called "open regionalism" is being promoted by the leaders of the Asia Pacific Economic Cooperation Forum (APEC). An open regionalism is one that increases "trade creation" without "trade diversion." See the Eminent Persons Group, *A Vision for APEC* (Singapore: Asia Pacific Economic Cooperation Forum, 1993). "Aggressive unilateralism" comes from the title of a book by Jagdish Bhagwati and Hugh T. Patrick (*Aggressive Unilateralism: America's 301 Trade Policy and the World Trading System* [Ann Arbor: University of Michigan Press, 1990]). It refers to the invocation of Section 301 of the U.S. Trade and Tariff Act to make unilateral demands or threats of retaliatory measures, especially involving reducing existing trade access to the U.S. market. This is done to obtain trade concessions by other trading partners.

2. MFN treatment refers to Most Favored Nation treatment. Under this policy, once a preferential tariff or other trade related treatment is established for one country, such treatment applies to all other countries. GSP means Generalized System of Preferences, the system that separates developing countries for treatment in trade with terms that are better than those for the developed countries. Thus, MFN-based GSP treatment means that all developing countries are equally getting preferential treatment in trade, and this treatment is better than that for the developed countries.

3. For discussions on various options the region can take in dealing with regionalism and multilateralism, see Soogil Young, "Globalism and Regionalism: Complements or Competitors?" in *Pacific Dynamism and the International Economic System*, ed. C. Fred Bergsten and Marcus Noland (Washington, D.C.: Institute for International Economics, 1993); and Yung-Woo Chun, "Regionalism and Multilateralism: A Strategy for East Asia," Institute Reports, East Asian Institute, Columbia University, New York, July 1994.

4. Carlos A. Primo Braga and Alexander Yeats, "How Multilateral Trading Arrangements May Affect the Post–Uruguay Round World," policy research working paper (Washington, D.C.: World Bank, 1992).

5. See Jefferey Frankel and Miles Kahler, eds., *Regionalism and Rivalry* (Chicago: University of Chicago Press, 1993), 3.

6. Braga and Yeats, "Multilateral Trading Arrangements."

7. The debate about whether an incoming FDI affects the host economy positively or negatively has continued for several decades, with neoclassical advocates of FDI opposing dependency theorists. This is still unresolved, partly due to the complexity of the issue. There are so many political, economic, social, and historical variables that affect the answer to the question. For the history of the debate and the variables on the bargaining side, see Theodore Moran, ed., *Investing in Development* (Washington, D.C.: Overseas Development Council, 1986), and idem, *The Impact of Trade-Related Investment Measures on Trade and Development* (New York: United Nations,

1991). For the variables on the sociopolitical and historical side, see Stephen Haggard, *Pathways from the Periphery* (Ithaca, N.Y.: Cornell University Press, 1990). Haggard addresses why East Asia benefited greatly from FDI and produced rapid economic growth, while Latin America did not produce a similar result despite the large size of FDI it received.

8. See Paul Romer, "Idea Gaps and Object Gaps in Economic Development," *Journal of Monetary Economics* 32 (1993): 543–573.

9. See Edwin Mansfield, "Intellectual Property Protection, Foreign Direct Investment, and Technology Transfer," International Finance Corporation (IFC) Discussion Paper No. 19, 1994.

10. Such examples abound. Consider VHS versus Beta, IBM versus Apple, digital versus analog technologies for high-definition television, Intel versus everyone else in computer chips, and Microsoft versus everyone else in personal computer software.

11. This idea of the condition for more restriction or more laxity had first been presented by Dale Murphy in his dissertation in progress at MIT's political science department.

12. For a discussion on the difference in the character of R&D consortia in Japan and the United States, see Gerald J. Hane, "The Real Lessons of Japanese Research Consortia," *Issues in Science and Technology* 10 (Winter 1993–1994): 56–62.

Chapter Four

THE INNOVATION TRIANGLE
Stimulating Innovation in
Private and Public Enterprises

Kee-Young Kim and Boong-Kyu Lee

What do Oleg Cassini, Christian Dior, Pierre Cardin, Pontiac, Caterpillar, General Electric, Northern Telecom, Mita, Acura, Sharp, and Toshiba have in common? These are all but a sample of the brand names whose products are supplied by a single Korean chaebol, the Daewoo Group.[1] From fashion to fighter jets, toothpaste to tankers, potato chips to computer chips, the breadth and range of the product spectrum for the Korean chaebols are truly astonishing. Korean firms are number one in world market share in such areas as dynamic random access memory (DRAM) semiconductors and container vessels; near the top in steel, videocassette recorders (VCRs), microwave ovens, and shoe sales; and respectable in countless other areas. In fact, Korea's automobile companies were among the very few global manufacturers whose domestic *and* foreign sales showed double-digit growth in 1993. So why is stimulating innovation in Korean public and private firms an issue?

The problem is that for each car made, 30 percent of the total technology cost is paid out in royalties to the foreign producers that provide the critical technologies. For each camcorder, 50 percent of the total technology cost; for each DRAM semiconductor made, 30 percent of the total technology cost; and for each notebook computer, 75 percent of the total technology cost is paid out in foreign royalties.[2] The average research and development (R&D) investment of Korea's so-called "Big Three" automobile producers—Hyundai, Kia Motors, and Daewoo—is a mere 6.2 percent of the U.S. Big Three (General Motors [GM], Ford, Chrysler) and 10.7 percent of the top three Japanese firms (Toyota, Nissan, Honda).[3] Moreover, Korean products are no longer cost competitive vis-à-vis their Chinese and Southeast Asian competitors. Labor costs, which have almost quadrupled during the period since 1989 without concomitant productivity gains, are not the only reason. Company financing costs are still at the double-digit rate, while transportation costs are skyrocketing because of underfunded investment in social overhead capital in recent years.

Korean products also suffer from a significant quality and image gap when compared to their Triad rivals (the world-dominating economic regions, that is, the United States, Europe, and Japan). Indeed, a Korean advertising agency has found that in the U.S. consumer electronics market, Korean products sell for a discount of up to 20 to 30 percent off average prices, while Japanese products enjoy a similar premium.[4] The combined assault from the cost, quality, and brand-name ends of the product spectrum are squeezing the Korean firms out of the global market.[5] Furthermore, with the passage of the Uruguay Round of the General Agreement on Tariffs and Trade (GATT) talks, Korea's chaebols can no longer count on a protected domestic market to make up for their razor-thin margins abroad. Korea's markets must be as open as those to which its firms wish to sell. On the other hand, the growth of regional trade blocs, including the formation of the European Community (EC) in 1992 and the signing of the North American Free Trade Agreement (NAFTA) in 1993, has formalized intraregion production requirements that penalize exports as a mode of foreign sales.

In the face of these negative trends, there is a growing consensus among Korea's corporate and bureaucratic circles that technology is the only way to restore Korea's competitive edge in global markets. Indeed, in various forums, Korea's President Kim Young-Sam has equated technology development with patriotism and has called science and technology (S&T) "the key to solving all of our socio-economic problems."[6] Yet, as examined in earlier chapters, the historical evolution of Korea's industrialization has imbued a production-oriented mentality among corporate managers, which, combined with a heavy-handed bureaucratic tradition, has hampered and discouraged Korea's technological innovation efforts.

This chapter explores how the Korean government can improve competitiveness through understanding the "innovation triangle," the interplay between technology, market conditions, and government policy. Our recommendations follow from our conclusion that the government should adopt an indirect policy posture that emphasizes the role of market competition as the primary driver of technological innovation. This new emphasis on market competition is an appropriate response to the growing trend toward liberalization of global trade.

TECHNOLOGY IN A DEVELOPING COUNTRY CONTEXT: A THEORETICAL FRAMEWORK

Technology-Development Process

In recent research sponsored by the World Bank, Kee-Young Kim and colleagues outlined five phases that Korea and other developing countries must undergo to improve their technological infrastructure.[7] The first phase consists of the import and implementation of foreign technologies. The major task of this phase is to get to the "know-what" as it is embodied in the technology. This is followed by the assimilation and reverse engineering phase. The major task here is the "know-how," particularly on the process technology side for the technology in question.

The third phase and fourth phase cover the "know-why" part of the technology-development process. During the third phase, countries modify technology to better serve local and international markets by introducing product differentiation strategies. Firms once dependent wholly on original equipment manufacturer (OEM) purchases thus attempt to grow out of their dependencies in marketing, design, R&D, and distribution.

Up to the third stage of the process, firms remain passive receivers of technological services. Public entities, in the third stage, begin to develop technology support institutions (TSIs), which bring together a wide range of institutions that support technical change and industrial and technological development through informational, scientific, technical, and standardization cooperation. TSIs include fully and partially government-funded research institutions, universities, economy-wide or industrywide institutions (e.g., venture capital firms), and standards-enforcement agencies. In the early stages of technological development, TSIs are primarily public in nature. Therefore, the government typically determines the content and quality as well as the planning and coordination of TSI–firm exchanges. Most local TSI activity at this stage is targeted for the small- and medium-size enterprises (SMEs), and large companies do not seek extracorporate technical support.

The fourth stage is characterized by the burgeoning of private TSIs, such as corporate R&D labs, and other types of increased high-technology activities. The importance of R&D in the frontier areas of technology and applied science is recognized. As the technological capabilities of the corporate sector develop, its technology requirements become more demanding. Embryonic R&D laboratories begin to be formed. Consequently, the R&D capabilities of firms reach a level significant enough to allow more of a two-way interaction between TSIs and firms. The exchange relationship is more collaborative.

Firms take the initiative in sponsoring and proposing new research projects, including joint information exchanges and research partnerships that can complement their technological needs. The role of government as the primary TSI shrinks as alternative TSIs, such as universities and foreign strategic collaborators, gain importance.

During the fifth phase, firms become technologically more confident and deepen their R&D activities, carry out collaborative and strategic research activities with foreign TSIs, and even begin the export of technologies to other developing countries.[8] The distinctiveness of these five stages tells us that the Korean government must determine the general status of technology development before it forms its policies for stimulating innovation. The five phases show that innovation stimulation results from a dynamic interaction between the technology, market conditions, and, in the case of developing countries, government policies. These three factors form the points of the "innovation triangle."

The Innovation Triangle: Technology Push, Market Pull, and Government Policies

Technology push is a broad concept encompassing the firms' perception of the technological pressures on them and the current level of their own technological abilities. *Market pull* refers to the strategic intention of companies to meet market competition. Finally, *government policies* induce the firms to develop technological capabilities through various incentive and support policies.

Out of the three forces, the first two determine the types of relationships formed between the government and other TSIs, on the one hand, and firms, on the other. The proper role of government can thus be found by examining the interactions among and between the technology and market factors.

As seen in Figure 4.1, the lower the market competition and technology capability, the greater is the need for TSIs and firms to form one-way, supportive relations that are initiated by TSIs. Technological-push forces motivate firms to improve their capabilities along the technological development process. The level of firm capabilities and competencies, in turn, determine the requirements of service and types of interaction required from the TSIs. If a company is not motivated or technologically able to develop the technology required, it most likely will not seek any services from TSIs.

Market competition is also an important force that induces firms to enhance their technology capabilities. With no competitive threats, a closed or monopolized industry will not be motivated to produce new products or technologies. Competition spurs innovation as a survival response to meet challenges and opportunities posed by new industry entrants.

Not surprising, in cases of high competition and high technology capability, firms are eager to receive as much support and service as possible through

Figure 4.1
Types of TSI/Government–Firm Relations

High

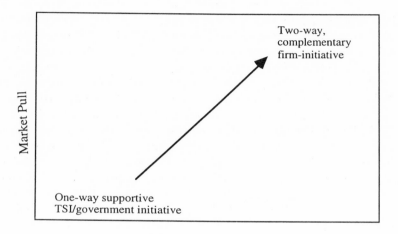

Low   Technology Push   High

Source: Kee-Young Kim, "Policies and Institutions for Industrial and Technological Development: A Korea Study," *World Bank Conference Paper,* Yonsei University, Seoul, 1994.

active cooperative R&D efforts with external TSIs. In this situation, the prevailing relationship between TSIs and firms is transformed into a two-way, complementary one.

Thus, as the innovation triangle matures, the role of government follows a trajectory from benefactor and source of technology guidance to equal partner and collaborator. As is further developed later in this chapter, we believe that Korean firms, especially the largest ones, are at a stage of high market competition and high technological capability. Therefore, the time for one-way support and direction from government for these firms has passed. Government must change from proactive to reactive incentive policies, moving from intervention and subsidization to regulation and environmental and consumer protection. SMEs still require more direct services.

Proaction–Reaction

Nascent industries and developing countries in general must develop policies creating a gradual transition from proactive to reactive support of firms and industries. This means that policy support should initially be formulated to first promote growth and self-sufficient competitiveness. Firms within industries can be supported through programs that reduce competition and provide for a rich environment. When these firms and industries have grown in size and sophistication, competition may be induced and subsidized resources taken away. Trade barriers that had previously provided protection may be taken down to allow competition within local markets. These latter policies can be thought of as reactive in nature. By transitioning from proactive to reactive policies over the development of an industry, the government can create incentives to induce firms to climb the technological ladder.

Proactive support relies on direct intervention to promote technological capabilities and innovation, thus decreasing the risk involved in venturing into areas where production functions are unknown. Such support is especially important during the inception and incubation phases of firm and industrial development. Policymakers may provide financial and tax incentives for trade, R&D, and training as well as noncompetitive procurement-based subsidies and support to industry. Such policies also lower the cost of importing the inputs or technology necessary for the industry in question. Along with scientific and technological support, human resource support may also be extended. At the same time, the state may raise barriers against the importation of the finished products of the targeted industry. The resulting industrial structure may tolerate monopolisitic and noncompetitive oligopolistic conditions to concentrate scarce resources and promote growth of domestic firms. Industrial sectors may even be carved out and allocated between a few privileged firms. In many respects, proaction provides a resource-rich environment for nourishing targeted firms and industries. These factors promote a pull condition for the inducement of coveted foreign technologies and practices for the targeted industry.

When the pertinent firms and industries become fairly well developed, policy support should generally turn indirect and reactive in nature. Firms and industries, as well as their technologies, are now expected to have reached international competitiveness and achieved self-reliance. Proactive and direct support may linger in these latter stages, but these will be relegated to those industries and sectors that have yet to reach competitive maturity, especially SMEs. Reactive policies take away much of the resources provided under previous proactive policies. This increases the costs and risks of doing business, forcing the firms to compete for scarce resources. High rates of innovative activities and performance are induced by firms scurrying to sustain a profitable niche in the newly competitive industrial structure.

Under a reactive policy, as the targeted industry gains competitiveness, import barriers are lowered and eventually removed. Other forms of protectionism, including those aimed at potential domestic entrants, may also be stopped. Reactive policies may eliminate tax and other financial subsidies, provide standards to which firms must conform, have competitive bidding for procurement contracts, and promote exports. The strengthening of export, design, manufacture, and environmental-control performance standards are other types of reactive policy instruments for the promotion of technology-innovation efforts. In addition, the required localization ratio may be increased to induce greater levels of indigenous technology development, while the liberalization rate for production or technology inputs may be increased to put competitive pressures on the local producers. Likewise, a more balanced growth of the industry may be promoted, with an added emphasis on the enforcement of fair trade and competition. This is achieved by strengthening the government's role as a regulator while weakening its interventionist tendencies.

Monopolies and noncompetitive oligopolies are no longer tolerated within reactive policies. In fact, policies that actively promote the entry of new and innovative firms and support the growth of small- and medium-size firms are introduced, creating market liberalization and increasing the presence of multinationals in the domestic market. In time, full liberalization of the market may result when firms and industries reach global competitiveness. By that time, traditional proactive policies may be more of an inhibitor than a promoter of innovation. Government investments should then be focused on science and engineering knowledge as well as human resource development. For a more comprehensive depiction of the ideas in this section, refer to Table 4.1.

Supply–Demand

The proactive–reactive conception can be enriched by adding supply and demand insights from Charles P. Kindleberger and Bruce Herrick, Won-Yong Lee, and Seong-Jae Yu.[9] Kindleberger and Herrick outlined several preconditions for the implementation of new structures for sharing innovative know-how: (1) innovator awareness of the potential for innovation, (2) optimism that innovation improves conditions, (3) willingness to accept associated risks, (4) ability to finance the innovation, and (5) availability of the necessary materials. Toward these ends, the state must design sectoral policies to effect the *supply* for the first, second, and fourth preconditions and *demand* of the third precondition. A successful combination of these supply–demand policies can create or shift comparative advantage to create a niche for the domestic economy in the international division of labor.

These supply and demand policies can be utilized under both proactive and reactive conditions.[10] Supply-side sectoral policies, for example, can develop the infrastructural requirements of a specific industry. The Korean government has relied heavily on government sponsorship of venture capital firms; commercial investment; selective university research; and national institutes for information, standards, education, and basic and applied research.[11] Infrastructure policies are generally created to support the development of industry by encouraging private-sector investment in R&D and technical capabilities. These sectoral policies have been directed at the training of technology-oriented

Table 4.1
Stage-Dependent National Innovation Framework

Time	1960s	1970s	1980s/1990s
Innovating Forces	Proaction-centered		Reaction-centered
Trade Environment	Market protection: Restriction on foreign Capital & products	Limited/selective Liberalization: Conditional imports	Full liberalization: Selective protection
Comparative Advantage	Labor	Mass production	Innovation
Industrial Structure	Monopolistic growth/ Oligopolistic diversification	Limited competition Conglomeration	Highly competitive Keiretsulization
Foreign Technology	Turnkey projects/	Foreign licensing	FDI/foreign licensing
Transfer Mode	FDI		
Industrial Policies	Import substitution/ export promotion National firms/ cross-investments	Production differentiation Rationalization/ competition	Innovation Small and medium-size firms
Industrial Policy Tools	Interventionist/ subsidies-centered	Interventionist/ regulative	Regulative environmental and consumer protection
Technology-Development Process	Import/ assimilation	Reverse engineering/ modification	Indigenous R&D
Firm Strategy	Growth/diversification	Conglomeration	Keiretsulization
Technology Policies	Generous subsidies Firm-specific	Industry-specific	R&D support only Project-specific
Firm-TSI Interaction	One-way flow via contract R&D	Two-way flow via joint R&D	Firm-initiated

Source: Kee-Young Kim, "Policies and Institutions for Industrial and Technological De-velopment: A Korea Study," *World Bank Conference Paper,* Yonsei University, Seoul, 1994.

personnel, the dissemination of technical knowledge to designated industries, and the creation of favorable R&D investment climates.

Supply-side policies also encourage the transfer of technology. Korean examples include the Development Promotion Act, the Foreign Capital In-ducement Act, and the Industrial Site Development Law.[12] Supply-side poli-cies—which are designed to reduce high risk, costs, and uncertainty—are effective in spurring the development of a knowledge base.

Demand-side policy instruments now in place in Korea include government procurements, industrial policies to increase competition, infant industry protection, and preferential financing offered to the purchasers of designated locally developed goods.[13] Whereas supply-side policies are infrastructural in nature and are often targeted at the entire economy, demand-side policies are more piecemeal, directed primarily at a particular industry. They are designed to induce the private sector to invest in R&D and increase their technology commercialization capability by creating a market for these potential innovators.[14]

Demand-side policies are more dynamic than supply-side counterparts because they are timed to encourage the development of a particular industry or technology. Exploiting such time-sensitive policies is essential for Korea to advance in industries or technologies that are in the declining stage of their life cycles in the more advanced countries. Timely procurement and infant policies can heighten potential profits, quickly solidifying the place of a key industry or technology. Supply-side policies help indirectly with subsidies and cheap funds, but demand-side policies can focus the attention of the entrepreneurs because of immediate positive impacts on the company's bottom line.

The present-day innovation triangle conditions for Korea, coupled with various changes in the international environment, call for a change in the Korean government's approach to government–firm activities to stimulate innovation and technology. A brief historical examination of Korean industrial technology development will enable us to make specific observations about Korea's industrial structure, leading us to make specific policy recommendations.

THE BEST PATTERN OF TECHNOLOGY DEVELOPMENT IN KOREA

In the process of their successful growth, Korean firms developed a standardized formula to acquire the technology they needed. They utilized the protectionist policies of the government as a wall within which to grow without threat from superior foreign competition. Without an indigenous technological backlog on which to rely, local companies had no choice but to look abroad for the technologies they needed.

Once the foreign technology was adopted into manufactured products, the Korean government provided incentives for adapting and improving the technology by imposing stringent export performance targets as a condition for access to the state-controlled financial system. In other words, the products had to be sufficiently advanced to compete on the world market. When certain levels of indigenous scientific and engineering capabilities were reached, the Korean government gradually relaxed these protective walls. Imported production and product-design technologies were quickly diffused within the country, accompanied by internal competition to improve the technologies and develop products. This process also, to a limited extent, advanced research and innovation.

This cycle is not unique to Korea. The early development of the Japanese automobile industry, for instance, from kit assembly to own-model production, bears many similarities to the Korean story; in fact, it may have been a model that Korean firms emulated. But the Japanese story differs with respect to the development of innovation.[15] The many innovations created by the Japanese industry (e.g., just-in-time production processes and lean production techniques) have signified the maturity of its technology-development process. The agenda for Korea lies in figuring out how to follow the Japanese example and move on to innovation.

In contrast to Japan, the concept of management in Korea has been historically defined largely in terms of production. One basis for Korea's technology development was the management of OEM sales. OEM sales provided Korean firms with a safe and relatively riskless way to quickly improve its production capabilities as well as to guarantee revenues. The OEM buyer—be it Sears, JCPenney, or Pontiac—supplied the required technology and equipment and often arranged financing for the funds needed for investment in the production facilities. Therefore, once a Korean firm secured a "buyer," its only concern was production at the lowest possible cost. Capital constraints notwithstanding, R&D was an extravagance that was neither necessary nor particularly helpful for the type of business in which the typical Korean firm engaged. Indeed, any unauthorized product modifications could result in rejection of the shipment by the foreign buyer. The government assisted by keeping manufacturing costs low through suppressing organization of labor into a collective bargaining entity.

The use of marketing under the OEM-based strategy was largely limited to the initial securing of the OEM order. A good marketing manager was one who traveled around the globe and picked up as many orders as possible. The foreign buyer did the actual "selling" of the product, including market development, advertising, and brand cultivation.

Under the OEM-driven business model, R&D for the creation of new products was also unnecessary for most firms. As a result, radical innovation was largely absent. A manager of a major Korean electronics concern expresses the rationale (Table 4.2):

What does it matter if we develop, like our local competitor has announced, a new laser disc standard that greatly increases sound fidelity and video capacity over the present version? Unless our foreign competitors, as well as the music software producers, accept our standard, it is useless. And since when did the Sonys and Phillips of the world ever follow the lead of a Korean firm? The several million dollars put into research becomes worthless.[16]

Korean firms have pursued incremental and process innovation quite actively and successfully, since they were competing primarily in terms of lowering total production costs. Several studies have shown production management to be one of the few functional areas in which Korea has maintained some measure of global competitiveness.[17]

Table 4.2
Reasons for Low R&D Investment Cited by Korean Firms

Factors Mentioned as Reasons for Low R&D Investment	Share (%)
1. Difficulty in ensuring sales	20.48
2. Low business prospects	17.62
3. Automated production facility investment has priority	17.38
4. Capital constraints	16.67
5. Low probability of development success	11.90
6. Not enough government policy incentives	10.48
7. Top management does not recognize the importance of R&D	5.47

Source: Federation of Korean Industries, "Technology Innovation and Industrial Policy,"
Seminar proceedings, Seoul, November 19, 1993.

Since Korea's labor costs skyrocketed in the past several years, the country as a whole is losing its attractiveness for OEM. The role of the OEM base has been assumed by China and Southeast Asian nations, and Korean firms have lost many of their traditional markets.

This situation leaves Korean firms in a difficult situation. Given their historical reliance on OEM sales, Korean firms are lagging behind in developing a brand identity of their own and in developing their own marketing channels. Most important, they have lost their source of technology, while failing to replace imported technology with its own technological innovations. All these trends are only aggravated by the increased protectionism of the advanced countries. Chastened by their experiences with Japan, U.S. firms are increasingly reluctant to supply their technology to a potential competitor. Naturally, Japan—itself a beneficiary of generous U.S. technology transfers—is even more vigilant than the Americans in regard to technology.

This combination of adverse environmental factors has meant that Korean firms are in desperate need of a new competitive advantage, and that advantage must be based on technology that enables them to make radical product innovations.

A PROFILE OF KOREAN INDUSTRY TODAY

Korea's industry can be classified into three main categories: small and medium firms, public enterprises, and chaebols.

Small and Medium Firms

In Korea, private enterprise firms are classified into small, medium, and large according to the regulations of the Basic Law for Small- and Medium-Size Enterprises. As in other countries, the stated purpose of this differentiation of firms is to protect and support small and medium firms. Although various and usually quantitative standards may be used in this effort (such as capitalization, asset base, and revenues), Korea uses the number of permanent employees as its primary legal yardstick (Tables 4.3 and 4.4).

In general, firms in the manufacturing, mining, transportation, and construction industries with less than 20 permanent employees are "small," while those with 21 to 300 permanent employees in the former three industries are classified as "medium." For construction, the standard for "medium" is 21 to 200 permanent employees. Retail and service industry firms are "small" when there are less than 5 permanent employees, and "medium" when there are 6 to 20 permanent employees. There are exceptions to this classification, however. For instance, in such labor-intensive manufacturing industries as automobile parts, the government acknowledges up to 1,000 permanent employees as the cutoff point for small and medium. Further exceptions exist for the asset base, an example being the suitcase and bag industry. Only those firms with less than 30 billion won in assets are considered small and medium.

Table 4.3
Definitions for Firm Classification: Korea, Japan, and the United States

Korea	Small	Mining, manufacturing, construction, transportation: less than 20 permanent employees; commerce and service: less than 5 permanent employees
	Medium	Mining, manufacturing, transportation: 21-300 permanent employees; construction: 21-200; commerce and service: 6-20
	Large	Mining, manufacturing, transportation: over 300 permanent employees; construction: over 200; commerce and service: over 20
Japan	Small	Mining, manufacturing: less than 300 permanent employees or a capitalization less than 100 million Yen; wholesale: less than 100 permanent employees or less than 30 million Yen; retail: less than 50 permanent employees or less than 10 million Yen
	Medium	Same as above
	Large	Enterprises that exceed the above scale
United States	Small	Very small: less than 20 permanent employees; small: 20-99 permanent employees
	Medium	100-499 permanent employees; retail: less than 100
	Large	Over 500 permanent employees

Source: Compiled from Byong-Rak Song, *Korean Economic Theory,* 3d ed. (Seoul: Bak Young Sa, 1992).

Table 4.4
International Comparison of Small and Medium Firms

	Korea	Japan	Taiwan	United States
	(1990)	*(1990)*	*(1990)*	*(1986)*
Total Firms (number)	68,872	435,966	157,965	497,740
Small and Medium Firms (number)	67,679	432,128	155,263	485,247
Share (percentage)	98.3	99.1	98.3	98.7
Total Output	*(billion Won)*	*(billion Yen)*	*(100 million NT$)*	*(million $)*
Total	175,234	323,129	37,136	1,960,206
Small and Medium Firms	74,634	167,232	20,063	1,054,146
Share (percentage)	42.6	51.8	54	53.8
Value-Added	*(billion Won)*	*(billion Yen)*	*(100 million NT$)*	*(million $)*
Total	70,935	118,910	10,258	824,118
Small and Medium Firms	31,432	65,947	4,828	441,184
Share (percentage)	44.3	54.9	47.1	53.5
Employees (number)	5 to 299	4 to 299	1 to 299	1 to 500

Source: Hankook Ilbo, August 11, 1993, p. 31.
Note: The total firms category reflects manufacturing concerns only. If service firms were included, the entry for total firms would be 128,700 for Korea, 6,512,000 for Japan, and 5,020,000 for the United States. This number for the United States does not include one-person firms with no employees, in which case the total would increase to 17, 499,000.

Exceptions are made to the aforementioned classification with respect to certain large corporations. Even though a firm may meet the employee standard for small and medium, if it is effectively controlled by a "large" parent company, it does not qualify for small and medium status. This also holds true for firms in any chaebol that have less than the prescribed number of permanent employees.

Public Enterprises

Public enterprises in Korea accounted for 9.4 percent of the 1990 Korean gross domestic product (GDP), which is not that different from the 8.3 percent share they had in 1975. The general definition used for a public enterprise here is any organization providing goods and services that is either owned or controlled via an ownership stake by a public institution. As of 1990, there were 120 such public enterprises controlled by the central government. At the local and provincial government level, the total was 187 for the same year. The former 120 are further classified according to the degree of control exerted by the respective central government institutions (see Chapter 8).

Government corporations refer to those functional organizations that are run as government ministries. These include the Korea Railroad Corporation, Korea Postal Service, and the Office of Government Supply. Government corporations are directly managed and staffed by civil servants.

Government-invested institutions are those organizations in which the government owns more than 50 percent of the shares. Among the twenty-three government-invested institutions are the Korea Development Bank, Korea Electrical Power Corporation (KEPCO), Korea Housing Corporation, Korea Telecom (KT), and the Korea Land Development Corporation. Government-financed institutions are those organizations in which the government holds a minority of the shares. In 1990, there were seven of these government-financed institutions, including Pohang Iron and Steel (POSCO) and the Korea Export–Import Bank. The subsidiaries of the government-invested institutions totaled eighty-six by 1990 and were founded in part as specific implementations of the government's industrial policy. Korea Heavy Industries is an example of this form of public enterprise. For instance, the Korea Development Bank owns twenty-five such subsidiaries, while Korea Electric Power has six.

Local government public enterprises are those organizations that are owned or managed by local administrative units, including those that supply water, gas, medical insurance, and housing to the citizenry. By 1991, there were 187 of these local public enterprises, with more than 25,000 employees and a budget exceeding 1.7 trillion won.

In appraising the dichotomy between private and public sectors in Korea, it may be instructive to remember a quote by Arthur Shenfield: "The difference between the public and private sectors was that the private sector was controlled by government, and the public sector wasn't controlled by anyone."[18]

Chaebols

Naturally, "large" firms are those that exceed the permanent employee standard for each industry. However, in Korea, perhaps as a result of the domination of the chaebols throughout the economy, the term *dae-gi-up* (the Korean phrase for "large firm") is often used interchangeably with the term that should be familiar by now, *chaebol*. This is because there are very few significant large firms that are independent of a chaebol in Korea. Indeed, when a firm gets to a certain size and becomes large, often the first thing it does is to buy or form various subsidiaries and create a *gu-roop* (the Koreanization of "group"), which is used as a synonym for chaebol. The term *ga-jok* (the Korean word for "family") is also used, more often by the chaebols themselves in self-references. The term *ga-jok*, which is supposed to evoke and promote a softer image, is preferred by the chaebols because the literal meaning of chaebol connotes a vaguely negative image of clans and just emphasizes the family-ownership aspects. Moreover, the term is a direct Korean pronunciation of the original Japanese concept (*zaibatsu*), which just aggravates the negative feelings that some societal sectors have for the chaebols.

The Korean government uses several clauses of the Anti-Monopoly and Fair Commerce Act to formally define a chaebol. It uses yet another phrase, "*dae-gyu-mo gi-up jip-dan* (large-scale group of companies)" to refer to the chaebols. Any group of companies with more than 400 billion won ($50 million at 800 won to the dollar) is classified as a chaebol. In 1986, there were a mere thirty that met this definition, thirty-two in 1987, forty in 1988, forty-three in 1989, fifty-three in 1990, and seventy-eight by 1992—hence the origin of the frequently used phrase, "the top thirty chaebols" (see Table 4.5), a similar concept to the *Fortune* 500 in the United States. (This comparison is especially apt when one considers the fact that most chaebols have in excess of twenty companies each.) There are two reasons for this continued increase. One, of course, is that as the economy grew; so did the number of large-scale company groups. The other is that, despite inflation, the Fair Trade Committee

Table 4.5
Specialization Areas of the Thirty Largest Chaebols

Areas of Specialization	Chaebols		Selected Companies	
	Number	*Share (percentage)*	*Number (#)*	*Share (percentage)*
1. Manufacturing	45	65.4	76	67.9
a. Chemicals	11	15.9	22	19.6
i. Petrochemicals			13	11.6
ii. Synthetic Textiles			6	5.4
iii. Miscellaneous			3	2.6
b. Food & Beverages	6	8.7	11	9.8
c. Automobiles	5	7.3	9	8.0
d. Energy & Resources	5	7.3	9	8.0
e. Electrics & Electronics & Information	5	7.3	6	5.4
f. Machinery & Equipment	4	5.8	6	5.4
g. Iron & Steel	4	5.8	6	5.4
h. Non Metals	4	5.8	5	4.5
i. Textiles & Clothing	1	1.5	2	1.8
2. Trade, Retail, and Transportation	16	23.1	24	21.4
a. Trade			9	8.0
b. Retail			7	6.3
c. Transportation & Storage			8	7.1
3. Construction	8	11.5	12	10.7
Total	69	100.0	112	100.7

Source: Compiled from Ministry of Trade, Industry, and Energy data, January 18, 1994.

did not increase the capital threshold. Why? To exert better and more effective control of the chaebols. There have been reports that the government is considering adding the concentration ratio of ownership as another criterion for chaebol classification. The stated goal is to use this information to prod the chaebols to dilute their ownership portion and lessen their considerable share of and control over the national economy (Table 4.6).

Controlling the Chaebols

After years of rapid growth, the chaebols are now as big as some of the biggest firms in the United States and Europe. Indeed, by 1993, twelve chaebols were included in the *Fortune* 500 list of the largest industrial companies in the world.[19] Yet, the chaebol-dominated structure of Korean business is a target of popular criticism by commentators and opinion leaders in the country. Criticisms may be grouped into two types: equity arguments and efficiency arguments. On the equity side, chaebols symbolize unequal income distribution and an enormous concentration of economic power. On the efficiency side, business groups are sometimes known to exercise monopoly power using their group structure, which naturally introduces inefficiencies into the free market–based competitive structure. As vertically integrated firms, chaebols can discriminate unfairly. A weak competitor in a business group can be subsidized by other member companies in the group through transfer-price manipulation. Critics argue that this represents an inefficient and unfair use of the limited investment capital of the nation. Responsive to these criticisms, the government has long sought out ways to reduce the economic concentration of the chaebols without damaging the country's economic performance.

Any government policy that aims to regulate the chaebols must examine whether chaebols are better suited than SMEs for the technologically intensive

Table 4.6
Economic Concentration Ratios: Top Six Company Groups in Korea and Japan

	Revenues (A)		GNP (B)		Concentration Ratio (percentage)	
	Trillion Won	Trillion Yen	Trillion Won	Trillion Yen	Revenues (A/B)	Value Added
Korea (1990, C)	87.5	16.4	168.4	31.6	51.9	14.7
Japan (1989, D)	---	236.5	---	406.2	58.2	19.0
Japan/Korea (D/C)	---	14.4 times	---	12.9 times	---	---

Source: Byong-Rak Song, *Korean Economic Theory,* 3d ed. (Seoul: Bak Young Sa, 1992).

industries of the future. In other words, which is better for technological innovation: large or small? The next few paragraphs are a brief aside on this question.

Without having to invoke the Chandlerian hypothesis that the history of the firm is one of continually increasing scale and scope economies, it is evident that the landscapes of mature industrial nations are dominated by large firms. For instance, in the United States, the top 100 companies account for 49 percent of the country's total corporate assets. Large size and scale enables economies in not only production but also distribution and R&D. In R&D, for instance, large companies have the luxury of making multiple bets on the future technology trajectory. In other words, they do not have to put all their eggs in one basket.

However, throughout the 1980s and early 1990s, a fetish of sorts has arisen among management theorists about the benefits of smallness. By becoming "lean and mean," it was argued, large companies could gain the flexibility needed to take advantage of a rapidly changing environment. Stumbles by Siemens, Digital, and others have shown the fallacy of bigness. Although bigness provides the resources and personnel to make a portfolio of investments, small and focused firms are often swifter and smarter than the "elephants." Large size may often lead to inertia and decision paralysis. Witness the so-called "curse of success," the tendency of firms to stick to the processes that brought them to success even when the competitive environment has moved on to a new dimension.[20] Slow and steady stability may have succeeded in the mass-production years of the past; but in the rapidly changing technological and competitive environment of the present, small and nimble firms are often better positioned to take advantage of new market opportunities. The difficulties encountered by incumbent firms attempting to create and adjust to radical innovations has been well documented in the management journals.[21] Indeed, research has shown that radical innovations often originate from outside the affected industry.[22] International Business Machines (IBM) and GM became symbols of the failed paradigm of bigness; and as these and other large companies shed their workforce by the tens of thousands, attention and admiration shifted to the small start-ups that seemed to create all the new technology and employment opportunities.

But if one considers that the large companies of today were the SMEs of yesterday and that the successful SMEs will become the large companies of tomorrow, it is evident that there cannot be a strict dichotomy between large and small. Furthermore, as IBM and GM recover from their 1980s doldrums—due, in part, to the strength of their backlog of technological expertise and managerial talent—a new sort of paradigm, "focused bigness," may be emerging as the next wave of the future. This entails forming a virtual corporation of sorts in which strategic alliances with previous competitors are formed to create an entity that is greater than the sum of its parts. Companies can then focus on what they do best—be it production, marketing, or research—and contract with others to fill in the missing parts of the value chain. This allows a firm to become big enough to create sustainable competitive advantages while taking advantage of the flexibility of a focused small competitor without unnecessary overhead.

Unfortunately, it is notoriously difficult in practice, as predicted by transaction cost theory, to create and maintain efficient and equitable contracts as required by a virtual corporation.[23] In Korea, financial liberalization as well as easy and sufficient access to capital in general, to say nothing of venture capital, are still a faraway goal. Technological innovation may, therefore, be better suited to the chaebols. It is probably true today that the Apples and Microsofts of Korea would either be starved for capital or absorbed by the chaebols, which have the larger pools of managerial talent and capital required to bring a new innovation into the marketplace.

The Korean government implemented a policy in January 1994 that does curb one aspect of bigness among the chaebols. This is a policy that curbs unwieldy diversification of chaebols to force them to innovate and excel in focused areas of specialization (see Table 4.5). This policy is also a new and significant weapon in the government's effort to stimulate R&D in Korean firms.

The new specialization policy is a way for the government to prod the chaebols into adjusting to a new international competitive environment. This policy, which was designed to force the chaebols to create their own competitiveness in technology, is not without serious faults. The first problem is the assumption that "big is beautiful." The specialization policy assumes that by focusing their resources on a single industry, the chaebols will become big enough to challenge the world-class firms. That is, by doing away with their insurance, credit card, advertising, shipbuilding, construction, and hospital businesses, Hyundai Automobile Company can compete against Toyota and GM on an equal basis. Yet Hyundai is one-eighteenth the size of GM, and GM invests more in R&D than all the firms in Korea combined.[24] That means that unless the whole country specializes into a single company, it would be nearly impossible for a Korean firm to bulk up to the size of the top world competitor.

There is another reason to believe that the bigness of the chaebols could help them to stimulate innovation. Although the underlying theory has been largely discredited in recent years, several insights from the Boston Consulting Group financial investment portfolio matrix may apply to the Korean situation. The chaebols can use a profitable subsidiary to fund a new business that may not be viable at the present but is foreseen to be important in the future (i.e., "cash cows" being milked for investment in "stars"). For instance, Samsung decided in the late 1970s to use its profits from its successful consumer electronics and insurance subsidiaries to invest in semiconductors. Although much criticized at the time, one can argue that the decision has proven to be a good one. Samsung is now the number one producer of DRAM chips in the world and seems well poised to succeed in future generation semiconductor products. It may be that only a chaebol, by balancing its investment portfolio, could have made the tremendous investment needed to become a player in semiconductors.

Chaebol bigness may be especially advantageous because of the current inefficient financial system in Korea. The government had—and, to a large extent, still has—direct or indirect control of the lending policies of the nation's banks. Only those loans that are within the policy guidelines promulgated by the Ministry of Finance are permitted. Interest rates, which have been completely determined, were often artificially lowered for favored investments by the government. The Korean Stock Market, also strongly regulated by the government, does not provide a constant and reliable source of investment capital. In addition, lending from abroad is only permitted with the government's approval. For instance, government approval is needed by Daewoo Heavy Industries to issue convertible bonds in the Eurocurrency market. Finally, foreigners are still subject to a 10 percent limit on the number of listed shares they can own in Korean firms, a policy which will be somewhat modified, according to government announcements.

In an inefficient financial environment such as this, the chaebol structure, using its portfolio investment principles, may have been an efficient method of financing new and promising ventures. Therefore, before the government mandates specialization and legislates for an eventual breakup of the chaebols, it must first create a financial environment that is fully liberalized. The financial justification of the chaebol structure will be defeated only when the firms can rely upon the financial system for investment capital.

The specialization policy may be unfair as well as inefficient, since it goes against the fundamental rights of business to enter into new industries as they see fit. Although the current policy allows multiple companies to be included in a specialized area, the loan regulations require that only companies with more than 70 percent of their revenues in a selected industry can receive relevant bank financing. This effectively forces the chaebols to select only mature businesses for investment. It rules out bank financing for promising new business areas, such as bioengineering or mechatronics. Although this is fine if the alternative financing mechanisms are robust, the Korean financial system, as we have pointed out, is still strictly regulated and controlled by the government. It remains difficult for businesses to receive financing in areas not included within industrial policy guidelines. Therefore, a significant risk exists that even if the policy works as planned, the chaebols will be transformed into big, bloated dinosaurs roaming in outdated and mature industries.

In summary, it seems that the government may be confusing the problem of economic concentration with economic efficiency. There are other ways to reduce the ownership portion of the chaebol-founding families, such as mandated listing on the stock market. Alternatively, the government could require that cross-shareholdings among subsidiaries be kept below a minimum of, say, 1 percent. Once the web of tangled cross-holdings is cleared away, the chaebols would be forced to look to the stock market to fill up the gap.

Specialization is a decision best left to the market and the chaebols themselves to decide. With the 1993 passage of the Uruguay Round of the GATT talks, the chaebols must soon contend with free foreign competition in the domestic market. Market competition will determine whether they can continue to exist in their current form. The Korean economy is too big now for the government to dictate industrial policy. The goal is admirable, but the devil is in the implementation.

We believe that the specialization policy should be withdrawn and canceled. Recent pronouncements by the newly appointed chief economic advisor to the president seem to echo our concern that excessive government regulation is unnecessary and less efficient than market mechanisms. Indeed, one should remember that the very phrase "excessive competition" is an oxymoron in light of neoclassical economic theory. Anything termed excessive competition would be called near the ideal of "perfect competition" in the economics textbooks.

POLICIES FOR SMALL- AND MEDIUM-SIZE ENTERPRISES

The first clause of the Basic Law for Small- and Medium-Size Enterprises defines SMEs in terms of their ability to "contribute to the balanced development of the national economy." There are several other important roles to consider, especially in the context of innovation and technology policy. Perhaps the most important role is to diffuse entrepreneurial spirit throughout the economy. In developing countries without a strong tradition of commerce, the very success of SMEs serves as a potent example of the fruits of entrepreneurship. The importance of this diffusion is underscored in Korea, where Confucian beliefs stunted the development of commerce as a respectable activity. Indeed, there is a phrase, "*sa nong gong sang*," which refers to the traditional Yi Dynasty (1392–1910) hierarchy of occupations from scholar to farmer to technician to merchant. The ruling classes spent their time in scholarly pursuits, leaving the "exchange of money" to the lower classes. It is probably this facet of Confucian ideology that caused Max Weber to dismiss the capitalist efforts of the East in favor of the Protestant West. Ironically, the importance put on education is now widely regarded as one of the key success factors of Korea's industrial experience.[25]

SMEs are a source of innovation in that they serve as a breeding ground for new ideas, products, and services that are not economical for large firms, which have minimal scale considerations. By virtue of their relatively small sizes, small and medium firms are often more flexible than their larger counterparts and more able to meet and adjust to new challenges in the market. New industries are often created by entrepreneurs with vision who dominate the emerging market until the competitive focus moves from uniqueness and quality to cost and broader market development.

In Korea, however, the good times end for the small entrepreneurs once the potential of the industry is recognized by the chaebols. The SMEs must walk a delicate balancing act: Be careful to avoid the competitive attention of the chaebols, but be visible enough to receive support from the government bureaucrats. It is a rare case, though, that the chaebols ignore a potential source of profit. Despite criticism from government agencies and the media, there are countless examples where chaebols muscled into promising sectors and forced their smaller competitors into retreat. For instance, the domestic electronics industry was once populated by many small and medium firms that specialized in particular product areas. One producer would focus exclusively on cassette radios, while another might concentrate on audio component systems. But these small firms were helpless in the face of the onslaught of chaebols such as Samsung and Goldstar, who used their superior base of capital and management to gradually encompass the entire product spectrum. Many industry pioneers such as Hwashin and Taihan Electric Wire were either bought out or forced into bankruptcy. Independent competitors in televisions, radios, semiconductors, and telephones have largely disappeared.

One way the government set out to protect the livelihood of the SMEs was to designate certain industries as off-limits to the chaebols. This policy direction was first espoused by what was called the Ministry of Trade and Industry in 1964, when all industries were classified into three categories. "A" industries were those that were designated as the exclusive domain of SMEs. In these industries, specialization and operational integration with the chaebols was pursued. At the same time, the chaebols were denied entry. "B" industries were those that should be developed into chaebol industries; entry by SMEs was denied. "C" industries were those that were targeted for gradual exit, and further investment was discouraged.

The classifications did not, in fact, work well. Industry boundaries were extremely porous and susceptible to chaebol lobbying efforts. Despite lip service, the reality was that the chaebols entered pretty much any industry they wanted. Their prestige and importance as top exporters who contributed greatly to the nation's economic growth was too powerful to deny. If an SME could not develop into a chaebol itself, the best way to ensure survival was to operate as a vendor to the chaebols.

SMEs can be classified by many standards. First are the SMEs that produce folk art or regional food specialties. These prototypical small firms also include those that produce for a limited local market (e.g., the neighborhood bakery). Second are those firms that operate as subcontractors to larger firms.

As in the case of the Korean automobile industry, there can be many tiers of subcontractors, which enable a medium-size firm to subcontract from several smaller firms, while, at the same time, subcontracting to a higher-level assembler. Third are those SMEs that compete directly against larger competitors with their own products and technologies. These firms are often at the crossroads, poised either to become large firms themselves or to succumb to the superior competition.

For this last category of firms, one promising strategy is consortium formation.[26] Firms could create a consortium according to the relevant legal provisions for providing primarily financial or marketing support. In financial consortia, firms cooperate in loan assessment and guarantee activities with the banking system. Banks lending to firms in traditional or nascent industries do not have the detailed insights that enable correct assessment of the viability of investment projects. When the investment is small, as is often the case for small and medium firms, it is not worthwhile for banks to develop their own expertise in the industry. They prefer to decide on the basis of collateral, usually property. Therefore, for entrepreneurial firms who need initial investments and do not yet have the required collateral, lending is nearly impossible.

By providing an objective insider's assessment of entrepreneurial ideas, financial consortia can replace the collateral function. For example, as a first step, firms in a consortium create an administrative process to pre-assess investment projects submitted by member companies. Those that pass are then forwarded to the banks with a loan guarantee issued by the consortium. This loan guarantee can be made possible by creating a fund comprised of consortium membership fees plus government contributions.

Marketing consortia are a way for small firms to pool their limited resources to share overhead and administrative expenses so that individual firms can concentrate on production. Market research, competitor research, design creation, export promotion, sales missions, information handling, and training facilities are several examples of the roles that such consortia can play. Existing information exchanges and national clearinghouses for the collection and distribution of new technologies might be better managed and funded at both the state and industry level. A good first step might be to establish a "technomart," where technology, technicians, patents, and foreign technology trend information would be shared among small and medium firms. Through these sorts of activities, small firms can maintain their independence from the chaebols by avoiding subcontracting. They also can possess the benefits of marketing economies of scale without growing undesirably large. Low overhead means that these firms can stay lean and remain flexible to change.

A stronger form of cooperation can be found in the growing international trend of networked firms. The network structure is an example of a coalitional mode, usually involving a small central organization that relies on other organizations to perform several, often critical, value-chain activities on a contract basis.[27] The network contrasts with the traditional hierarchical firm by this high degree of flexibility and its concentration on its core competencies. Enabling factors have included the rapid development of information technology and, in international settings, the globalization of finance. For example, a fancy-goods (i.e., gift shop items aimed at a teen market) firm in Korea claims that it does "manufacturing without factory" by concentrating on design and marketing, while leaving the production to its long-term suppliers. The fad or fashion component of the industry requires rapid adjustment and flexibility, which is enhanced by this type of arrangement.[28] Value chains in a network increasingly link independent firms into extended production complexes. Once consortium activity is institutionalized and trust among the partners develops, networks can and should be created in Korea.

All these types of arrangements must be predicated on the existence of technology. If the small firms do not have competitive products that are accepted by the market, the form of organization is immaterial. Small and medium firms are also faced with the same general threat from Chinese and Southeast Asian competitors in the international market. Moreover, with market liberalization, imports from these less-developed countries are driving labor-intensive domestic manufacturers (e.g., wooden chopsticks, processed plastics) out of the market. This price threat is even affecting the "model" case of Italy, where there are currently calls for higher levels of specialization, quality control, and innovation.

Unfortunately, the trend for R&D investment is not going in the right direction for development of small and medium firms (Table 4.7). According to a 1993 survey reported in the Korean press, the total proportion of these companies that invested in R&D fell from a paltry 14 percent in 1985 to an alarming 5.4 percent in 1991.[29] The proportion apparently grew to 15.6 percent in 1986, 15.7 percent in 1987, and 18.5 percent in 1988 before it started to fall

Table 4.7
Reasons for Shortages in R&D Personnel in Small and Medium Firms

Reasons Cited for Shortages in R&D Personnel	Percentage
1. Absolute shortage in the national pool of talent	36.2
2. Low wages	34.1
3. Poor working conditions and lack of welfare benefits	26.5
4. Preference for chaebols	48.1
5. Headhunting by competitors	15.1
6. Distance from urban areas	10.8
7. Transfer to construction and service industries	11.4
8. Lack of job security	17.3

Source: Industrial Bank of Korea, *Korea's Small and Medium Corporations* (Seoul: Industrial Bank of Korea, 1992).
Note: Respondents were allowed to give multiple answers.

to 10.3 percent in 1989, recovering slightly to 10.5 percent in 1990. This means that a whopping 94.6 percent of the SMEs in Korea invested *nothing* in R&D in 1991. The total SME R&D investment in 1991 was 283 billion won, or 0.24 percent of sales. Per company, this works out to less than 57 million won, a mere $81,000 in 1991 U.S. dollars. This figure is in marked contrast to Taiwanese and Japanese SMEs that invest 5 to 10 percent of their annual revenues in R&D.

There is a Korean saying, *"bal-deung-eui bul,"* which can be literally translated as "the fire on top of the foot." It refers to the immediate and urgent task that must be attended to, implying that anything else is secondary and postponable. Korea's SMEs often cite this saying to explain their lack of R&D investment. They also echo the reasons cited by the chaebols, which include difficulty in ensuring sales, low business prospects, low probability of development success, and not enough government incentives (see Table 4.2).

It is important for Korea's SMEs to look inward for the seeds of their revival. That is, unless they are satisfied to remain as an easily replaceable, labor-based subcontractor to the chaebols, SMEs must invest in technology to ensure their independent survival. Yet, the former strategy is not sustainable, as the chaebols are increasingly using cheaper foreign suppliers, especially in the labor-intensive stage of production. The conclusion? Like the chaebols, Korea's SMEs must invest in technology so that they can compete on quality rather than price. Tables 4.7 to 4.11 cover various important informational tables and statistics on Korea's SMEs.

POLICIES FOR PUBLIC ENTERPRISES

Previous government efforts to stimulate innovation in state enterprises have focused on changing the management evaluation standards. Managers of state enterprises are being audited on a variety of performance measures. The rationale goes that if government included and gave high weight to a measure for innovation, the managers would redouble their efforts in this area. But this kind of thinking represents the way bureaucrats think within the existing system. The frame of reference itself must be changed.

First, the assumptions behind the "public" nature of many public areas have been increasingly challenged. When many of these enterprises were begun, there were no viable private-sector sources of investment. With industrialization, however, the capitalist institutional structure has matured to the point where this is no longer true. Private-investment sources represent a more efficient alternative to public expenditure and management. Furthermore, the range and breadth of government enterprises have grown to encompass many private-good areas. Once again, the time for government to directly participate in sectors such as ginseng, textbooks, construction, and sightseeing has passed. Similar arguments can be made for the financial system, where the environment for innovation has radically changed.

Table 4.8
R&D Support Policies for SMEs in Selected Advanced Nations

Nation and Support Type	Major Highlights
United States	
Regional Manufacturing Technology Center (RMTC) of National Institute of Standards and Technology (NIST)	• Free loans of donated machinery and equipment to be used at five regional centers for advanced manufacturing technology
	• 50% funded by the federal government, the rest from universities and other non profit organizations
Small Business Innovation Research (SBIR)	• SBIR Law passed in 1982; federal government budgetary support for the development and commercialization of R&D in technologically intensive small businesses
United Kingdom	
Small Manufacturing Awards for Research Technology (SMART)	• Financial rewards given for successful technology development cases
	• 1st stage: idea implementation funding of up to 75% or a maximum of 45,000 pounds
	• 2nd stage: 70% of 1st stage firms selected for up to 50% in initial expense funding or a maximum of 120,000 pounds
France	
Regional Technology Transfer Support Fund sponsored by the Ministry of Industry and regional assemblies	• Support for small business research institutes and university contract research; up to 200,000 FF, total budget is 60 million FF
Researcher Employment Support Fund (ANVAR)	• Supplementary funding for full-time researchers employed in small businesses; up to 200,000 FF, total budget is 100 million FF
Japan	
Technology Training Supplementary Fund	• Support of technology training for small businesses at municipalities and universities (235 million Yen in 1993)
Industrial Technology Institute Regional Testing Station R&D	• Support of collaborative research between small businesses and regional technology stations (3.496 billion Yen in '93)
Regional R&D Incentive Program	• Creating new products using national testing institute and university research for regional small businesses
R&D-intensive Business Incubator Program	• Non collateral loan guarantees for advanced R&D-intensive small businesses

Source: Small and Medium Industrial Promotion Corporation (Seoul: Ministry of Trade and Industry, 1993).

These considerations have led to the announcement of privatization of government enterprises, using three methods: (1) sell shares directly into the stock market, (2) initial public offering with delayed listing, and (3) public tender auctions, with the spoils going to the highest bidder.

Table 4.9
Technology Level of SMEs in Selected Nations

Type of Technology	U.S.	Western Europe	Japan	Korea	Taiwan
Foreign Expert Opinion					
Production	100	94	103	67	66
Design	100	97	96	64	59
Product Development	100	93	95	63	59
Local Expert Opinion					
Production	100	93	112	72	72
Design	100	98	92	57	57
Product Development	100	98	96	66	58
Automation	100	93	109	68	59

Source: Small and Medium Industrial Promotion Corporation (Seoul: Ministry of Trade and Industry, 1993).

Table 4.10
Reasons for SME Participation in Industry, Academia, and Research Institutes

Reasons	Government-Funded Research Institutes	Universities	Firms
Risk-dispersal through shared capital outlay	8.1	0.3	18.7
Utilization of superior research personnel	23.1	37.1	3.9
Use of research facilities and equipment	11.9	10.2	5.5.
Enhanced research results	5.6	22.5	11.9
Shortened R&D cycle	3.3	6.4	10.3
Use of key technological information	10.4	11.4	10.6
Market creation for developed products	2.5	0.3	14.8
Entry into a new area	2.9	5.8	4.5
Increased success rate for R&D efforts	2.9	2.6	9.4
Difficulty in obtaining advanced technology from abroad	5.8	1.8	4.8
Participation in government-support funds and programs	23.5	1.5	4.8
Total	100.0	100.0	100.0

Source: Korean Industrial Research Institute, *1993 Industrial Technology White Paper* (Seoul: Korea Industrial Research Institute, 1993).

GENERAL POLICY RECOMMENDATIONS

To recap the primary principles of a reactive policy regime: Excessive regulation as well as overt forms of protectionism, including that aimed at potential domestic entrants, should be removed. A reactive policy regime should eliminate tax and other financial subsidies, provide standards to which firms

Table 4.11
Utilization and Effectiveness of Tax-Support Policies

Tax-Support Policies	Utilization	Effectiveness
•Technology-development preparatory funds	2.8280	3.4810
•Technology and human resources development tax exemption	3.5437	3.7579
•Tax exemption or special amortization of research or testing facilities investment	3.4040	3.8621
•Asset investment tax exemption or special amortization for new-technology firms	2.3253	3.2154
•Tax support for technology income	1.8974	3.1552
•Income exemption for technology service projects	1.8961	3.0167
•Regional tax exemption for land used for corporate R&D sites	2.7065	3.6538
•Customs duties exemption for research materials	3.6667	4.0333
•Special consumption tax exemption for research samples	2.6154	3.5433
•Application of temporary special consumption tax rates for vanguard technology items	1.9589	2.8889
•Reduction of technology payments	2.0390	3.0984
•Income tax exemption for foreign technicians	1.9873	2.7313
•Support for technology-intensive new SMEs	1.6301	3.1311

Source: Korean Industrial Research Institute, *1993 Industrial Technology White Paper* (Seoul: Korea Industrial Research Institute, 1993).
Notes: Survey used both the top 100 R&D-investing large firms and SMEs, respectively. (Unit: 5-point scale; 1 is none, 3 is average, and 5 is very high.)

must conform, ensure competitive bidding for procurement contracts, and promote exports. Export, design, manufacture, and environmental-control performance standards are other types of reactive policy instruments that are useful for promoting technology innovation. A reactive policy may also mean increasing the required localization ratio to induce greater levels of industry indigenization, while the liberalization rate for production or technology inputs may be increased to put competitive pressures on the local producers. A reactive policy can promote a more balanced growth of the industry when there is an added emphasis on the enforcement of fair trade and competition. This is achieved by strengthening the government's role as a regulator while weakening its interventionist tendencies.

Promote Strategic Alliances with Domestic and International Competitors

Ever-shortening product life cycles and correspondingly increasing R&D expenditures are making managers realize that merely keeping pace with technological and marketing breakthroughs is becoming a difficult proposition in itself. Moreover, in order to succeed as international players, firms are being required to participate in previously unknown markets, shift out of declining and into growing industries, and stay on top of the most recent technological trends to adjust to changing environmental conditions. To many firms, multinational contractual agreements that allow the participants to share information, resources, markets, and risks have been a popular coping strategy.[30] Indeed, Kenichi Ohmae, the management consultant, has been quoted as saying that "no company can stay competitive in the world today single-handedly."[31]

Korean firms are no exception to this trend. Indeed, Korea's firms have enjoyed and continue to benefit greatly from joint ventures with foreign companies as they competitively upgrade. Mention a major international player in any industry, and chances are that you will likely find a Korean joint venture with that firm. Samsung–Hewlett Packard, Goldstar–Alps, Daewoo–Carrier, and Lotte–Canon are but a few examples. The beneficial effects of multinational OEM relationships for Korea's technology acquisition and development have also been discussed. Yet, it is ironic that intra-Korean strategic alliances are few in number and rarely successful.

As Table 4.12 shows, there are many reasons for this situation. Korean firms often complain about the potential for partner conflict, unwanted diffusion of proprietary information, the creation of possible future competitors, and the difficulties in achieving harmonious cooperation and ensuring equal effort. These reasons are of a transaction cost nature, which is ironic because multinational partnerships possess equal, if not more, problems. If multinational joint ventures can be structured and operated successfully, so should domestic ventures.[32]

Korean antitrust regulation is not as strict as that of the United States, and there is considerable leeway in arranging cooperative alliances among heretofore competitors. Along with joint production, mutual part and component purchase, and joint marketing agreements, there exist some rudimentary technology alliances among the Korean chaebols (Table 4.13). Naturally, these alliances should be encouraged and promoted.

The government may assist in this process by acting as an honest broker for the alliance partners. It may also promote alliances by providing seed money for research or guarantee purchase, as was the case in the telephone digital exchange (TDX) telephone switching system or the Taicom computer-development project.

Table 4.12
Problems in Collaborative Research Cited by Korean Firms

Factors Mentioned as Problems in Collaborative Research	Share (in Percentage)
1. Conflicting interests (e.g., views on the utilization of development results)	22.86
2. Reluctance to mutually exchange technology	22.14
3. Difficulty in achieving harmonious cooperation	19.29
4. Difficulty in ensuring equal effort	16.43
5. Product market competition dulls collaborative instinct	11.43
6. Low possibility of success	7.85

Source: Korea Industrial Research Institute, *1993 Industrial Technology White Paper* (Seoul: Korea Industrial Research Institute, 1993).

Table 4.13
Selected Strategic Alliances among Domestic Firms

Category	Form of Alliance	Participants	Content
Technology Alliance	Patent sharing	Goldstar Co. - Samsung Electric	2,000 television-related patents
	Joint development	Goldstar Industrial Electronics - Kia Machinery	Domestic robot development
	Joint system management	Orion Electric (Daewoo) - Korea Tungsten Mining	Tungsten alloy wire development
		Samyang - Pusan Pipe	Joint use of computer system
Production/ Sales Alliance	Joint production/sales	Samsung Electronics - Goldstar - Daewoo	Joint production of white goods
	Mutual parts and components purchasing	Samsung Heavy Industries - Daewoo Heavy Industries	Purchase of crucial parts
	Joint marketing	Hwasung - Kukje - Kolon	Joint foreign retail operation
Cooperation for Foreign Entry	Participation in international bidding auctions	Hyundai - Daewoo - Samsung	Awarded Saudi oil tanker bid
	Foreign construction contracts	Hyundai Construction - Ssangyong Construction	Awarded Singapore construction contract
Public-Private Sector Joint Research	Joint development	ETRI - Samsung - Goldstar - Orion Electric	Development of high-definition television braun tube
		ETRI - Samsung and other industry participants	TDX switching system development

Source: Korea Industrial Research Institute, *1993 Industrial Technology White Paper* (Seoul: Korea Industrial Research Institute, 1993).

Once alliances are embedded in the industrial system, true and unforced specialization can occur. Firms can concentrate on the areas where they perform best, using that expertise to create a cooperative whole with their similarly specialized partners in mutually exclusive areas. Chaebols may then leave areas in which they are second- or third-best and concentrate on their specialties.

Most of the existing cases of strategic alliances among Korean firms are at the chaebol level. Past alliances between chaebols and SMEs were prone to failure, often as a result of the unequal power balance in favor of the former. Naturally, smaller enterprises became wary of tie-ups with the chaebols. Once again, the government can use its influence as an honest broker between the contracting partners to ensure that the weaker firms are protected.

Reduce the Bureaucratic Red Tape and Regulations That Strangle the Innovative Efforts of Korean Firms

On January 3, 1994, the government launched yet another new blue-ribbon committee to study ways to improve Korea's national competitiveness. But this time, the task was one of reduction rather than creation. Rather than having the government devise new policies to structure industrial activity, this committee examined how to do away with existing regulations. Why? For one thing, more than thirty years after the first economic development plan was implemented, the Korean government still exerts near total control over general business activities. Entry regulations; factory location and approval; production, marketing, and export control; price control; environment; workplace safety; health and welfare; and quasi-taxation regulations are still prevalent throughout the Korean industrial landscape. Confusing, contradictory, and overlapping regulatory bodies exert control over all industrial activity.

For example, a survey has found that 26.8 percent of all new businesses take more than two years to incorporate. Of this delay, 26 percent is attributed to the complicated certification and approval procedures. Indeed, there are reports that it takes over 100 "chops" of approval from local, provincial, and national bureaucracies to build a new factory. The many laborious steps required in the approval process make the system prone to abuse. Petty corruption accumulates, causing "lobbying" expenses that often equal actual construction costs. The costs to efficiency are nearly incalculable.

The complex regulatory structure is often cited as a contributing factor to the retardation of SMEs in Korea, since usually only large firms have the administrative structure necessary to pursue bureaucratic approval. This bureaucracy also negatively affects the entrepreneurial spirit needed for innovation. If it takes two years to just set up a company, why bother? The Small and Medium Enterprises Promotion Corporation, as well as the Ministry of Science and Technology (MOST), have established entrepreneurial incubator systems as a way to combat this problem. But the key to success must lie in achieving true and fundamental deregulation.

An episode in the domestic automobile industry provides another illustration of the negative impacts of excessive regulation on innovation. In January 1994, the major automobile producers announced a 200,000- to 300,000-won average increase in prices, the first official increase in seven years. The 1987 democratization of society had freed up labor union activity, which led to factory wages quadrupling in less than five years. Yet, government officials concerned with inflation prevented the automobile producers from raising their prices, in accordance with a regulation that requires Ministry of Trade, Industry, and Energy (MOTIE) approval for industrial products that are controlled by an oligopoly. Initially, the automobile producers wanted a 1,000,000-won average increase; but they settled for the more modest amount to encourage regulatory approval. Despite this, the government forced the producers to rescind their price increase, once again citing inflationary concerns. As an added measure, the Fair Trade Commission announced that it would be looking into possible collusion, with the unspoken threat that, unless the prices stayed at their previous levels, a negative ruling might be handed down. Forced to maintain their razor-thin profit margins of less than 1 percent of revenues, Korea's automobile manufacturers do not have the wherewithal to invest in facility automation, let alone R&D. Once again, they have *bal-deung-eui bul* to worry about.

Liberalize the Financial Sector

Another area where regulation should be reduced is the financial system. Despite several stages of liberalization, Korea's bureaucrats still exert significant control over interest rates and continue to use differential rates to promote their policy goals. Indeed, the major enforcement tool for the government's top thirty chaebol specialization policy is their control over the bank lending system. Conditions for stock and bond offerings are overly strict, which has stunted the growth of Korea's capital market as a viable alternative to bank financing. As a result, most chaebols are amazingly leveraged, and 200 to 500 percent debt/equity ratios are distressingly common.[33] This high leverage is another way that the governments exert control over the chaebols. Since the government controls the banking system, it can call in loans to chaebols at any time.

An example of this kind of power can be found in the overnight demise of the then-seventh-ranked chaebol, Kukje, when they ran afoul of the top political leadership in the mid-1980s. Within several months, all the various companies that comprised Kukje were sold or merged into other chaebols by the banks that held the debt.[34]

Regulatory approval is also required for stock or bond offerings overseas, which is unnecessarily limiting the sources of capital and investment of the cash-hungry chaebols. Naturally, R&D investment, with its long-term and uncertain impact, often bears the brunt of this government meddling. A positive step to alleviate this problem can be found in the aforementioned privatization policies targeted at the government-invested banks, but further measures must also be implemented.

Promote R&D by Making It Fully Tax Deductible and Provide Unimpeded, Low-Interest Financing

In December 1993, the Korea Economic Research Institute reported several findings about the government's R&D policies (see Tables 4.11, 4.14, and 4.15).[35] Among the fifteen existing R&D support funds in four categories—government

Table 4.14
Current State of Technical Personnel–Support Policies

Mode	Support	Support Content	Support Scope
Tax Policy	Technology Development Preparatory Fund	Training expenses for developing human resources both in-house and at domestic and foreign institutions	Total expense treatment
	Tax Exemption for Technology and Human Resources Development	On and off-site training expenses for improvement of technological skills; job-training funding, human resources development & technology guidance expenses for SMEs; human resources development expenses for productivity improvement	5% of spending treated as expenses; 10% of SMEs
	In-House Technology University	Operating expenses for in-house technology university; introduction of training materials	5% of expenditure treated as expenses; 90% of custom duties reduction
Financial Policy	Korea Development Bank (KDB) Technology Development Fund	Construction costs of training facilities for technical personnel	Up to 100% of required costs; repayment within 8 years (with up to 3-year deferment of interest); 11.4%-12.4% annual interest; no limit of loan amount
	Industrial Bank of Korea (IBK) Technical Personnel Support Fund	Off-site training expenses for the improvement of the R&D capability and skill level of SME technical personnel	Loan limit: 10 million Won per company; loan period: 3 years (with 1-year deferment of interest); annual interest rates: 7.5%; loans for 100% of required costs

Table 4.14 (continued)

Mode	Support	Support Content	Support Scope
<u>Support and Recruitment of Human Resources</u>	Military Exemption for Research Personnel	Selection of private corporate R&D institutes that meet certain qualifications to serve as host organizations for those receiving military exemption as researchers	5-year term of service required to offset military duty
	Recruitment of Overseas Korean Scientists	15-day to 6-month temporary invitations for overseas Korean and foreign researchers in basic science and advanced technology	Overseas Korean scientists: airfare + living expenses (900,000 Won/month); foreign scientists: airfare + living expenses (1.5 million Won/month)
	Post-Doctoral Training Overseas	Domestic and overseas training for new scientists within 5-years of their degree or under 40 years of age	Support period: 1 year; university training: 1 million Won/month; research institute training: 350,000 Won/month
	Brain Pool	Employment referral for those with foreign Ph.D.s (Japan) from the Korean Institute of Science and Technology; employment referral for science and engineering Ph.D.s from the Korea Academic Promotion Foundation	Employment support in government-funded research institutes and industry; employment referral for university faculty
	Science and Technology Personnel Information	Creation of database for domestic and foreign scientists and researchers	Supply of personnel information through KRISTAL network

Source: Federation of Korean Industries seminar, "Technology Innovation and Industrial Policy," Seminar proceedings, Seoul, November 19, 1993.

Table 4.15
Problems in Research Personnel–Support Policies

Policy Type	Current Status	Problems
Military Exemption for Research Personnel	• Selection criteria for host organization: more than 5 master-level researchers: by MOST	• Same criteria for SMEs and regionally-located firms as the chaebols
	•Selection criteria for research personnel: master- or- higher level researchers in the natural sciences and engineering	•Increased hiring costs for SMEs
	•Distribution of personnel: decided by the Military Exemption Advisory Committee	•Exclusion of private sector participation
	•Foreign travel for exempt researchers: prior recommendation and approval required	•Excessive time requirements for recommendation
	•Limit on job transfer: 3-years after exempt status begins	•Job transfers prohibited even within same corporation
	• Selection of host organization: by Minister of Science and Technology	•Dual jurisdiction over host organizations
	•Limits on specialty fields and majors: limited to electrics, electronics, telecommunications, and aerospace majors	•Limited and unrealistic view of future technologies
	•Limits on foreign training: technical training for 18 months at most	•Examples of forced mid-term return of researchers
In-House Technology Institute	•Graduates receive exemptions on only electronics and computing subjects in the national college equivalency examination	• Nonrecognition of academic credentials
		•Prohibition of industry-wide technical institutes
Recruitment of Overseas Research Personnel	• On the initiative of the inviting organization	•Non-support of housing or education for dependents
Brain Pool	•Supply of Japan-trained Ph.D.'s to government-funded research institute •Employment referral for those with foreign PhDs (Japan) from the Korean Institute of Science and Technology; employment referral for science and engineering Ph.D.'s from the Korea Academic Promotion Foundation •Creation of database for domestic and foreign scientists and researchers	•Limited candidates and scope •Employment support in government-funded research institutes and industry; employment referral for university faculty •Supply of personnel information through KRISTAL network

Source: Korea Foreign Trade Association, "Status and Utilization of Strategic Alliances, in *Research Volume* 93–99 (Seoul: Korea Foreign Trade Association, 1993).

investment, policy funds, banking funds, and venture capital—only four were used. The remaining eleven kinds of support funds were completely untapped by companies that presumably are starved for R&D investment capital.

Why? The reason was unfortunately a familiar one: oppressive regulation. Surveyed companies cited excessive paperwork requirements, complicated application procedures, and artificial interest-rate correction by the lending banks. The final point needs elaboration. Despite the fact that the banks are required to follow the government's technology policy directives for the provision of preferential interest-rate loans, their managers are also responsible for the performance of the bank itself. As a compensatory policy, the banks often force the companies that are receiving the loan to redeposit a portion at a low interest rate. This artificial interest-rate correction, or *"gguk-gi,"* restores the so-called "policy rate" to the market rate. Once again, this is an example of government regulations interfering with the will to innovate in Korean business.

On a positive note, the Ministry of Justice, which is in administrative control over the Korean commercial code, has announced plans to allow companies to deduct all R&D expenditures from taxes.[36] Currently, the tax deduction depends on the type of R&D expense.

Alternative Investment Vehicles That Are Speculative and Nonproductive in Nature, such as Real Estate and *Zaitech*, Should Be Discouraged

Korean businesses have a long and storied tradition of investing in land. The following set of statistics provide an explanation. Starting in 1974 and at a base of 100, the growth index of companies as a function of their investment decisions reveals that those businesses that invested only in facilities grew to 331 in 1987. Those firms that invested 50 percent in facilities and 50 percent in land grew to 612, and those that invested 100 percent in land grew to an amazing 1,004.[37] This, of course, reflects the incredible appreciation in land prices over the period of Korea's industrialization. But why did the land appreciate so much?

One reason is the correlative effect of land prices and an increase of the general wealth of the country. As noted, Korea's per capita GNP has grown nearly 7,000 percent since industrialization began in 1961. But that fact alone does not account for the entire rate of appreciation. The remaining key can be found in the lending policies of the Korean commercial banks. The total loan outlay of the five major commercial banks and the KorAm Bank was more than 34.3 trillion won in 1993. Of this total, only 40.9 percent were loans extended on a pure credit basis, while the rest were backed by collateral put up by the lendee companies. And the most important and preferred form of collateral is land. The reasons are simple: Land prices have almost never depreciated and are simple to manage because land requires no oversight.

Land is an attractive investment for firms because using land as collateral enables them to obtain bank loans. Then, another type of snowball effect occurs. That is, with the loan, firms buy more land, which they use to get more loans. As this process repeats itself, firms increase their land possessions as well as their lines of credit. Furthermore, since land prices are continually appreciating from the demand created by similarly thinking businesses, the value of their land increases as well. It is an easy way to make money.

Why should Korean firms invest their profits in necessarily risky R&D when they can invest in land, a sure bet? There are two main reasons. One is that the continual cycle of land appreciation based on speculative demand cannot go on forever. As the current case of Japan's prolonged recession shows, once investors start to lose their firm belief in the valuation of land, the bubble bursts and the market collapses.

Furthermore, when the bubble bursts, Korea will be left with diminished productive capability. As long as rent-seeking activities that contribute not to the nation's industrial well-being but to the bubble economy are not regulated, the capital flows into R&D will be limited in favor of better-yielding investments. The appreciation of land prices is ultimately based on the assumptions of productive use for that land. Land in itself does not produce anything. If the businesses continue to invest their capital in land to the detriment of productive capability, their competitiveness will erode, while their asset base may increase. This asset base itself will disappear when the artificially inflated paper profits disappear and land loses its worth.

The government can respond to this situation in three ways. The fundamental solution is to break the link between land and banks. In 1992, only 44.4 percent of the total loan amount extended in Korea was on credit terms. This should be increased to at least the level of the 61.7 percent figure for Japan (1992) or the 59.2 percent of the United States (1993).[38]

Next, the long-term effects of R&D investment should not be penalized by an outdated tax system. Although there have been efforts to overhaul the tax system to penalize real estate speculation, the effectiveness has been questionable because of the halfhearted nature of the implementation. In the late 1980s, frustration over ever-rising land prices spurred a serious attempt to introduce a "land as a public good concept" and solve the problem with socialist means. A less radical proposal is taxation at prohibitive levels so that speculation can be discouraged.

The government should also promote alternative forms of collateral. The government's policy of forcing the commercial banks to extend low-interest, "policy-backed" loans to favored companies and industrial sectors has saddled the banking industry with a large amount of nonperforming loans, distorted financial markets, and led to a chronic overdemand for money. Recent liberalization measures, by dint of their halfheartedness, have allowed banks to require more stringent collateral requirements for any new loans, and especially what the banks perceive as "risky" R&D expenditures. Therefore, in line with other R&D incentives, firms should be allowed to utilize their technology base and development potential as a new form of collateral. These may include a firm's reputation or mutual guarantees among consortia companies.

Another interesting policy alternative is to promote evaluation of a firm's technology base. That is, the bank puts a value on the store or prospects of a lendee firm's technology. This is not as far-fetched as one might think. Venture capital firms operate on a similar principle, although the firm's equity serves as another form of collateral. A precondition is that banks must significantly upgrade their capabilities to accurately value a firm's market and technology prospects—the process for which the government can provide support.

Intellectual Property Rights Must Be Better Enforced to Allow Appropriation of R&D Efforts

Academic researchers, especially in the economic tradition, have long debated the interrelated nature of innovation, appropriability, and patent enforcement.[39] A general consensus exists that strong patent protection is a crucial precondition for the motivation of firms to innovate. Korean society, however, expresses the contrary concern that the benefits of innovation be disseminated widely so that scarce resources are not "wasted" through "needless" duplication. As discussed, Korea's government has had an explicit policy for promoting diffusion. Since the technology previously acquired was of a standardized nature and was sourced from existing foreign sources, this policy was not an issue. Firms importing technology accepted its diffusion, since they expected the favor to be returned the next time.

But as the backlog of foreign technology dried up, this policy of easy diffusion has become a stumbling block for the innovative efforts of Korean firms. To say nothing of foreigners' complaints about lax intellectual protection, this policy has retarded the development of an innovative corporate culture. Potential entrepreneurs are discouraged, which also exacerbates the weak condition of Korea's SME development.

Software, a prototypical industry for entrepreneurs and small business, exemplifies this problem. Some estimates say that up to 90 percent of the software used in Korea is illegal. This has prompted complaints from the major foreign manufacturers. More critically for Korea, software piracy has discouraged the development of local software houses. Given the widespread assumptions that the future will be dominated by information-based industries, it is high time that the government steps in to strictly enforce intellectual property rights.

As a remedy to the increased need for patent protection, the government has announced plans to transfer the technologies developed by the government research institutes to small and medium businesses free of charge.[40]

Furthermore, MOST will use its Science and Technology Promotion Fund to support up to 80 percent of the firms' commercialization efforts for these technologies with low-interest loans (6.5% for up to seven years with a three-year grace period. The current market rates are about 16%). MOTIE will also make available loans for facility investment and operating expenses.

Meanwhile, however, the research institutes are complaining bitterly that the technical training expenses for the 245 technology projects will be taken out of their research budgets. Naturally, the research institutes feel that this is just another example of the traditional discrimination against S&T personnel in favor of the industrialists. So as the Korean saying says, the government is "adding a mole, rather than removing one." A systematic cohesion among government policies must be achieved for all "moles" to be removed.

The Government Should Continue Its Role as a Market for New Products and Services so That the Market Risk for R&D Can Be Reduced

With 20 million subscribers, Korea now ranks eighth in the world in terms of telephone switching capacity. Only twenty years ago, it took several months for subscribers to get a new line. Now there is true same-day service. There used to be less than one line for every 100 people. Now there are thirty-eight per 100, soon estimated to become fifty per 100. The key to this upgrade in the national telecommunication capability was the development of the TDX advanced switching system.

There were two keys to the successful development of the TDX system. One was the fruitful collaboration between the Electronics and Telecommunications Research Institute (ETRI) and local firms, such as Samsung, Goldstar, and Daewoo. Private and public sources split the development costs equally and shared the resulting patents and technology, which was commercialized independently by the firms.[41] But the more important factor was that the government guaranteed a market for the developing firms by guaranteeing procurement.

Broadly speaking, there are two kinds of risk and uncertainty in R&D. First is the risk of development, or whether the desired technology can be created. The other is market risk, or whether the technology can be sold. The collaboration between the private and public sector lessened the former risk. The latter risk was lessened by the market guaranteed by the government. Without both conditions satisfied, the firms would not have had sufficient motivation to spend scarce capital on this ambitious project.

After honing and perfecting the technology in the local market, the Korean producers are now actively selling the TDX systems abroad. In 1993, for instance, Samsung exported $321.4 million worth of TDX-related products to the Philippines, Nicaragua, Ecuador, Russia, Poland, and China. Goldstar exported $106 million to Vietnam and Romania. Korea is now, by some estimates, ahead of Japan in this crucial technology of the future information age. In order for there to be many more similarly successful examples of local technology development, the role of the government as a market must continue.

Try to Manipulate the Fierce Competition among Triad Companies to Gain Strategic Advantages

A classic bargaining strategy is to play one bidder against another. When a potential seller wants to receive the highest possible price, it is best to create a competitive bidding situation and jack up the price. It is also an advantage, however, for potential buyers to force sellers to compete with one another. This point certainly holds true for buying technology, and Korea remains an important technology purchaser from the Triad. An example of competition between technology sellers can be found in the famous VHS versus Beta wars in the late 1970s to early 1980s. Sony developed and commercialized the Beta standard well before Matsushita came up with their own VHS standard for the VCR. Yet despite the first-mover advantages of Sony, Matsushita was able to ultimately prevail by implementing a liberal licensing strategy in which their technology was transferred to any competitor agreeing to its standard. This contrasted with the strict patent protection policy of Sony. Eventually, the critical mass achieved by Matsushita convinced the software producers to drop Beta and go with the more popular and widespread VHS standard. Once this lesson was learned by the global consumer electronics industry, future product standards that were developed competed to enlist supporters to their banner. Korean consumer electronics firms have and should continue to take advantage of this competition in standards to acquire the technology they need. Similarly, Korean firms have increasingly been creating alliances with U.S. and European firms by presenting themselves as a counterweight to the dominating Japanese competitors.

Take Advantage of Undercapitalized, Small, or Venture Capital–Financed Triad Companies

By buying into or taking control of small, but technologically sophisticated, firms abroad, Korean firms can quickly come up to speed in cutting-edge technologies. An interesting phenomenon to be encouraged is the trend of Korean chaebols to take advantage of the capital needs of the innovative and entrepreneurial U.S. start-ups and trade new technology for funding. In short, provide latter-stage venture capital in return for a shortcut to new technologies. The design divisions of Korea's automobile and semiconductor companies have greatly benefited from such transactions. As permitted by GATT, expenditures of this nature can be encouraged through preferential government-sponsored loans or tax incentives.

A recent application of this strategy can be found in the 1994 acquisition of Maxtor (a top U.S. hard disk drive manufacturer) by Hyundai Electronics. Maxtor was ranked in the global top five, but it ran into financial difficulties while keeping up with the fierce industry competition. By stepping in, Hyundai gained access to world-class technology and brand recognition in one swoop to become a global player overnight. Samsung's stake in AST and LG's takeover of Zenith can be seen as similar implementations of this strategy.

CONCLUSION

"Businessmen go down with their businesses because they like the old way so well they cannot bring themselves to change. . . . Seldom does the cobbler take up a new fangled way of soling shoes and seldom does the artisan willingly take up with new methods in his trade."[42] The preceding quote by Henry Ford is an eloquent restatement of the problems facing Korea today. Within a generation, Korea has gone from abject poverty to the brink of advanced status as a nation. The institutional structure that was created with the drive for modernization has enabled Korea to transform itself from an agrarian society to an industrial one. The government acted as a benevolent but strict taskmaster for Korean businesses to force them into an operational mode appropriate for exporting mass-produced and technologically standardized products on the world market. The production-oriented mentality, based on OEM sales, has helped Korean firms become feared competitors in many global industries.

However, Korean firms are now, in effect, victims of their own success. The evolution of the competitive environment has made past modes of business obsolete (Table 4.16). Labor costs are averaging $1,144 per month, among the highest in Asia outside Japan. Triad competitors are not as liberal in their technology-transfer policies. The domestic market is no longer isolated from global competition. Direct subsidization from the government has been ruled out by the passage of a new world trading regime. If Korean firms persist in the old ways of doing business, their future will be a limited one. A new competitive strategy based on innovation must replace the old. The time for quantity has passed, and the age of quality has arrived.

Chaebols must specialize, small and medium firms must join together in a networked future, and public enterprises must be privatized. And the government has to let go. The growth of the Korean economy and its sheer size may have made any fine-tuning of micro-issues obsolete. Perhaps the time has come for the government to take a more traditional neoclassical role and limit itself to the horizontal dimension of policymaking (i.e., R&D credits, investment credits, worker training subsidies) rather than any sectoral "picking of winners." In a movie metaphor, the government would remain as a producer who provides the stage on which the actor–chaebols direct themselves toward the final product. Indirect and reactive policies should be implemented so that firms can compete in a rich and viable environment that is supportive of innovation-

and technology-development efforts. Rather than HAN (Highly Advanced National) or G-7 projects, government should concentrate on educating and training a top-notch human resources pool. Instead of direct industry subsidies, it should create and nurture a comprehensive and efficient information and computer network that enables communication and collaboration among domestic and foreign researchers. Rather than creating unnecessary and innovation-stifling regulation, the government should enhance and take care of the transportation infrastructure. In short, the time for one-way government support is gone; and two-way, symbiotic interaction between firms and the public sector should be the replacement.

Table 4.16
Korean World Competitiveness in Major Industries

Industry	Level of International Competitiveness
Iron & Steel	1. # 6 in the world in terms of total production 2. Net production cost of cold-rolled steel versus Japan -- 75.7% (1988) ---> 89.3% (1993)

Machinery	1. Lower cost competitiveness versus Taiwan, China, Southeast Asia
	2. Lower-technology competitiveness versus Triad
	  -- design, processing, assembly skills: 40%-50% versus Triad
	  -- production, quality control skills: 70-80% versus Triad
	3. Low level of indigenization for key components

Consumer Electronics	1. # 2 in the world in terms of production level
	2. Global market share (in import terms) of color televisions declining
	  -- U.S.: 6.8% (1990) ---> 4.5% (1992)
	  -- Japan: 58.6% (1990) ---> 27.6% (1992)
	  -- Germany: 6.8% (1990) ---> 4.3% (1992)
	3. Technology competitiveness versus Triad: 70%
	4. Rising labor costs
	  -- 1985-1991 labor cost appreciation rates: Korea (143%), Japan (18%), Taiwan (76%)

Computers	1. U.S. market share (in import terms) declining
	  -- 11.8% (1990) ---> 6.8% (1992)
	2. Cost competitiveness declining versus Taiwan
	  -- 386SX personal computer export price: 108%
	  -- notebook computer export price: 128%
	3. Technology level in computer peripherals less than 50% of Triad
	4. Defect rate three times that of Japan

Semiconductors	1. # 2 in total production
	2. # 2 in DRAM production (Samsung is # 1 producer in the world)
	  -- world market share 14.0% (1990) ---> 24.3% (1992)
	  -- equal or better price competitiveness versus Japan
	3. Low levels of technology in semiconductor materials, equipment, and non-memory products
	4. Own-brand exports: 70%

Table 4.16 (continued)

Industry	Level of International Competitiveness
Automobiles	1. Low levels of productivity and automation -- assembly hours per vehicle: Korea (30.3), Japan (16.8), U.S. (25.1) -- process automation rate: Korea (21.7%), Japan (38.3%), U.S. (30.6%) 2. Royalty share of sales increasing -- 0.38% (1990) ---> 0.41% (1992) 3. Low non-price competitiveness versus Triad -- new product development skills: 60%, domestic supply of components: 70% 4. Poor levels of quality (in terms of defects per ninety days after 100 cars sold) -- GM: 169 (1989) ---> 136 (1992); Ford: 149 (1989) ---> 129 (1992) -- Toyota: 117 (1989) ---> 83 (1992); Honda: 113 (1989) ---> 106 (1992)
Shipbuilding	1. # 2 in world market share in terms of billings 2. Low technology competitiveness versus Japan -- production skills: 75%; design skills: 71%; administrative skills: 68% 3. Poor process automation rate -- design: Korea (35%), Japan (80%) -- operations management: Korea (10%), Japan (35%)

Source: Korea Development Bank, *Industries of Korea* (Seoul: Korea Development Bank, 1993).

The following is a quote attributed to Abraham Lincoln: "The worst thing you could do to those you love is to do for them what they can and should do for themselves." This perfectly captures how the Korean government should direct its efforts to promote R&D.

NOTES

1. A *chaebol* is a family-owned diversified industrial conglomerate.
2. Federation of Korean Industries seminar, Seoul, Korea, November 19, 1993.
3. *Joongang Ilbo*, August 23, 1995.
4. In a related note, at a March 1993 Harvard seminar, Dr. Soon-Hoon Bae, president (current chairman) of Daewoo Electronics, explained that he must price his products an average of 17 percent lower than Sony.
5. Korean managers refer to this phenomenon as the so-called "sandwich effect," a metaphor that describes the threat to the viability of Korean firms caused from the simultaneous attack from Triad and later-developing foreign competitors.
6. *Hankook Ilbo*, February 17, 1994, p. 4.

7. Kee-Young Kim, et al., "Policies and Institutions for Industrial and Technological Development: A Korea Study," World Bank Conference paper, Yonsei University, Seoul, 1994.

8. See Kee-Young Kim and Ku-Hyun Chung, "A Technology-Transfer Model for a Firm in a Newly Industrializing Country," in *Proceedings of the International Conference of the International Business Study* (Toronto: 1988), and Linsu Kim, "Stages of Development of Industrial Technology in a LDC: A Model," *Research Policy* 9, no. 3 (1980): 254–277.

9. Charles P. Kindleberger and Bruce Herrick, *Economic Development*, 3d ed., Economics Handbook Series (New York: McGraw Hill, 1977); Won-Yong Lee, "Science and Technology Policy in Korea," in *Industrial Development Policies and Issues*, ed. Kyu-Uck Lee (Seoul: Korea Development Institute, 1986); Seong-JaeYu, "Korea Electronic Enterprises," in *Management behind Industrialization: Readings in Korean Business*, ed. Dong-Ki Kim and Linsu Kim (Seoul: Korea University Press, 1989).

10. A third category, linkage policies, is also commonly used in the supply–demand framework. However, its use here is limited, since these policies are less clearly defined and, in many cases, indistinguishable from supply policies. The linkage concepts are discussed and included under the supply-side policies.

11. Won-Yong Lee, "Science and Technology Policy."

12. Ibid.

13. Ibid.

14. Linsu Kim, Jangwoo Lee, and Jinjoo Lee, "Korea's Entry into the Computer Industry and Its Acquisition of Technological Capability," in *Management behind Industrialization: Readings in Korean Business,* ed. Dong-Ki Kim and Linsu Kim (Seoul: Korea University Press, 1989).

15. Michael Porter, *The Competitive Advantage of Nations* (New York: Free Press, 1990).

16. Dr. Soon-Hoon Bae, (then-president of Daewoo Electronics) CSIA seminar, Harvard University, March 1993.

17. For example, the *Hankook Ilbo*, a Korean daily newspaper, reports in its October 29, 1993 issue that the production technology of Korean videotape recorder manufacturers is equal to that of their Japanese competitors. However, in all other categories, such as design, brand image, and supplier quality, the Koreans fall far behind.

18. Quoted from Margaret Thatcher's memoir, *The Downing Street Years* (New York: HarperCollins, 1993), p. 6.

19. *Fortune*, July 26, 1993, p. 77. The twelve are (with their rankings) Samsung (18), Daewoo (41), Ssangyong (87), Sunkyong (90), Hyundai Motor (170), Pohang Iron and Steel (190), Hyundai Heavy Industries (232), Hyosung (236), Goldstar (307), Kia Motors (333), Honam Oil (357), and Doosan (390). *Fortune* rankings differ from the Korean rankings in that they sometimes list the entire group, as in the case of Samsung and Daewoo, and at other times separate out individual member companies. For instance, both Goldstar and Honam Oil are part of the LG (Lucky–Goldstar) Group.

20. See, for instance, William J. Abernathy and James M. Utterback, "Patterns of Industrial Innovation," *Technology Review* 80 (1978): 40–47; James M. Utterback and William J. Abernathy, "A Dynamic Model of Process and Product Innovation," *Omega* 33 (1975): 639–656.

21. See, for instance, Rebecca M. Henderson, "Successful Japanese Giants: A Major Challenge to Existing Theories of Technological Capability," unpublished working paper, Sloan School of Management, Massachusetts Institute of Technology, Cambridge, 1991; Rebecca M. Henderson and Kim B. Clark, "Architectural Innovation: the Reconfiguration of Existing Product Technologies and the Failures of Established Firms," *Administrative Science Quarterly* 35 (1990): 9–30; Rebecca M. Henderson, "Underinvestment and Incompetence as Responses to Radical Innovation: Evidence from the Photolithographic Alignment Equipment Industry," unpublished working paper, Sloan School of Management, Massachusetts Institute of Technology, Cambridge, 1990.

22. See, for instance, Michael L. Tushman and Philip Anderson, "Technological Discontinuities and Organizational Environments," *Administrative Science Quarterly* 31 (1986): 439–456; Michael L. Tushman and Elaine Romanelli, "Organizational Evolution: A Metamorphosis Model of Convergence and Reorientation," in *Research in Organizational Behavior*, vol. 7, ed. L. L. Cummings and Barry M. Staw (Greenwich, Conn.: JAI Press, 1985).

23. See, for instance, Boong-Kyu Lee, "Joint Ventures in Korea: A Transaction Cost Analysis of a Multinational Advertising Joint Venture," unpublished S. M. thesis, Sloan School of Management, Massachusetts Institute of Technology, Cambridge, 1993.

24. The total R&D investment of all firms on the Korean stock exchange was 1.8 trillion won in 1992. This total is about 40 percent of GM's $5.917-billion investment in R&D for the same year. One must note that GM is the firm with the most R&D investment in the world, followed in order by Siemens ($5.322 billion), IBM ($5.083 billion), Ford ($4.332 billion), and Hitachi ($3.907 billion). *Chosun Ilbo*, September 29, 1983.

25. Yet, in terms of personnel, the societal norms toward science and engineering professionals must be corrected so that an equally rewarding and beneficial dual ladder that runs parallel to management is developed. Too many advanced-degree holders succumb to the temptations of the skewed rewards of administrative positions and give up promising years of research. At a lower level, the government should take charge of the development of more skilled technicians through liberal establishment policies for technical institutions. At the firm level, in-house training centers should be further cultivated and encouraged by generous incentive schemes. At the universities, research should be better linked to industrial efforts, with the rewards of commercialization accruing to the schools as well.

26. Michael H. Best, in his book, *The New Competition: Institutions of Industrial Restructuring* (Cambridge, Mass.: Harvard University Press, 1990), describes the so-called "Third Italy" region as a case in which small firms have joined together to form a collective competitive entity.

27. Raymond E. Miles and Charles C. Snow, "Organizations: New Concepts for New Forms," *California Management Review* (spring 1986): 62–73; Jeffrey Pfeffer and James N. Baron, "Taking the Workers Back Out: Recent Trends in the Structuring of Employment," in *Research in Organizational Behavior*, vol. 10, ed. Barry M. Staw and L. L. Cummings (Greenwich, Conn.: JAI Press, 1988): 257–303; Peter F. Drucker, "The Coming of the New Organization," *Harvard Business Review* (January–February 1988): 45–53.

28. Benetton of Italy, with its small central core for design and finance and count-less independent suppliers, is a famous application of the network. Similar arrange-ments can be found in SMH of Switzerland, which produces Omega and other brand-name watches.

29. *Hankook Ilbo*, August 11, 1993, p. 31.

30. Farok J. Contractor and Peter Lorange, eds., *Cooperative Strategies in Inter-national Business* (Lexington, Mass.: Lexington Books, 1988).

31. "Are Foreign Partners Good for U.S. Companies?" *Business Week*, May 28, 1984, pp. 58–60.

32. B. K. Lee, "Joint Ventures in Korea."

33. An implication of this type of balance sheet is that while total return on assets are often less than 1 percent, the chaebols manage a more robust 15 to 30 percent re-turn on equity.

34. An interesting postscript to this example is that in 1993 a court ruled that the decision to breakup Kukje was unconstitutional. Although the government has ap-pealed this decision, the former owners of Kukje are already demanding that their companies be returned to them. It goes without saying that the current owners of the Kukje companies are refusing to even consider this turn of events, pointing out that they had acquired the companies through a legal bidding process. The question is yet to be resolved.

35. *Hankook Ilbo*, December 1, 1993, p. 30.

36. *Chosun Ilbo*, March 15, 1994, p. 27.

37. *Hankook Ilbo*, March 23, 1994, p. 1.

38. Ibid.

39. For instance, see David J. Teece, "Profiting from Technological Innovation: Implications for Integration, Collaboration, Licensing, and Public Policy," *Research Policy* 15 (1986): 285–305. Also, Kenneth J. Arrow, "Economic Welfare and the Al-location of Resources of Invention," in *The Rate and Direction of Inventive Activity* (Princeton: Princeton University Press, National Bureau of Economic Research, 1962).

40. *Hankook Ilbo*, May 8, 1993, p. 39; *Chosun Ilbo*, May 7, 1993, p. 10.

41. "Digital Switching Systems: Cutting Edge Technology," *Korea Economic Re-port* (April 1994): 31.

42. Henry Ford, with S. Crowther, *My Life and Work* (Garden City, N.Y.: Doubleday, 1922).

Chapter Five

SHIFTING STRATEGIES
From Cost-Advantage to Superior Value

Kwang-Doo Kim

In its steady, strenuous efforts to industrialize and compete in world markets, Korea has relied on hard-working workers, low wages, imported foreign technology, and an undervalued currency. From the 1960s until recently, that development strategy worked well. However, Korea has started to face new domestic and foreign challenges. Now it is experiencing higher labor costs, a stronger currency, the reluctance by developed countries to transfer their know-how to developing countries, and greater attempts by Korean workers to avoid dangerous, difficult, and dirty jobs. Korea has simultaneously endured declining exports, a sluggish economy, and growing fears that it might lose its competitive edge.

The endogenous and exogenous environments have been changing (as discussed in Chapters 3 and 13). Exogenously, the settlement of the Uruguay Round in December 1993 is challenging Korea's industries, along with the possible arrival of the Green Round, Blue Round, and Technology Round. On the other hand, wage hikes and declining work attitudes are weakening Korean international competitiveness. Korea must find its way out of this dilemma and re-launch itself into full industrial development.

This chapter begins by reviewing Korean development strategy since the 1980s. Next I describe a new alternative strategy, one that shifts from factor- and investment-driven development to an innovation-based economy. I then discuss the various internal and external obstacles that Korea must face in its transition to the new economy. Finally, I examine how the new strategy alternative will affect specific industries.

THE HISTORY OF KOREAN DEVELOPMENT STRATEGIES

The history of Korean modern economic development since the 1960s can be roughly divided into the following three periods: (1) 1962–1972—the period of the export-led growth strategy; (2) 1973–1981—the period of the heavy and chemical industry drives; and (3) 1982–1992—the period of stabilization and liberalization. (For further discussion of these periods, see Chapter 2.)

The Korean War (1950–1953) had nearly ruined the Korean economy. In the 1950s, the Korean savings rate was very low, but the gap between domestic investment and savings was made up by foreign aid. The Korean government adopted an import-substitution policy, developing goods for domestic use to replace imports to reconstruct the economy. Since the domestic market was small and the investment projects needed too much credit, the import-substitution strategy reached its limits. Inheriting this economic condition, the new government realized that the Korean economy was limited by scarcities in natural resources, skilled labor, and domestic market capacity. Fortunately, the Korean government then turned its focus toward the world market by taking the outward-looking development strategy of the 1960s and early 1970s (1962–1971).

This development strategy resulted in very fast economic growth. However, Korea's success in the 1960s was possible because workers were well educated and hard working due to the Confucian cultural background; entrepreneurs were eager to play their new roles and strengthen the country's industrial base; government forged its role as a coordinator; and world and domestic economic environments were also favorable.[1]

In the early 1970s, the establishment of U.S. diplomatic relations with China provoked the fear among Koreans of possible U.S. troop withdrawals from their country. The first oil crisis then hit the Korean peninsula, revealing to the Korean people the importance of economic self-sufficiency. In addition, other developing countries such as China started using cheaper labor to supply labor-intensive manufacturing products to the international markets. Following these important events, the Korean government realized that its economy was vulnerable to external shocks. Therefore, national economic security became one of its most important national goals. To accomplish this goal, the Korean government selected heavy and chemical industries as potential import-substitution industries. This might be called the second stage of import substitution because Korea completed the first stage of import substitution in the 1950s. It should be emphasized that in developing this new economy, some of the heavy and chemical industries were promoted not only as a means of import substitution but also as a means of export expansion.[2]

The average annual rate of Korean economic growth from 1972 to 1981 was 7.5 percent, and capital was quickly accumulated. However, the easy monetary policy and suppressed interest rates resulted in extremely high inflation, which most seriously afflicted the real estate market. The negative results of the heavy and chemical industry drive included heavy external debt, high constant inflation, greater inequality in income distribution, economic concentration by the chaebol, and an excessive dependence on oil prices and other conditions within the global economy that were beyond Korea's control. The second oil crisis revealed all of these problems. Since its capital-intensive growth strategy required heavy international borrowing, Korea's external debt was very vulnerable to fluctuations in the world economy.[3]

Regarding export promotion, the economic policies in the 1960s worked much better than those of the 1970s. While protecting markets of domestic industries, the government boosted the private sector's exports through various incentives. The industrial policy of the 1960s was results oriented; and at this time, the private sector made a major contribution to economic success. In contrast, the industrial policy in the 1970s was process oriented, retaining the goal of export expansion by promoting selected industries, usually through government intervention. As a result, the Korean economy of the 1960s outperformed its results of the 1970s.

To cope with the economic problems inherited from the 1970s, the Korean government decided in the early 1980s to move the economy toward stabilization and liberalization. To suppress inflation, it cut public spending drastically and managed a very tight monetary growth policy.[4] These policies were successful. The government simultaneously adopted a liberalization policy in various areas of the economy that successfully promoted competition and enhanced the efficiency of the market mechanism.

From 1986 to 1988, Korea experienced a major economic boom as a result of the so-called "Three Lows" (low oil prices, low interest rates, and low exchange rates). In spite of this favorable macroeconomic development, the growing balance-of-payments surplus caused rapid monetary expansion, generating inflationary pressure and growing trade friction. The period of 1986 to 1988 could thus be called one of macroeconomic adjustment to the current balance-of-payments surplus. However, since the exchange rate was not adjusted optimally, it generated too much external surplus from 1986 to 1988; it made the current account surplus decrease in 1989; and it created a deficit for 1990 and 1991.[5] In addition, Korea experienced high wage hikes associated with work strikes, a decline in labor productivity that began in 1987, and a variety of serious political problems stemming from the transition to democratization. These factors all contributed to Korea's loss of its competitive edge.

In summary, since the 1980s, Korea has rapidly modernized its industrial structure by promoting capital investment and technology development, a policy designed to spur industrial adjustment toward high value-added and technology-intensive products. In the 1980s, the economic development strategy shifted from strong and extensive government intervention in specific industries to the more liberalized and open market mechanism. In line with this industrial policy, the technology-intensive industries became more important. However, Korea's policy of adjustment to the trade surplus was excessive. As a result, from 1986 to 1990, the unit labor cost (in dollars) for Korean workers increased too much relative to those of Japan and Taiwan. Therefore, the country's industrial competitiveness seriously deteriorated.

THE SEARCH FOR A NEW STRATEGY

Midway through the 1990s, new external and internal changes are challenging Korea's economic success and demanding new strategies for development. The exogenous changes are discussed in Chapters 3 and 13. We next examine the recent changes within Korea in the 1990s and try to predict some future prospects for the Korean economy.

Korean Manufacturing Firms

Korean manufacturing firms usually have a small scale of production relative to the world market, with low levels of technology and factory automation. They often experience excessive competition or excess production capacity as a result of new firms entering the industry and because of the limitations of domestic demand and lack of knowledge about foreign markets. Korean firms performed well in the world market in the past, but they mainly relied on original equipment manufacturer (OEM) exports under foreign brand names. In other words, they neglected to cultivate their own brands and new markets. As a result, Korean technological competence remains invisible to the outside world.[6]

Labor and Wage-Related Problems

Since the late 1970s, Korea has faced growing conflicts between economic classes as economic concentration is increasing. A few large conglomerate firms contribute the majority of manufacturing gross national product (GNP). Once praised for their diligence in spite of low wages, workers are increasingly asking for a larger proportion of the economic pie. Labor costs are increasing too rapidly (see Tables 5.1, 5.2, and 5.3), so Korean industries are losing their price competitiveness. From 1986 to 1990, the increase in the annual nominal wage rate in the manufacturing sector was 19 percent, while labor productivity jumped by only 4.6 percent annually. According to M. Ishaq Nadri, labor productivity is decreasing.[7]

When changes in unit labor cost and exchange rate are combined, from 1986 to 1990 Korea's unit labor cost (in dollars) increased at an annual rate of 20 percent. In contrast, that for Japan and Taiwan increased only by 2 percent and 13 percent, respectively. As a result, Korea's export competitiveness has sharply deteriorated. Meanwhile, labor unions have strengthened their

Table 5.1
International Comparison of the Unit Dollar Labor Cost Price

	1976	1977	1978	1979	Annual Change 1976-79 (Percentage)
Korea	131.8	161.6	194.8	273.3	27.5
Taiwan	104.0	116.8	122.1	136.2	9.4
Singapore	89.3	88.9	102.1	100.1	3.9
Japan	104.6	123.2	166.3	155.7	14.2

Source: Sung-Hee Jwa, 1991, p.25.

Table 5.2
Historical Performance of the Korean Economy

	Growth Rate (Average Percentage per Year)		Per Capita GNP Current U.S$	As a Percentage of GNP (Current Price)	
	Labor Force	Real GNP		Investment	Savings
1962-1966	2.84	7.8	104	15.6	8.7
1967-1971	3.05	9.7	210	29.4	18.8
1972-1976	4.39	10.1	523	27.2	20.5
1977-1981	2.41	6.0	1,546	32.5	26.6
1982-1990	2.57	10.0	3,165	31.3	32.4
1982	0.52	7.2	1,824	29.8	25.0
1983	0.32	12.6	2,002	29.7	28.1
1984	-0.95	9.3	2,158	30.9	30.3
1985	3.80	7.0	2,194	30.3	29.5
1986	3.38	12.9	2,505	29.7	33.5
1987	4.70	12.8	3,110	29.9	36.9
1988	2.56	12.4	4,127	30.7	38.1
1989	3.38	6.8	4,994	33.5	35.3
1990	2.87	9.0	5,569	37.1	35.3
1962-1992	3.03	8.7	–	–	–

Source: Bank of Korea, *Economic Statistics Yearbook, and Monthly Statistics of Korea,* various issues.

positions, sometimes staging strikes. Frequent labor disputes over the past few years have substantially undermined the international competitiveness of Korean industries. A vicious spiral of wage and living expenses has recently developed that is directly linked to skyrocketing housing costs. In response to these labor-wage problems, Korean industry needs productivity growth from automation and a restructuring toward high value-added products.

A change in attitude among Korean workers has created added burdens as Korea strives for a more productive economy. Korean workers have traditionally

Table 5.3
Trend of Unit Labor Costs in the Manufacturing Sector for Korea

	1985	1986	1987	1988	1989	1990	Rate of Change (1986-1990)
Nominal Wage	91.6	100.0	111.6	133.5	166.9	200.6	19.0
Labor Productivity	92.3	100.0	102.9	110.4	110.4	119.6	4.6
Unit Labor Cost	99.2	100.0	108.5	120.9	151.2	167.8	13.8
Won-dollar Exchange Rate	98.7	100.0	93.3	82.9	76.2	80.3	-5.3
Unit Labor Cost in dollars	100.5	100.0 (0.1)	116.2 (16.2)	145.8 (25.5)	198.4 (36.1)	208.9 (5.3)	20.2
Export Unit Price	97.9	100.0 (2.1)	110.1 (10.1)	123.1 (13.6)	137.3 (9.7)	136.9 (-0.3)	8.2

Source: Sung-Hee Jwa, 1991, p. 45.
Notes: Period average.
   The number in parenthesis is the rate of change over the previous year (percentage).

been praised for their hard-working attitudes in spite of low wages. However, they are now avoiding difficult, dangerous, or dirty jobs (so-called 3D jobs), asking for higher wages and shorter working hours, and seeking more comfortable working conditions. The hard-working spirit of Korean workers is disappearing. If this dedication to hard work cannot be recovered, as seems unlikely, Korea will have to find another way to reform its economy to be competitive in the world. It seems unlikely that Korea can rely on its traditional culture to recover the needed worker spirit. Incentives for productivity and added value, such as those used in other countries, will have to play an increasing role.

A NEW KOREAN DEVELOPMENT STRATEGY

   Korean competitiveness has been declining, at least when compared to other rapidly developing countries.[8] Which development strategy should the Korean government take to turn this trend around? The new strategy should be centered on the acceleration of innovation, both to increase productivity and to give Korea unique sources of competitive advantage. This, in turn, requires the development of Korea's capabilities in science, technology, and their forms of exploitation. As we will next consider, a new strategy must take into account the future prospects of the Korean economy and the role of specific industries.

The future prospects for the economy will be determined in part by the New Five-Year Economic Development Plan (1994–1998) prepared by the Korean government in 1993, which emphasizes improving Korea's international competitiveness. It optimistically predicts that from 1993 to 1998, the average rate of economic growth will be 6.9 percent, and per-capita current GNP will be U.S.$14,076 in 1998. The government is staking out even bolder goals for the future. In 1996, the Korea Development Institute issued a report at the request of the finance minister entitled the "Vision and Development Strategy of the Korean Economy in the 21st Century." These goals, displayed in Table 5.4, are even more ambitious. They project a threefold real increase in per-capita GNP by the year 2020 and seventh-place ranking in world GNP. Most significant for Korea's innovation-based strategy is the assumption that in 2020 the rate of technological advancement will be making a 30-percent contribution to GNP (Table 5.4).

The government will try, under the plan, to encourage technological and managerial innovation to stimulate the growth potential of the Korean economy. The current Five-Year Plan also attempts to increase the building of necessary social infrastructure and to expand industrial sites. It also plans to ease labor shortages, especially in the manufacturing industries. The government aims to realign the social and economic systems according to free-market principles and to ease economic concentration. To promote greater industrial competitiveness and innovation, the government will attempt to simplify and deregulate administrative procedures.

In addition, the New Five-Year Economic Development Plan intends to improve social welfare and socioeconomic fairness. In light of the Uruguay Round's impact upon the agricultural sector, the government plans to increase off-farm incomes in rural areas. It also intends to expand housing supply by increasing the availability of housing loans. The New Five-Year plan emphasizes financial liberalization, although the Organization for Economic Cooperation and Development (OECD) requirements for opening financial markets have generated some questions in Seoul about the merits of postponing OECD membership.

At Korea's current stage of development, access to and mastery of technology may be the major constraint to the achievement of industrialized country status. Indeed, the New Five-Year Plan points out technology development as the most crucial of all issues.

The Status and Tasks of Manufacturing Industries

Since the 1960s, the Korean manufacturing sector has led the economy, achieving more than 10 percent annual growth. In most Korean manufacturing

Table 5.4
New Long-Term Economic Plan

Year	1995	2000	2010	2020
GDP (current, billions of U.S. dollars)	456	872	2107	4081
World rank in GDP (U.S. dollars)	11th	9th	8th	7th
Per capita GDP (U.S. dollars)	10,163	18,200	41,300	80,600
Per capita GDP in constant 1995 U.S. dollars	(10,163)	(13,700)	(22,000)	(32,000)
Industrial Structure (percentage):				
Agriculture and Fisheries	6.6	3.9	3.0	1.6
Manufactures	26.9	27.4	26.9	26.8
Services	66.2	68.6	70.2	71.9
R&D Expenditures as Percent of GNP	2.7	3.6	4.0	4.0
High Tech Industry as Percent of Manufacturing	14.8	19.0	31.6	44.5
Contribution of Rate of Advance of Technology to GNP Growth	13	17	22	30

Source: Korea Development Institute, "Vision and Development Strategy of the Korean Economy in the 21st Century," Seoul: Korea Development Institute, July 1996.

industries, excluding high technology, mass production has been established. However, Korea has a relatively small supply capacity in the global market; and its products often suffer a quality gap compared with those of developed countries. Korean heavy and chemical industries have not passed beyond the low value-added stage, continuing to use imports for critical components and equipment. More than 40 percent of industrial equipment is imported. Labor-intensive light industries, once major exporters, are now losing their price competitiveness, inducing a sustained deficit by current accounts and a share loss in traditional export markets such as the United States.

Korean industry, in general, is narrowing the technology gap between itself and industry in developed countries. However, Korean industries are weak in technology related to high technology, high value-added products, and core parts of manufacturing technology.

The future opportunities for growth of the Korean economy lie in two areas: the advancement of heavy and chemical industries through process-technology improvements and, in selected light industries, emphasizing high value-added products. Process-technology advances can come through development of the world's top-class machinery, parts, and materials technology. To strengthen competitiveness in light industry, the focus should be on the production of high value-added products through design technology and the development of high-grade materials.

Neither Japan nor the United States could dominate high-technology markets without a rich, competitive, indigenous collection of small- to medium-size enterprises (SMEs) specializing in some area of technology—tools, instruments, materials, services, software, and the like. Korea's industrial structure is very thin in this respect. The chaebols are well organized to exploit technologies that they acquire from abroad. However, if they want to innovate independently, they need access to a variety of good ideas and clever components, materials, and services from small and medium firms. This is a basic necessity. In this sense, cooperative relationships between large firms and their small- and medium-size counterparts should be strengthened and reorganized.

FROM FACTOR-DRIVEN DEVELOPMENT TO AN INNOVATION-DRIVEN ECONOMY

The role of the Korean government has always been decisive and important in its country's economic development. Even in the 1970s, the Korean government heavily intervened in allocating economic resources. Autonomous market mechanisms should now be enhanced at the expense of market regulation. Simply deregulating markets is not desirable because of possible market failures. Therefore, the content and the quality of regulation should be changed. The government should provide a vision for future economic prospects, providing the national goal to private-sector firms, while leaving implementation decisions to the firms.

A country's level of technology will determine its competitiveness, since this factor correlates with increases in labor productivity. Since importing technology becomes more difficult and less satisfactory as a nation reaches technological maturity, the country must develop its own technological capacity. Technology, in turn, relies on the level of a country's science. The task of both the Korean government and private firms is to develop science and technology (S&T) together. Basic science should be emphasized and subsidized by both government and industry.

Thus, the development of S&T should be the main target of Korean policy through the end of the 1990s. This implies that the policy focus of Korean development strategy should be changed from factor-driven and investment-driven development to a more innovation-driven economy.

How can Korea move toward a high-technology and high value-added oriented economy? Effective ways to improve the industrial structure depend on the stage of development of each industry sector, its ability to absorb and acquire technology, and its international position. The Korean industrial structure can supplement its high technology and become more value-added by making interindustry or intra-industry adjustments. The interindustry adjustments can be made by placing more weight on the capital goods industry, especially machinery. Intra-industry adjustments must be accomplished mainly within the automobile, electronics, and shipbuilding industries.

Korea has made interindustry structural adjustments over the past thirty years, ranging from agriculture to light industry, from light industry to materials, from materials to heavy and chemical industries, from heavy and chemical industries to process assembly–based heavy industry. In most developed countries, the machinery industry plays the most important role in the manufacturing sector. In Korea, however, the machinery industry is a very small part of manufacturing production. The weakness of this industry is the main cause of the trade deficit, resulting in heavy imports, especially from Japan. Thus, the development of machinery industry is the most important factor in interindustry adjustment.

The need to develop machinery industry requires changes in how the market and the government relate to each other, especially in the early stages of an export-oriented development strategy. Lack of demand and weaknesses in technology suggest a government role in promoting the precision, durability, and quality of the machinery industry's products. This industry also needs additional training of highly skilled engineers.

For interindustry adjustment, the relationship between supplier firms and product integrators is critical. This is the most rapid area of change in the U.S. industry structure as firms focus on core competence, look to alliances with suppliers for specialized technologies, and prepare for what is called "agile manufacturing." Thus, competitors are going to be much more effective at exploiting the synergy between large firms with strong market access and their suppliers, who are being granted more freedom to innovate, while receiving more help from their larger customers. Unfortunately, Korea has a weak small- and medium-size manufacturing economy. Chapter 10 compares Korea with Taiwan, arguing that a strong small- to medium-size high-technology–firm sector accounts for how Taiwan is pulling ahead of Korea. Thus, Korea should strengthen the SME sector and reestablish the cooperative relationship between the SMEs and large firms.

The direction of intra-industry adjustment should also be considered. Korean industrial structure partially approaches the industrial structure of developed countries. Although the textile industry has a relatively high share of the economy, and machinery constitutes a relatively low proportion, the Korean manufacturing sector has moderate shares of electronics, automobiles, chemicals, steel, and shipbuilding in comparison with the industrial balance in the manufacturing sectors of developed countries. However, when we compare the absolute level of Korean and developed countries' industries, we can easily notice the gap between Korea and its competitors. Most Korean products are still middle leveled or low leveled because of the nation's limited design and marketing abilities and production technology. Korean intra-industry adjustment should be directed to increase local sources of core parts; ensure strong product design and development technology; develop Korean brands; improve marketing abilities; and especially focus on automation, on improving information, and on internationalization.

Intra-industry adjustments, including deepening the internal structure of large-scale industries, such as automobiles, electronics, and shipbuilding, will be the main force in restructuring Korean industrial structure. These changes will increase the amount of machinery production relative to assembly-based heavy industry. To shift Korean production toward high-technology or high value-added products, design technology and reverse engineering ability should be well developed among Korean firms.

Promotion of Science and Technology Innovation

How can Korea strengthen its international competitiveness? In one word, innovation. Many Koreans believe that Korea has neglected the importance of innovation. Innovation is very important because it has spillover effects on other industries. The Korean government is pushing to boost the national spending on research and development (R&D) to between 4 and 5 percent of GNP by the year 2001, up from 2.3 percent in 1989. The majority of this increase will have to come from the private sector. However, government investment spending should be oriented toward the development of the S&T base most conducive to encouraging innovation.

Korea's great strides in semiconductors drew world attention, perhaps creating a misleading image of the country as a high-technology haven.[9] In fact, Korea had to purchase its photolithography masks, production equipment, chemicals, and design tools from Japan and the United States. Overall, the proportion of imports used in Korean production is decreasing because of increased local sourcing. However, the manufacturing sector still depends on imports that account for more than 30 to 40 percent of its manufacturing costs.

The importance of technology as a production factor becomes greater as technology protectionism rises among the developed countries. In other words, whether a country has a source of its own technology is a crucial factor for economic development. Korea should exert itself to increase the proportions of homemade products in the manufacturing output to make Korean industry structure high value-added. To do this, technology development in the parts and materials sector is absolutely necessary. This development places special emphasis on the small- to medium-size firms.

Because of recent changes in the domestic and foreign environments, Korea can no longer depend on its imported technology to continue to grow. Furthermore, it cannot continue to depend on a production structure in which middle-level or low-level quality products are its primary export goods. Korea should transform its production structure toward high value-added and high-technology products such as industrial equipment and innovative parts. It is also very important that firms have source technology, which induces the growth of technology-development capacity. The source technology may come from the country's own R&D development. The proportion of homemade products should eventually increase as the import dependence declines.

Nadri concludes that Korean industries have benefited greatly from their R&D investment.[10] The rate of return on R&D investment in the manufacturing sector has been very high compared to that in the Japanese and U.S. sectors. R&D investment has played a major role in narrowing the gap between levels of labor productivity in the Korean and Japanese manufacturing sectors.[11]

Role of the Korean Government in the New Development Strategy

In a market economy, the functioning of firms is the most important factor for economic development. However, the responsibility of government economic policy is to provide fair rules and encourage open-market competition. The government must support product standardization and technology development. It should also give firms institutional support for the internationalization of business activity and for strategic rearing of the core parts and intermediate goods industries.

The Korean distribution system for agricultural and fishery products should also be rationally reformed to lessen its heavy and burdensome costs to producers and consumers.

The government should also support technology development, cultivation of a proper labor supply, and efficient financing. It must promote labor education and factory automation to avoid a shortage of skilled labor. Financial markets must efficiently allocate funds, particularly for smaller firms that have difficulty competing with the chaebols for investment funding. It would help to have a vigorous system of highly competitive domestic commercial banks, all vying with each other for investments from innovative but smaller firms that yield high returns. The government also must provide a support system for firms' technology development. For internationalization of the industry, government may help firms' foreign direct investment or foreign marketing efforts. It should encourage cooperation among firms, universities, and research institutes.

As technological protectionism expands all over the world, autonomous technology development has become very urgent. R&D investment, research personnel and facilities, and technological information services should be extended. Such investments not only strengthen Korean indigenous capability but also increase Korea's bargaining power for importing the high technology it needs. The center of the R&D effort is the individual firm's responsibility, but the government should seek to induce each firm's autonomous S&T development efforts.

As the industrial structure advances, firms may reach toward larger scale and globalization of their businesses. As innovation rates in the world market accelerate and product life shortens, consumer demands are becoming increasingly diverse. Under these circumstances, investment risk may increase and competition may become fierce. Firms are likely to encounter difficulty in their internationalization. Therefore, at the government level, cooperation among countries is necessary to minimize international investment risk. Especially in the case of automobile industry, the correct timing of a government decision to allow the importation of foreign-produced automobiles is crucial. Liberalizing automobile importation too quickly may jeopardize the automobile industry, while appropriately speedy import liberalization may promote competition among domestic, oligopolistic automobile producers.

Let us look at some other industries. In the chemical industry, the government should orchestrate a proper balance between supply and production capacity by coordinating competition among chemical firms. In the shipbuilding and aircraft industries, government may take a role in building a pan-national research system. It should improve the existing shipbuilding finance system and work to create new shipbuilding financing tools favorable for the shipbuilding industry.

In summary, the proper role of the government is to provide a long-run vision, to support the nation's S&T base, to encourage the development of parts and intermediate capital goods, to stimulate the competitiveness of SMEs, and to help the firms' globalization effort of their businesses.

The Role of Korean Firms in the New Development Strategy

Korean firms should seek research partnerships among domestic and foreign firms. They can also pursue business globalization through international cooperation with world-class firms.[12] These companies should develop their own brands, make the appropriate marketing efforts, and increase domestic sourcing of parts. The growth strategy of Korean manufacturing firms may include technology development, globalization, and diversification.[13] Korean manufacturing firms should concentrate on their own S&T development to gain competitive advantage from technological factors rather than relying on the low wages of skilled, dedicated workers. In summary, Korean firms must develop their own sources of technology through R&D investment in their own organizations, in new high-technology SMEs supplying the OEMs, and through alliances with foreign enterprises.

NOTES

1. At that time, the philosophy of free trade surged around the world. Domestically, Korea's inflation was also low enough to offer favorable circumstances.

2. For example, shipbuilding and machinery could achieve significant levels of exports within a short period of time.

3. In fact, Korea's foreign debt grew quickly. This was also due to the rising trade deficit, the second oil crisis, and the sharp increase in international interest rates.

4. For example, the government froze its budget in 1984. It also removed various subsidies and tax incentives to heavy industries and the like. Therefore, the overall fiscal deficit greatly decreased, from 4 percent of GNP in 1981 to about 1 percent a few years later. On the other hand, the money-supply growth dropped to about 10 to 15 percent in the mid-1980s, compared to about 30 percent in the late 1970s.

5. In 1986 and 1987, Korea's exchange rate was depreciated in real terms. This caused overly successful economic performance from 1986 to 1988, which resulted in the large and rapid appreciation of the exchange rate in 1988 and 1989.

6. Americans know that Korea produces cars, but they assume that there is only one car company—Hyundai. However, there are six Korean automakers in Korea, some of whom export their cars to the United States under brand names such as Ford or General Motors (GM). For example, Daewoo Motors company exports Leman under the name of GM Leman, and Kia Motors sells its Pride in the United States under the brand of Ford Festiva.

7. M. Ishaq Nadri, *Output and Labor Productivity, R&D Expenditure and Catch-up Scenarios: A Comparison of the U.S., Japanese, and Korean Manufacturing Sector* (Seoul: Korea Economic Research Institute, 1993).

8. World Economy Forum and IMO have reported the competitiveness of the industry in many countries. According to its recent report (1994), Korea is ranked as seventh among eighteen developing countries. However, Korean competitiveness has declined from its previous rank of third in 1991, fifth in 1992, and sixth in 1993. In 1994, Korea was behind Singapore, Hong Kong, Malaysia, Taiwan, Chile, and Thailand.

9. In August 1994, Samsung electronics reported itself as the first successful developer of a 256-megabit memory chip in the world. However, Samsung still needs to import many components of that chip.

10. Nadri, *Output and Labor Productivity*.

11. Ibid. Nadri predicted that the Korean manufacturing sector could overtake the Japanese sector in productivity within four to five years if it can sustain the high growth rate of traditional input experienced in the 1980s. However, he pointed out that such high rates of growth of inputs are not likely to be sustainable because of the slow growth of population, rising wage rate, and the slow pace of autonomous technological progress. Thus, he argued that only high-level R&D by the Korean manufacturing sector could offset the technological gap between the Korean and Japanese sectors. It could also considerably shorten the catch-up period as Korea faces a lower growth of traditional inputs.

12. Cooperative international specialization between developed countries and developing countries seems to be increasing. The globalization of product markets is unavoidable because the lifestyles and behavior of each country's consumers are becoming more homogenous.

13. Firms should try to diversify their business, for example, by increasing the volume of products they produce, enlarging their market share, and increasing their market regions. These approaches are necessary for maintaining the growth of firms.

Part Two

KOREA'S CURRENT RESOURCES FOR INNOVATION

Chapter Six

PROMOTING THE CULTURE OF SCIENCE AND INNOVATION

Seong-Rae Park and Hak-Soo Kim

Korean citizens need to learn how to create a culture based on scientific and technological innovation. In fact, innovation is a key to accomplishing President Kim Young-Sam's ambitions for national reform. His political slogan, "*Shin Hankook* (New Korea)," is apparently aimed at re-creating Korea by emulating technologically and economically advanced countries such as the United States, Japan, and Germany.

Although scientific and technological innovation may be the key to Korea's economic success, Koreans are pessimistic about the country's development and potential in this area. According to a 1991 survey conducted by Korea Gallup, Korean adults judged that the nation's science and technology (S&T) lagged 30.46 years behind the United States and 23.35 years behind Japan.[1] When the respondents ranked six countries in order of scientific and technological development, the United States was ranked, on average, 1.52; Japan was 2.42; Germany was 3.07; Russia was 3.37; Korea was 4.98; and China was 5.62.[2] Lack of research-and-development (R&D) investment was ranked as the primary reason why Korean S&T had lagged behind advanced countries (Figure 6.1).

This perception was also quite similar to the views of most professional scientists and engineers. According to a 1992 survey sponsored by the Korea Science Foundation (KSF), about 80 percent of the respondents thought that

Figure 6.1
Korean Public Opinion Poll: Primary Reasons for Korea's Underdevelopment in Science and Technology (in Percentage)

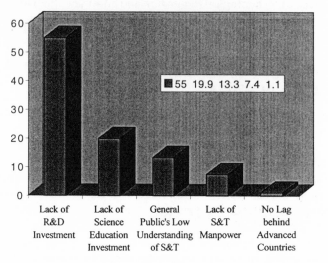

Source: Korea Science Foundation, "The Survey Report of Public Understanding of Science and Technology," conducted by Korea Gallup, April 1991.

Korea's level of research in basic sciences was low relative to the world level.[3] When Korea's research capacity was compared to the world leaders, 74 percent of the respondents ranked it low in energy-related sciences, 68.5 percent in advanced sciences, and 41.8 percent in other applied sciences. Among the scientists and engineers in this poll, 96.2 percent believed that lack of interest in technology development by managers of Korean enterprises was a major obstacle to improving S&T. They named several additional roadblocks: lack of capability of Korean scientists and engineers (88.1%), inadequate support from the government (98.6%), lack of cooperation between industrial sectors and research institutes (90.5%), the general public's lack of confidence in domestic technology (79.9%), and inadequate R&D investment (98.5%). These results indicate that professionals were more critical of Korea's level of S&T than the general public. They believed that all the key factors indispensable to developing S&T were seriously deficient.

These two surveys showed that Korean people had not paid much attention to technological innovation until 1992 because they believed that they lacked innovative capability and the appropriate conditions for mobilizing the required capability. In short, technological innovation seemed quite remote to Korean people.

This chapter first examines the history of scientific and technological development in Korean culture to help identify problems that the nation must address. Next, we describe how the Korean people are gaining awareness of the importance of technological innovation and how the culture of innovation has been promoted in Korea. Finally, we suggest some options for promoting innovative culture.

THE HISTORY OF SCIENCE AND TECHNOLOGY IN KOREA

Feelings of apathy and helplessness among Koreans with respect to their capacity for innovation are understandable when one examines cultural history over the past few hundred years. Two features stand out: First, internal development of S&T was not as strongly encouraged as in the West because of Korea's cultural and social values. Second, Korea lacked contact with western scientific thinking until the seventeenth century because missionaries virtually ignored the remote country in favor of China and Japan.

However, the early history of Korea is not without evidence of both a strong interest in scientific observation and a few outstanding examples of technological achievement. In the area of printing, the first known example of movable metal type technology in the world was in place from the early thirteenth century, during the Koryo Dynasty. This advance, utilizing bronze technology, followed a printing tradition that probably included the world's first example of wood block printing.

Early Japanese records show that Korea had a wide array of its own scientific innovations as well as those it borrowed from China. Korean expeditions to Japan were responsible for nearly all of the S&T in Japan in the Nara and early Heian periods. According to the *Nihon shoki*, the Japanese history compiled in the early eighth century, all Chinese learning, including the Chinese characters and major classics such as the Confucian Analects, were known to the Japanese through Korean scholars visiting Japan. In 554 c.e., Paekche sent Korean doctors, herb specialists, calendar specialists, and diviners to Japan. In 602 c.e., Kwalluk, a Paekche monk, was dispatched to deliver books on astronomy, calendar-making, geography, and divination to Japan, where he stayed to train Japanese students. Paper and writing ink, as well as the flour mill, were also introduced to Japan from Korea. With the rise of Buddhism in Japan, all the important techniques related to the building of temples, pagodas, and temple bells were learned from the Korean Buddhist scholars and technicians.

Koreans showed early interest in astronomical observations, as evidenced by the building of a unique star-gazing tower, *Ch'omsongdae*, in 633 c.e. Korea's great scientific interests continued throughout Korean history. The *Samguk sagi* (the *Annals of the Three Kingdoms Period*), for instance, has recorded about a thousand natural phenomena as integral parts of its entries. The next major historical source in Korea, the *Koryosa* (the *History of the Koryo Period*), includes about 6,500 such records on natural phenomena. According to records from the *Sillok* (the *Veritable Records*) compiled by one of this article's authors (Seong-Rae Park), about 8,000 observations were noted during the first century of the dynasty (1392–1510).

The great concern for astronomical or "heavenly" phenomena was based on the traditional belief that Heaven serves as a sort of mirror for earthly government and politics. Any phenomena, such as solar eclipses and stars shining during daylight (infringing on the sun's normal brightness), were omens of a danger to the throne.

Early Korean interest in earthly matters equaled attention paid to the heavens. Geomancy, a method of divination, began with a Buddhist monk named Toson toward the end of the Unified Silla period. Ever since the Koryo Dynasty, geomancy has played an important role in the daily lives of the people as well as in national politics.

Great strides in S&T were made under the reign of King Sejong (reigned 1412–1450), the best-known cultural hero in Korean history. Perhaps the most important inventions were the many ingenious instruments of astronomy and horology (the science of timekeeping), including a self-striking water clock built by King Sejong and a half dozen different kinds of sundials. During his reign, King Sejong also built the Royal Observatory in his main palace in Seoul. Around the lake of Kyonghoeru in the Kyongbok Palace, he prepared a series of astronomical and horological devices, including a simplified armillary sphere, the self-striking water clock, a "jade clock," and a forty-feet high bronze gnomon to measure the exact altitude of the sun. During his tenure, a rain gauge was invented that, for the first time in the world history, precisely measured rainfall. In addition, under King Sejong's reign, the Korean alphabets were invented; herbal medicine was successfully accommodated to the local conditions of Korea; and important technological advances were made regarding printing and gunpowder.

In 1442, Korea made its greatest strides in astronomy when the Korean version of traditional calendrical sciences was compiled into the *Ch'ilchongsan* (*On the Calculations of the Seven Luminaries*). This book helped Koreans calculate and accurately predict all the major heavenly phenomena, such as solar eclipses and other stellar movements. The first Japanese calendar, created by the astronomer Shibukawa Harumi, was made possible by the Korean version in the Sejong period.

The Sejong period witnessed one of the finest inventions in Korean technology, a great warship called the turtle boat. Built during the Hideyoshi invasions (1592–1598), the boat covered and thereby protected the sailors on board. Iron spikes were nailed over the cover of the boat to prevent the landing of enemies. Under the brilliant leadership of Admiral Yi Sunsin, the turtle boats led to a succession of legendary victories for both the Koreans and the Japanese.

During this period of Japanese invasions, Dr. Ho Chun (1546–1615) compiled his medical masterpiece, the *Tongui pogam* (*Mirror of Korean Medicine*). The Koreanization of the dominant Chinese medicine in Korea had begun in the late Koryo period with a succession of medical books titled *Korean Medicine*, which continued to be published until the early Choson period. The *Hyangyak chipsongbang* (*Compendia of Korean Pharmacopeia*) in 1433 was perhaps the most celebrated of these books. Dr. Ho's *Mirror* was the most important successor of the tradition. It has been republished many times in Korea, Japan, and China and is still in print.

All the aforementioned achievements in S&T during premodern Korean history offer proof of the culture's capacity for innovation. Before we look at Korea's contemporary morale problems regarding its capacity to develop its S&T, we will examine Korea's first encounters with western science.

THE INTRODUCTION OF WESTERN SCIENCE

The introduction of western sciences and technologies into Korea was later and more indirect than in China and Japan, since Korea was north of the routes that western missionary scientists took to China. Thus, few westerners visited Korea before the opening of the country in 1876. Beginning with Ambassador Chong Tu-Won's return from China to Korea in 1630 and Crown Prince Sohyon's trip to China in 1644, Korean scholars attempted to stay informed about western science in indirect ways, especially through its contacts with China.

Western science's influence on Korea became quite obvious beginning in the nineteenth century. Ch'oe Han-Gi (1803–1877) used western scientific concepts in his writings, which first introduced the western writing system to Korean readers. In 1886, western languages were first taught in Korea with the opening of the Royal English School. Although the Japanese had been translating western scientific books since 1774, Koreans did not begin their translations until the nineteenth century. Thus, Korea was relatively isolated from western scientific concepts until its opening to the West in 1876.

Between 1876 and 1910, science education in Korea was limited to the intermediate levels. The Korean government started some professional schools, which did not survive annexation by the Japanese in 1910. When the Japanese opened Korea's first university, the University of Seoul, in 1926, there were no science or engineering departments. These were not added until 1941.

SCIENCE AND TECHNOLOGY AFTER LIBERATION

When liberation came to Korea in 1945, Korea had to start to build its modern S&T from scratch. There were a few dozen college graduates in natural S&T at the time of the liberation, but only several of them had Ph.D.'s (see Chapter 7). This very limited workforce in science was divided into two camps because of the immediate North–South division of Korea. Poorly trained and under-degreed Korean scientists and engineers had suddenly become college professors and research leaders of the nation on both sides of the 38th Parallel.

Only after the armistice in 1953 did the two Koreas begin their development of modern S&T, largely with help from their more advanced allies. They were very diligent in introducing western S&T, at least in their form, if not the content.

Under President Syngman Rhee, Korea created a high government office in charge of the S&T of the nation. The Office of Atomic Energy, opened officially in 1959, was meant to be the national center for S&T, notwithstanding its name. Financial support came from the Atoms for Peace program of the United States under President Eisenhower.

It was largely through this program, supplemented by other similar ones— including the Agency for International Development (AID), the United Nations Development Program (UNDP), and the Colombo Plan—that many young Koreans found their way to America and to European countries for studies in modern science and engineering—the first such venture in Korean history. A total of 189 Korean students were dispatched under scholarships through the Atoms for Peace program alone from 1956 to 1963. The Minnesota Program enabled some of the Seoul National University professors in applied sciences to receive training at the University of Minnesota from 1954 and thereafter. Thus began the modern training of college teachers in science and engineering as well as the introduction of basic instruments necessary for science experiments.

This rapid introduction of western S&T took place without the benefit of in-depth discussions, controversies, or intellectual scrutiny before the 1960s. Until environmental problems from technology emerged for public discussion in the 1980s, scientism, or the absolute belief in S&T, reigned in Korea. In fact, western S&T never became "naturalized" within Korean culture.

The basis for Korean attitudes toward western science might be explained by two strains within its cultural tradition: Confucianism and Chungin-ism. Among the major three Far Eastern countries, Korea was the Confucian society par excellence. As such, Koreans had a deep-seated disdain against anything technical and scientific, for these issues seemed to have nothing to do with humane values. The Confucian value system put its highest mark on the political participation of learned people, and this has been very well reflected in the recent history of Korea after the liberation. This value system might well remain subconscious; but when it appears on the surface, it simply overrides everything.

Politically oriented Confucianism has been closely tied to economic aspirations, and the country's hierarchy of leadership follows these values. The country has been led by politicians first and by businessmen second. In Korean politics, there have been no places for scientists and engineers; and politicians control science. Until the rise of the Korean high-technology industry, Korean scientists and engineers had always been employees of the government or worked in institutions financed and controlled by the government, no matter what their nominal positions were. Even today the situation has barely changed. Whether in a university or research institute, Korean research funding is almost totally under government command.

This subordination of scientists closely resembles Choson society, where the ruling *yangban* were not allowed to do what was considered to be demeaning work, including technical work such as mathematics, astronomy, medicine, and law. Instead, a lower, strictly hereditary social class, the *chungin* (middle people), was established for such work. The *chungin*, though political outsiders, were better off economically than the *yangban* people.

Just as the *chungin* were political outsiders, scientists are in the same position in Korea today. And just as the *chungin* in the Choson times had been economically well treated, Korean scientists and engineers are comparatively well paid today. The complete lack of critical spirit among the Korean science circle during the military rule is reminiscent of these historical class differences.

FOCUSING ATTENTION ON INNOVATION IN KOREA TODAY

A number of efforts are taking place in contemporary Korea to reconcile historical attitudes with the need to develop an S&T-based culture. Government efforts in the early 1990s have raised public awareness about the value of scientific and technical innovation.

The focus of President Kim's reform drive on contemporary economic problems elevated the public's interest in S&T, since innovations are considered fundamental to Korea's economic resurrection. The term *innovation*, rather than *reform*, began to be widely used with the Taejon International Exposition, held from August 7 to November 7, 1993. Some 108 countries and 33 international organizations took part in Taejon Expo '93, which was the first Bureau of International Exposition–sanctioned event ever to be held by a developing country. The event drew about 14 million people, including 600,000 foreigners. Its major theme was "The Challenge of a New Road to Development," with two subthemes: "Traditional and Modern Science and Technology for the Developing World" and "Toward an Improved Use for and Recycling of Resources."

The Taejon Fair signaled a new beginning for the nation, since it was a good opportunity to promote S&T to the general public. The importance of innovation, a term usually applied to the field of S&T, was first mentioned. Most exhibits at the Taejon Fair were focused on demonstrating diverse innovations that aroused great curiosity, such as electric cars and electronic inventions.

The government highly publicized the Taejon Fair through mass media so that a huge number of people could attend it. When the Korea Gallup surveyed the public's views on the fair about fifty days before its opening, 94.1 percent of the Korean adults knew about it, and 72.3 percent believed that it would be successful. The most interesting finding was that more than half of the total respondents expected that the event would positively affect the development of S&T (Figure 6.2).[4] Both youths and highly educated people believed the expected effect more strongly.

In another survey conducted just a few days before the Taejon Fair ended, 57.9 percent of the Korean adults believed that the fair created positive effects overall, while 38 percent thought that it brought negative effects.[5] However, when concrete items were questioned, the evaluation of diverse effects was different (Table 6.1).

Although it is not easy to judge whether the Taejon Fair will prove to be greatly worthwhile in the long term, it clearly enhanced the public's interest in S&T and served as the first step by the government to promote scientific and innovative culture in Korea.

Figure 6.2
Proportions of Support by Respondents for Each Expected Effect of the Taejon Fair (in Percentage)

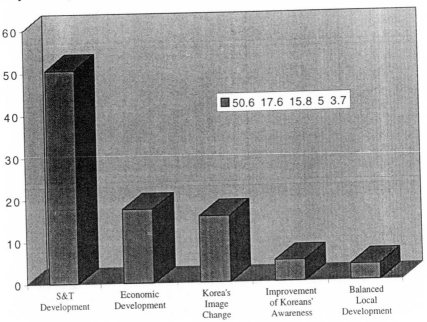

Source: Korea Gallup's Public Opinion Poll, July 13, 1993.

Table 6.1
Public Evaluation of the Taejon Fair's Future Contributions (in Percentage)

Evaluation	Great Contribution		Some	Little		None
Development of Advanced S&T	21.2 ———+——— 67.3			9.7 ———+——— 0.7		
		88.5			10.4	
Economic Development	12.4 ———+——— 61.0			22.9 ———+———3.1		
		83.4			26.0	
Balanced Development of Local Land	21.5 ———+——— 56.0			19.3 ———+———1.3		
		77.5			20.6	
Culture and Artistic Development	22.5 ———+——— 61.2			13.9 ———+———1.3		
		83.7			15.2	
Improvement of the Nation's International Prestige	24.8 ———+——— 51.9			20.2 ———+——— 1.9		
		76.7			22.1	

Source: Institute of Asian Studies Public Opinion Poll, November 1993.

Public concern for the Taejon Fair had faded away by November 1993, but a second event soon brought popular attention to the need for innovation. Media coverage focused on the Korean government's interest in the Final Act of the Uruguay Round of Multilateral Trade Negotiations, a proposal initiated in 1986 to enlarge the spirit of free trade found in the General Agreement on Tariffs and Trade (GATT). At an Asian-Pacific Economic Cooperation forum (APEC) meeting held in Seattle in November 1993, President Kim delivered a keynote speech stating that the Korean government would like to conclude the Uruguay Round Final Act within 1993. His Minister of Agriculture and Fishery then declared it inevitable that Korea would permit imports of rice.

The mass media interpreted the Uruguay Round agreement in terms of global competition and linked it with the need for innovation. They reported that as each nation's trade barriers were eliminated, a new global competition for goods and services should accelerate and quality products would assume ever-greater importance. This situation, they stated, would demand continuous innovation for Korea's survival.

A 1994 survey provides a measurement of how, in late 1993, the Taejon Fair and the Uruguay Round negotiation affected the public's concept of innovation in S&T. This survey showed the public believing that the government was quite interested in developing S&T (Table 6.2).[6] Older people held this view most strongly.

Meanwhile, the same survey revealed public opinion that private corporations were not making many efforts to develop technology (Table 6.3). Younger persons had the most critical views of corporate efforts. These results indicate that it is time for corporations to demonstrate their commitment to innovative efforts, since the public and the government are full of the spirit of

Table 6.2
Public Opinion of the Government's Interest in Developing Science and Technology

	Frequency	Very Much	Pretty Much	Little	None	Don't Know/No Answer	Total
Total	(700)	23.2 percent	46.8 percent	23.6 percent	2.6 percent	3.3 percent	100.0 percent
Sex							
Male	(346)	22.7	45.3	26.9	1.8	3.4	100.0
Female	(354)	23.6	48.4	20.4	3.5	4.2	100.0
Age							
20	(249)	19.6	47.4	28.5	3.6	0.9	100.0
30	(176)	17.3	47.0	29.9	2.4	3.5	100.0
40	(111)	22.2	52.1	17.5	2.9	5.31	100.0
50	(164)	35.5	42.2	13.5	1.3	7.5	100.0

Source: KukDong Research Institute's Public Opinion Poll, February 22, 1994.

Table 6.3
Public Opinion of the Private Corporate Efforts to Develop Technology

	Frequency	Very Much	Pretty Much	Little	None	Don't Know/No Answer	Total
Total	(700)	17.8 percent	39.1 percent	35.8 percent	4.4 percent	2.9 percent	100.0 percent
Sex							
Male	(346)	15.5	36.0	40.1	6.3	2.0	100.0
Female	(354)	20.1	42.1	31.5	2.5	3.8	100.0
Age							
20	(249)	9.6	36.6	47.8	5.0	1.0	100.0
30	(176)	13.8	38.8	39.0	4.9	3.5	100.0
40	(111)	17.3	44.4	31.2	5.8	1.3	100.0
50	(164)	35.0	39.6	17.1	2.1	6.2	100.0

Source: KukDong Research Institute's Public Opinion Poll, February 22, 1994.

innovation for S&T. The survey data also show that the concept of innovation was brought to the Korean public's focus of attention by media coverage of the national events. Since the culture of innovation cannot grow without education about innovative practices, we need to examine what polices are available in Korea to promote this new culture.

PRACTICES FOR CULTIVATING
INNOVATION IN KOREA

To promote the culture of innovation and, more generally, of S&T, a non-profit organization called the Korea Science Foundation (KSF) was established in 1967. (The KSF is different from the Korea Science and Engineering Foundation [KOSEF], which supports scientific research.) It is focused largely on cultivating scientific interests among youths, since they are likely to become the agents for future innovation. However, as we shall detail, the KSF is an organization for influencing overall public opinion on S&T in Korea. KSF activities are in five areas: public education through electronic media; use of books, games, and science fairs to interest young people in science; sponsoring international activities to learn how foreign countries promote scientific innovation in their cultures; educating the public about nuclear technology; and helping scientists communicate their creative ideas among themselves.

The KSF, whose budget is provided mostly by the government's Ministry of Science and Technology (MOST), had five major programs directed toward the general public in 1993.[7] It has tried to introduce or distribute many kinds of print media to the general public, and it has distributed a list of literature abstracts to educational and research institutions and mass media. The KSF operates a library of periodicals and books related to the culture of S&T. It also translates a United Nations Educational, Scientific, and Cultural Organization (UNESCO) journal, *Impact of Science on Society*, into Korean and distributes it to about 1,500 institutes and laboratories. The KSF sponsored two groups of scholars to write introductory books on informatics and genetic engineering for the general public, published 2,000 copies of each book, and distributed them to educational institutes and the mass media.

The organization has also produced and distributed audiovisual media related to promoting the culture of S&T. It produced one entertainment movie covering science in Korea in the twenty-first century, making 164 copies to be distributed to cinema houses in all parts of Korea. It also sponsored the Educational Broadcasting System (EBS, similar to the U.S. Public Broadcasting System [PBS]) to produce and broadcast three documentaries on optics, microorganisms, and robotics. EBS is a good channel for promoting the culture of innovation for S&T, since it targets the intellectual public and youth. The KSF purchased fifty-two films to demonstrate various types of scientific knowledge and twenty-nine nature documentaries, mostly imported from foreign countries such as the United States, Canada, Germany, Britain, France, and Japan. They all were arranged to be broadcast by EBS.

In 1993, the KSF held a seminar on science and the arts to entice artists to the science world. It also sponsored two public lectures for housewives so that they might foster the culture of science at home. About 570 housewives attended the events to listen to lectures on health, information systems, and environmental protection.

To develop new alternatives to encourage public acceptance of science-based culture, the KSF commissioned four studies in 1993. The first study recommended setting up a comprehensive plan for promoting scientific and technological culture. The second study examined how to develop games that helped young people value and utilize scientific knowledge. The third program investigated about 100 domestic historical heritages focusing on S&T, published a book explaining them with photographs, and distributed them widely. The fourth study examined how to publicize a notable scientist and valuable role model from Korean history, Mr. Chun Lee, who had led a group that developed a new form of printing in the early Lee Dynasty (C.E. 15).

Aside from all these efforts directed toward the general public, the KSF undertook major campaigns aimed specifically at young people. In 1993, the KSF held a science contest in which about 1,200 primary and high school students participated. The event required students to apply scientific knowledge to build a model plane, assemble a science box, and experiment with electronics. The KSF dispatched four science buses to 162 primary schools in the country, two summer camps, and eighteen event locations. Those buses were designed to demonstrate some scientific experiments and show science films.

The KSF also distributed science books to 3,400 primary and junior high schools recommended from every local board of education. Among those books were fourteen science fiction novels translated into Korean, five popular science magazines, and forty new quality books appropriate for youths. In addition, the KSF held three conventions to inform science teachers of current trends in science education. Each convention attracted more than 300 participants. The KSF arranged for scientists to visit their old primary schools and serve as one-day science teachers. In 1993, sixty-nine noted scientists participated in the program, each delivering a special speech, demonstrating a scientific experiment, having a talk with pupils, and donating some scientific instruments or books.

When the Ministry of Education named 1993 the "Year of Science Education," the KSF staged a campaign to make Korean adults realize the importance of the culture of science, to help science education for youths, and to create a trend toward reading science books among students. The program included raising funds for donations of science books to primary and secondary schools. About 30,000 adults joined the campaign, largely contributing to their old schools, providing a little more than 300 million won.

The KSF also launched a program to enhance international cooperation in exchanging ideas and developing a world culture based on S&T. In 1993, a troupe of Chinese officials from the Department of Science Popularization, China Association for Science and Technology, were invited to visit the KSF to discuss mutual cooperation in science popularization activities. The KSF also sent its representatives to the International Conference on the Public Understanding of Science and Technology, hosted by the Chicago Academy of Sciences.

In addition, a delegation visited the U.S. American Association for the Advancement of Science as well as the Scientists' Institute for Public Information. All these visits helped the KSF learn how to popularize science in Korea.

Realizing that public antagonism toward the hazards of nuclear technology was clouding overall acceptance of S&T in Korea, the KSF launched a campaign to develop an understanding of nuclear energy and wastes. It distributed booklets during tours of science buses and presented films to forty-three local communities.

Finally, the KSF has tried to help professional scientists working at the Daeduk Science Park, the Mecca of Korea's R&D, by publishing a monthly newsletter communicating creative scientific work. The newsletter, with a circulation of 5,500, is also distributed to Korean scientists living abroad.

Despite all the work and ambitions of the KSF, its effectiveness is limited by inadequate funding. Its 1993 budget amounted to only 2.5 billion won, and 20 percent of this covered personnel expenses. Thus, neither government, industry, nor the nation as a whole has provided an all-out effort to support the development of a scientific and innovative culture.

SUGGESTING AN ALTERNATIVE
FOR INNOVATIVE CULTURE

Much more substantive work needs to be done to promote innovation in Korea. Many of the current government efforts are poorly publicized or are undertaken halfheartedly. For example, April is known informally in Korea as the "Month of Science," supported by a few activities undertaken by MOST. In 1994, national science museums and science educational centers held a variety of exhibitions, films, speeches, and demonstrations of experiments. Some science institutions, such as the Korea Institute of Science and Technology, the Korea Atomic Energy Research Institute, and the Central Meteorological Office, held open houses for the general public.[8] However, these events were little known to most people because of lack of publicity. A nationally declared Day of Science, marked as April 21 in commemoration of the formation of MOST, is nearly meaningless in terms of effects upon the population at large.

The general press still hesitates to cover progress in S&T, so the public has little sense of overall progress and the excitement that accompanies such achievements. As of 1993, only 6 out of the nation's 100 daily newspapers had a regular page covering S&T. Only 9 general dailies had formal departments of S&T within their newsrooms. This area is often merged with sections covering lifestyle or environmental issues (Table 6.4).[9] The number of science journalists in either news agencies or broadcasting is very limited.

These facts indicate that the nation is conditioned to apathy when it comes to innovation in S&T. Korea needs an all-out government campaign, as com-

Table 6.4
Number of Science Journalists in Daily Publications

Name of Daily	Han-Kook	Han-Kyoreh	Kukmin	Kyunghwang	Joong-Ang	Chosun	Segye	Dong-A	Seoul
Name of Department	Living/ Science	Living/ Environmental	Living/ Environ mental	Living/ Science	Science	Science	Science	Science	Science
Number of Science Journalists	8	9	7	10	5	4	5	4	5
(Total Journalists)	(315)	(195)	(227)	(353)	(254)	(300)	(284)	(292)	(237)

Source: Survey by author, Hak-Soo Kim.

mitted in this area as in its social reforms, to build an innovation-based culture. Such a campaign would itself be innovative in terms of public communication because of the variety and amount of publicity it would require.

As one measure for stimulating interest, the government should "officially" declare April as "National Science Month" and should hold an annual national science festival. Both public and private organizations in S&T would be encouraged to prepare their own events for the general public during that festival. This is likely to attract the whole nation's attention for one month and contribute greatly to science popularization.

The festival should meet two goals: educating the public about scientific methodology and providing scientific knowledge. The former seems to be more important than the latter, since people familiar with scientific methodology can understand scientific knowledge and apply it to their own circumstances and their roles as citizens.

Most of the world's science festivals focus on providing scientific knowledge. For example, the U.S. National Science Week and Britain's Edinburgh International Science Festival advocate a particular theme every year. Examples include "Global Environmental Change" (United States, 1990), "Curiosity Is the Frontier" (United States, 1991), "Food" (Edinburgh, 1990), and "The Body" (Edinburgh, 1991). These festivals concentrate on delivering scientific knowledge rather than educating people about how to become scientific. The culture of science cannot grow without learning and utilizing scientific methodology.

In addition, Korea should establish an association of scientists and nonscientists to support the culture of S&T. This would be the equivalent of the British Association for the Advancement of Science. The association would enable scientists to interact with nonscientists in the festival's events and thereby enhance the national science festival.

The government should provide wide and advanced national publicity for all the events of the festival. It could follow the example of the Japanese government's Science and Technology Agency, which publishes a booklet introducing the events of their National Science Week and distributes it to every part of the country.

Which branch of government should be the focal point for ensuring the success of national efforts to promote innovation? The KSF can be the operating institution to implement it, but the Blue House must be involved. The Presidential Council on Science and Technology might be especially helpful. While supporting the president's declaration of National Science Month, it can highlight the importance of innovation from the highest level of government.

Given Korea's history and the strains of pessimism in Korean culture about the country's ability to innovate, moving the country toward an S&T-based culture will be a long-term effort. Nevertheless, government initiatives and efforts by national cultural leaders can turn Korea into an important player in the new international economic order.

NOTES

1. From March 25 to April 3, 1991, the Korea Gallup conducted face-to-face interviews with 2,000 nationwide respondents eighteen years of age or older and used the multistage stratified sampling method.

2. The figures from the Korea Gallup survey are the mean scores of the actual results.

3. From June to July 1992, the Korea Science Foundation conducted face-to-face interviews with 419 professional scientists and engineers using the purposive sampling method. Respondents were employed by universities and public or private research institutes.

4. From June 15 to 22, 1993, the Korea Gallup conducted face-to-face interviews with 1,500 respondents, who were twenty years of age or older, using the multistage stratified sampling method.

5. From November 3 to 4, 1993, the Institute of Asian Studies conducted telephone interviews of 1,000 respondents twenty years of age or older, also using the multistage stratified sampling method.

6. On February 21, 1994, the KukDong Research Institute conducted telephone interviews with 700 respondents, who were twenty years of age or older, using the multistage stratified sampling method.

7. The Korea Science Foundation 1993 annual report, Seoul 1994.

8. *The Science Weekly*, no. 544 (April 11, 1994): 16.

9. Hak-Soo Kim, "A Comprehensive and Stepwise Plan for Scientific and Technological Culture," final report of a research project sponsored by the Korea Science Foundation, 1993.

Chapter Seven

INNOVATION AND THE ROLE OF KOREA'S UNIVERSITIES

Young-Gul Kim

Korea must depend on its universities as a major source for the ideas and trained workers who will build the innovation-based economy of the future. In the past, government research institutes have accepted large responsibility for creating the country's innovative capacity by way of their research results (see Chapter 8). However, the need for innovation is rapidly increasing in an evolving, technology-based world economy. As stated throughout this book, Korea's past rate of economic growth, based heavily on imported tools and technology, stands in stark contrast to the fundamental weakness of its scientific and technological foundations. The university, if properly reformed, can and must strengthen these foundations. Korea has several research universities that maintain high academic standards, but their research capabilities are more limited than their rivals in the United States, Europe, and Japan.

In this chapter, we examine the relation between the academic research enterprise and the direct contribution of academic research toward innovation. We do not deal with accomplishments but with concerted efforts that are being made. We use this analysis to determine what Korea must do to help its universities supply the innovative resources for the future. We also look at the problems industries face in collaborating with universities.

Other nations have struggled in various ways with how academic–industrial collaboration can best take place.[1] Within a given society, these interactions have evolved greatly over time. It is not universally acknowledged that universities should make a direct research contribution toward the development of industrial technologies. In fact, there is an active debate in many industrialized nations about the importance and appropriateness of this link between industry and university. Last, we examine the situation for Korea and offer some options, taking into account the experiences of various industrialized countries.

UNIVERSITY RESEARCH IN KOREA

The end of World War II left Korea with very few industries in the modern sense and no technical personnel pool. Indeed, in 1945 Korea had only a dozen or so university graduates who held a B.S. degree in physics. Postwar social confusion was followed by the Korean War, which left the country in ruins. Political instability following the cease-fire eventually led to the military coup in 1962 and the subsequent military government. At this point, economic development began in earnest.

We need not recount this phase of Korea's recent developmental history (see Chapter 2) except to mention that until about the mid-1970s, Korea's industries had little need for advanced technical personnel. During the 1960s and the 1970s, the period of greatest dependence on imported technology, most of the manufacturing plants were imported on a "turnkey" basis, and the primary need for technical personnel was for people who could operate the imported equipment by following instructions given in the manuals. Industries had no need for workers with a university level of education in science and engineering. However, strong basic education of the workforce was important in these early stages of Korea's industrial development.

A 1993 report by the World Bank identifies general literacy and a good basic education in the East Asian countries as the major elements responsible for creating the "miracle" of Asian economic development.[2] It concludes, however, that higher education contributed relatively little to this progress. Statistics on educational expenditures of Korea and Venezuela show a striking contrast. In 1985, Korea allocated 83.9 percent of its total education budget to basic (primary and secondary) education and only 10.3 percent to higher education. In Venezuela, the corresponding figures stood at 31 percent and 43.4 percent, respectively. Although Venezuela spent a higher percentage of gross national product (GNP) on education (4.3 percent) than Korea (3 percent), the percentage of GNP spent on basic education was higher in Korea (2.5 percent) than in Venezuela (1.3 percent). One might infer from these figures that Korea's economic development during the two decades beginning in the mid-1960s owes much to its concentrated efforts on basic education.

THE BEGINNING OF
GRADUATE EDUCATION IN KOREA

In the late 1960s, the Korean government recognized the need for advanced training for scientists and engineers in preparation for the development of indigenous technologies. This recognition was a farsighted one, considering that at least a decade would pass before the developed countries, fearful of the "boomerang" effect, initiated restrictions on licensing technologies to Korea.

A survey of advanced scientific personnel in the universities yielded bleak news. In 1969, there were only about 600 full-time graduate students in all science and engineering fields in all of South Korea, and they were scattered among 152 departments in twenty-two schools.[3] Such fragmentation meant that very few departments could offer viable graduate programs. In most cases, the graduate program was nothing more than an appendage to the predominantly undergraduate education. The training offered by these graduate programs was held in such low esteem by industrial firms that the starting salaries for the master's degree holders were the same as those of bachelor's degree holders. In fact, both were subjected to identical selection procedures with identical standards. Obviously, something had to be done quickly both to increase the number of scientists and engineers with advanced training and to upgrade the standard of graduate education.

In 1972, the government set up a new graduate school of engineering and applied sciences, the Korea Advanced Institute of Science (KAIS), to meet this challenge.[4] Created by a special presidential decree, many of its features were unique among Korean institutions of higher learning. First and foremost was the provision that exempted prospective students from the compulsory, three-year military service and guaranteed full financial support while in school (including tuition, room and board, and incidental expenses). In exchange, the graduates were obligated to serve in Korea for three years in some science and technology–related work. This ensured that many of the best college graduates from the entire nation would vie for admission to the institute. The government provided funding for salaries at more than twice the prevailing rates and the state-of-the-art research facilities, which proved to be strong enough incentives to attract top-quality faculty from among Korean scientists and engineers living overseas.

The government wisely placed the new institute under the jurisdiction of the Ministry of Science and Technology (MOST), which freed it from the rules and regulations of the Ministry of Education (MOE) that often stifled innovative approaches in education. With this autonomy, the institute was free to establish its own admissions and graduation standards, curricula, allocation of research funds, faculty promotion and tenure policies, and academic governance. Drawing students from the top 1 percent of the nation's college graduates, and providing adequate research funding and time for research (an average teaching load, one course a semester), serious research activities took root for the first time in a Korean academic institution during the mid-1970s.

The presence of KAIS (later renamed KAIST, with the addition of "and technology" to the name) in Korea's educational scene had a tremendous impact on the country's level of graduate education. Its secondary effect on undergraduate education was no less significant. It also improved the situation for university faculty members, which led to raising the salaries of other science and engineering research workers.

The multiplier effect of KAIS on the nation's graduate education as a whole is evident in statistics compiled from the annual reports of MOST and MOE. The numbers of M.S. and Ph.D. degrees granted in science and engineering from 1970 to 1985 were 754 in 1970, 1,282 in 1975, 2,662 in 1980, and 7,502 in 1985.

THE INADEQUACIES OF GRADUATE EDUCATION

There is an implicit mandate for universities to supply well-trained scientists and engineers for the nation's needs. However, the first instance of the Korean government asking any university to contribute to industrial development occurred in 1977, when the deputy prime minister and the minister of the Economic Planning Board (EPB) asked the administrators of KAIS to start a special program to train professional engineers. These graduates had to be capable of creating original designs of manufacturing plants. The initial target was the petrochemical industry, but the machine industry was soon to be included. At this time, the government was preparing to make Korean engineering firms the prime contractors when granting engineering contracts, and a survey had showed an insufficiency of high-level technical personnel to institute this policy.

Universities were slowly improving then, largely through the International Bank for Reconstruction and Development (IBRD) loans used to procure badly needed laboratory equipment. MOE, which controlled enrollment in higher education by strictly imposing quotas on individual colleges and universities, was pressured by the EPB to increase the quotas for science and engineering departments. However, the improvements in quality did not keep pace with the increase in enrollments. Rapid economic growth during the 1970s had led to a scarcity of scientists and engineers, resulting in salary increases that were deemed unacceptably high by the government. To add to the supply of scientists and engineers in Korea, the university enrollment quota was increased. This proved quite convenient to the administrators of private universities (which accounted for 75% of all the institutions of higher learning). They solved the financial difficulties of their schools by taking in additional students without a proportionate increase in faculty size and capital investment.

At present, there are more than 150 four-year colleges and universities in Korea. A majority of them offer graduate programs in science and engineering, with a total enrollment of more than 100,000 students. This figure is comparable to the enrollments in Japanese universities, which stood at 78,914 as of 1987.

When one considers that Japan has three times the population of South Korea and that its GNP is twelve times greater, Korea's enrollment figures are unusually high. However, the majority of the institutions are quite inadequate by the standards of developed countries. Even today, only a few universities in Korea meet a reasonable requirement for quality graduate education in science and engineering.[5]

The proliferation of substandard graduate programs was caused largely by inadequate government investments in higher education over the past thirty years. The military-dominated government needed to establish its "legitimacy" rapidly by investing in projects, including manufacturing plants and public works that visibly raised the nation's living standard from near poverty to a reasonably high level. In contrast, substantial investment of the nation's scarce resources into higher education would not have shown visible results in under a decade.

Instead of boosting universities under a long-term plan, the government gave "entrepreneurs" sufficient incentives to turn the building of private universities into an attractive "business" venture. These private universities, once established, financed themselves almost entirely from tuition and fees collected from the students. It soon became apparent that a certain minimum enrollment was required to be self-sustaining, and that the humanities and social sciences required much less capital investment compared to science and engineering.

Until recently, MOE wielded nearly absolute power over all phases of higher education, including curriculum, entrance and graduation requirements, faculty qualifications, tuition and fee determination, and regulations on university governance. MOE adopted a policy that required increases in science and engineering enrollment to accompany any increases in other, less costly disciplines. Universities were forced to comply with this ruling as they grew, regardless of how it affected their overall financial conditions.

Since Koreans attach the highest value to educating children, higher education became a business that could not lose. The government used these conditions to increase the supply of trained technical personnel without making great investments in higher education. Korea is likely to pay for this short-sighted negligence for a long time. The quality of education has suffered in universities and throughout the educational system, from the primary school up to the graduate school.

The Emphasis on Numbers and Its Disastrous Consequences

This policy of increasing enrollment without regard to quality continues to this day. Owing to this misguided policy, Korea has a glut of poorly educated scientists and engineers at all levels. If the current "inventory" is a serious waste of potential human resources, the continuously increasing "output" is even more damaging.

The problem is exacerbated by the fact that the vast majority of Ph.D. degree holders prefer an academic position as their first career choice. In the deep-rooted Korean cultural heritage, the "scholar" class was at the top of social prestige for many centuries. Not only does the academic position command higher social esteem, but the financial reward is also greater than for many other starting jobs. Many research scientists and engineers employed by industries or government-funded research institutes are looking for positions in universities, even at those universities unable to offer any meaningful research opportunities. When these Ph.D.'s do find jobs in universities, they naturally produce clones of themselves—graduates with advanced degrees—rather than producing talented workers with the skills and training to address societal needs at the level that matches their potentials. The academics demand a share of the scarce R&D resources from the national treasury to turn out these new graduates and perpetuate the vicious cycle.

A minister of science and technology stated that there were more than 450 unemployed Ph.D.'s in science and engineering trained within Korea during the past several years. There are many more job-seeking Ph.D.'s in science trained abroad, mostly in the United States, waiting to return home. Korea "boasts" one of the highest numbers of students enrolled in colleges and universities per capita in the world. From 1965 to 1985, the enrollment in undergraduate science and engineering programs soared from 46,000 to 376,000, while the enrollment in graduate programs increased twentyfold, going from 900 to 18,000. This trend has continued to the present. The operating budgets of private universities, derived mostly from tuition fees, are grossly inadequate to equip and run expensive science and engineering laboratories. However, if all these substandard science and engineering programs in private universities were to be closed, a serious shortage of scientists and engineers would result. A major task facing the policymakers entails determining how to mobilize the nation's scarce resources from both public and private sectors to selectively upgrade the quality of viable research universities without resorting to wasteful across-the-board resource allocations.

Korea's national R&D enterprise is heavily skewed regarding two major R&D resources: personnel and funds. About 70 percent of the Ph.D.'s in science and engineering are employed by universities, but these researchers have access to only meager funding. Meanwhile, the industries that command most of the material resources for R&D lack commensurate brain power. Only 7.2 percent of the national R&D budget was expended by universities from 1992 to 1993.[6] This is less than half the figures reported for the United States, Germany, the United Kingdom, and France.

Korea's research system also suffers because it is skewed geographically, overwhelmingly concentrated in and around Seoul. Seoul and its surroundings contain 30 percent of the South Korean population, more than half of Korea's major universities are located there, and most of the country's main cultural events also take place in this city. Corporate research laboratories and government-funded research institutes have been largely decentralized. However, the heavy concentration of universities in Seoul, accompanied by a maldistribution of research personnel, poses a serious problem for developing an integrated research enterprise. In the early 1990s, the national government began strengthening engineering education outside the Seoul area, selecting eight universities in the provinces for concentrated support over the next five years. Each of the selected engineering colleges will receive about U.S.$12 million per year to upgrade its engineering training. In December 1995, MOE also designated several university departments with potential strength in selected areas to inaugurate innovative graduate programs in science and engineering. These departments will receive concentrated five-year support ranging from U.S.$25 million to $30 million. Such selective support will continue in the future.

Only a few academic institutions in Korea provide anywhere near sufficient research support. In most universities, a newly recruited professor must start with an empty laboratory space and very meager university support for expendable supplies and equipment.

Two research foundations, supported by MOST and MOE, respectively, provide the primary sources of outside financial support for basic research. These research funds pay for expendables, computer and analytical instrument usage, limited domestic travel, and allowances for graduate students that meet about one-third of the students' minimum needs. Capital equipment is mostly beyond the reach of the research grants from these foundations. Once every few years, universities apply for government loans, which are packaged into an IBRD educational loan. These loans are the primary sources of capital equipment for most universities, but they are neither steady nor dependable. Hence, industrial patrons are sought by academics. This leads to a dilemma: Industrial contracts help build their laboratories and support research staff, but the results often do not advance scholarly careers in the academic system.

Lessons from Industrialized Countries

What lessons can Korea draw from the experience of developed nations to direct its university research activity toward national development? Each nation has its own unique system, but a common thread runs through them.[7] The universities are well-established institutions that combine teaching with research and prize academic excellence. Industrial–university links in developed countries take many different forms, and the lessons they provide can be confusing. Korea must selectively transplant those features from the highly industrialized countries that best suit its particular condition.

The U.S. model depends on the existence of a research infrastructure in the universities, together with a tradition of funding research and granting professors time away from teaching to do this work. This system encourages faculty to compete for research grants, which improves research quality and output.[8] The strong tradition of university linkages to industry further acts to guide university research priorities, while preserving university autonomy. Although these conditions are not well met in Korea at present, the U.S. system is worthy of emulation. The use of competitive grants, such as those awarded by the Korea Science and Engineering Foundation (KOSEF), is valuable for setting a fairly uniform standard of quality on all university research competition for grants.

The industry-led Japanese model depends on strong industrial leadership in the R&D phases of activity.[9] However, Japanese industry, which contributes 80 percent of the national R&D outlays, must exercise a more active leadership role in creating a balanced national research enterprise. This applies particularly to large corporations, many of which have not yet responded to their need for strong support from university research. It is encouraging that Korea's chaebols show increasing interest in establishing R&D outposts within major research universities. If they continue on this path, an industrial–university partnership that is quite unlike that of Japan can emerge.

The strong scholastic tradition found in Germany is lacking in Korean universities. Unless higher education, in general, and graduate programs, in particular, are reformed, it would be difficult for Korea to follow Germany's example and use the university as a major component of the national R&D enterprise.[10] The close ties between the high-caliber government-funded research institutes, such as the Max–Planck Institutes, and universities provide a glimpse of what Korea's government-funded research institutes should evolve to after industry assumes the more pressing task of developing technologies.

The U.K. model, with shrinking government support and consequent demoralization of universities, cannot serve as an example to emulate at this time.[11] Although the academic quality of British universities is uniformly high, their contribution to innovative technologies is not commensurate with their potential. Korea should learn a hard lesson from the United Kingdom: Strength in basic science capability does not necessarily lead to capabilities for innovative commercial technologies.

Korea should study the French system of national research because the two countries share a similar starting point.[12] Given the large number of unproductive (in terms of research output) and substandard universities in Korea, investments for upgrading university research capabilities must be done very selectively. However, the political climate following the inauguration of the first civilian president in over three decades would work against the politically unpopular measure of selecting a few institutions for concentrated financial support.

The French used the National Center for Scientific Research (CNRS) to reinforce existing university laboratories or create new ones. This approach would obviate the need to support all engineering or science colleges within a given university. The Korean MOST's initiation of Science and Engineering

Research Centers—centers of excellence designed to reinforce high quality departments at selected universities—is a start in this direction. The late Professor Frederick Terman of Stanford University, the "founding father" of Silicon Valley, noted that the creation of "steeples of excellence" within a given university can be a catalyst for improving the quality of the surrounding disciplines as well.

The relationship between CNRS and the university suggests a possible symbiosis between government-funded research institutes and universities in Korea. In recent years, some of these institutes have formed partnerships with major research universities to share the facilities and research expertise to improve graduate education. This arrangement shows great potential for Korea.

INDUSTRIAL–UNIVERSITY LINKS IN KOREA

Many academics in Korea ignore the contributions that they can make toward the development of industrial technologies for two reasons. First, the vast majority of Korea's top scientists and engineers in leadership positions were trained in the United States during the post–Sputnik decades, when American academics were almost exclusively engaged in basic research. Naturally, these Korean scientists and engineers would emulate the mind-sets and habits of their U.S. mentors. They have perpetuated this preference for fundamental science in Korea since their return, although circumstances are vastly different in the two countries. Whereas most U.S. industries have enough in-house R&D capabilities for their immediate and medium-term needs, Korean industries (with some exceptions) are far from possessing such capabilities.

The second reason is more deeply rooted in Korean culture, and many Koreans may not even be conscious of it. In Korea, the traditional hierarchy of occupation or social status has been in this order: scholars, farmers, artisans, and merchants (see Chapter 6). The scholar class was actually the ruling class, whose "scholarly activities" consisted of learning oriental philosophy and Chinese classics. They led the life of cultured elites without much relevance to anything practical, which was considered to be demeaning. Many academic scientists, who, in the old days, might have been relegated to the artisan class, subconsciously identify with the "scholar" class of the feudal periods. Even in the United States, where universities have a long tradition of links with industry, such elements exist. John A. Armstrong, vice president for science and technology of IBM, wrote in 1990:

There is, however, one aspect of this problem [industry–university collaboration] where the universities could be of major help in the long run: that is, in helping Western culture to get rid of, once and for all, the intellectual hierarchy in which "pure" is somehow better than "applied," in which physics is better than chemistry, both are better than engineering, and the discipline and intellectual content of manufacturing is hardly valued at all.[13]

INDUSTRY–UNIVERSITY COLLABORATIONS

Recent developments show that major corporations are beginning to recognize the need for collaboration with universities to develop technology. Increasing numbers of large corporations are establishing footholds in universities to tap their research capabilities. In some cases, they have created their own technical institutions of higher education.

The POSCO–POSTECH–RIST Linkage

The Pohang Iron and Steel Company (POSCO), established in 1968, is the world's second-largest and one of the most competitive companies in its field. While R&D activities begun in the late 1970s provided adequate in-house technical capabilities, POSCO was unable to carry out central research work required for a forward-looking modern corporation. The company was seeking business diversification, anticipating the inevitable decline in the steel-making activities of Korea in the early years of the coming century.

POSCO made a bold move by creating a first-rate, research-oriented university of science and engineering, then integrating it with POSCO's own central research laboratory.[14] The new institution, Pohang University of Science and Technology (POSTECH), was established in July 1985. This was only seventeen months after MOE approved its establishment. The first freshman class of 250 was drawn from the top 2 percent of the nation's pool of high school graduates, and a graduate school begun in 1988 drew more than fifteen applicants for each slot.

POSCO's central research laboratory was made autonomous by reorganizing it into the Research Institute of Industrial Science and Technology (RIST) in March 1987. Sharing the campus with POSTECH, RIST absorbs the old technical service function along with its new mandate of serving as both the research arm of the POSTECH and the corporate research laboratory of POSCO. This POSCO–POSTECH–RIST linkage constitutes a community with a built-in industry–university collaboration mechanism. The company has had a number of successful results that have helped improve its existing manufacturing processes as well as generating future-oriented technologies. POSCO has invested more than U.S.$1 billion for POSTECH since 1985. This is a unique experiment, not likely to be duplicated by other major corporations. However, POSCO's success in single-handedly creating a foremost research university in less than a decade has been a tremendous stimulus to industries. Many firms will emulate this work, although on a more modest scale, in the years to come.

The Ajou University–Daewoo Group Linkage

A few years ago, the Daewoo Group, Korea's fourth-largest business group (chaebol), established the Institute for Advanced Engineering to link the manufacturing companies of the Group with selected departments of the Ajou University. The institute serves as an education center for Daewoo research staff on forefront manufacturing technologies, bringing them into contact with world authorities in their respective fields. It also houses joint research between the Ajou faculty and the Daewoo research staff, the results of which will eventually be used by Daewoo in their various manufacturing activities.

Centers of Excellence

Another hopeful sign for Korea's future is the government's creation of centers of excellence through KOSEF, an equivalent of the National Science Foundation in the United States. Since 1990, twenty-two engineering research centers (ERCs) and sixteen science research centers (SRCs) have been created. While SRCs are expected to raise the standard of research in selected universities to an international level, ERCs have an added mandate to contribute toward the development of industrial technologies. The awards are being granted preferably to universities with demonstrated research competence. For example, three major institutions—Seoul National University, KAIST, and POSTECH—have been awarded about two-thirds of all the centers. It will be interesting to observe whether this stratification will continue, or whether the government will bow to strong social pressures for equalization and distribute the centers more widely across geographical areas. Many of the ERCs have acted as catalysts for bringing academics and industrial researchers together for joint work. Early successful case histories should breed more successes soon.

Industry–University Consortia

In response to urgent needs, a large number of industry–university R&D consortia are mushrooming around major university campuses throughout Korea. Corporations have become generous in donating funds for building laboratories for joint research. However, it is too early to tell whether collaborative research will yield results within a time frame that is acceptable to industry's management, thereby sustaining the initial momentum for these collaborations.

REFORM OF HIGHER EDUCATION AS THE ESSENTIAL STEP

Educational reform is currently one of the most pressing items on Korea's national agenda. MOE, which is responsible for basic education at the precollege level, does not appear to comprehend the seriousness of the problem. The reform being proposed here must be understood within the context of Korean cultural tradition and the peculiar practices that have prevailed over the past several decades.

Cultural Background

Korea's culture emphasizes harmony in society. Critical evaluation of existing institutions is discouraged, and it takes a person of rare courage and sound judgment to come out for concrete diagnosis and remedy. In 1976, this chapter's author wrote an article in a major weekly news magazine, observing that Korea's mix of harmony versus efficiency as an operating principle of society seems to be the reverse of how many western nations operate.[15] In the West, they would say about a capable but abrasive individual that "he is hard to get along with, but he is capable," and his talent is utilized. In Korea, they would say, "He is very talented, but unfortunately he is hard to get along with," and he is excluded.

In Korean society, apparent or superficial credentials may triumph over substantive quality. A person with a university degree, even with limited abilities, commands more "respect" from society than a high school graduate with a high-level, useful skill. Thus, there is a built-in drive in the entire society that pushes high school graduates toward the university without regard to one's innate ability to benefit from higher education. A family that can afford to send a son or a daughter to a university will stop at nothing to get him or her admitted to a university, regardless of the person's ability. If the young person fails to get into a prestigious university, the entire family will feel the shame. An opinion poll taken in Korea in 1990 showed that 96.5 percent of parents want their sons to have a university degree; a similar poll taken in Japan in 1991 showed that 54 percent of parents wanted their sons to go to a university. A person with a technical high school education and essential skills for gainful employment is made to feel inferior to his unemployed or unemployable peer who has a college degree but nothing else.

Contrast this with the German case, where the pursuit of excellence is held up as a high virtue; excellence on the shop floor by a master craftsman gives as much satisfaction to him as excellence in the Nobel-caliber laboratory. Korea lacks a tradition in which craftsmen compete with each other for excellence and take pride in their accomplishments, a tradition in which society grants as much respect to such achievements as to high scholarly achievements in universities or notable accomplishments in business.

Korean society must turn away from valuing the meaningless chase after the ephemeral "prestige" of the university degrees and value instead a genuine university education with its ability to develop intellectual capacities. Otherwise, any educational reform will meet with almost insurmountable obstacles. The financial resources at the disposal of this society are simply not great enough to provide quality university education to all those who seek it.

Another malady afflicting industrial as well as government-funded research laboratories in Korea is the preference of many research personnel for "managerial" positions. Many industries are trying to correct this problem by instituting a dual-ladder system, whereby the technical and managerial careers are given equal treatment. However, Korea's cultural milieu, in which management posts carry much social recognition, often works against this solution.

Specific Remedies for Education Reform

MOST attempted to institute a "master" system during the 1970s that encouraged experienced master craftsmen without university degrees to aspire to professional prestige and reward comparable to a professional engineering and research career. However, the jurisdiction for implementing the system was later transferred to the Ministry of Labor; and the system was reduced to a meaningless one. A concerted national effort is needed to resurrect the original spirit of this system, which would allow institutions of higher education to focus on educating those who can best benefit from and use their education.

Specific remedies for reforming the university system must begin by diversifying university functions based on available educational resources: faculty quality and size, student quality, availability of physical facilities, and the financial resources at the disposal of each university. In particular, the ability of a university to provide graduate education involving quality research must be objectively assessed; and each university should be classified as one of the following: research university with full M.S. and Ph.D. programs, university with only M.S. programs, and teaching university awarding only B.S. degrees. The loss of graduate programs would affect the majority of universities, both public and private. Universities deprived of income from graduate students' tuition fees might be offset by increasing the undergraduate enrollment quota.

To implement these reforms completely, many competent research-minded faculty members should be relocated to selected research universities. To effect this draconian solution, a new government agency capable of managing higher education would be needed. This "Ministry of Higher Education" would have the task of completely overhauling the higher-education system. It would rigorously assess the capacities of existing universities to regulate the size of each graduate program.

Although the creation of a new ministry runs counter to the current political trend toward streamlining government, higher education has such a far-reaching impact on the fundamental fabric of the society that it must have a new voice in the highest council of the nation. A strong national consensus exists that MOE, as currently constituted, is totally inadequate to deal with higher education.

If higher education could be reformed merely by building up the research infrastructures of universities and distributing research funds more efficiently, MOST might conceivably absorb jurisdiction over higher education. However, the administration of higher education is too far-reaching for MOST to assume as an added responsibility.

Basic versus Applied Research

How should Korea decide to divide its limited resources between basic and applied research at universities? Some in the scientific community claim that since the university's function is the creation of new knowledge, basic research should be its major focus. They claim, with considerable cogency and often quite vocally, that Korea has concentrated too long on short-term projects to achieve immediate results at the expense of long-range, basic research. Others believe that basic research is a luxury that Korea cannot yet afford. It takes too long and is too costly to begin with basic research and use the outcomes to develop industrial technologies. Basic research results are available in the public domain worldwide, and efforts should be concentrated on applying them to industrial uses until Korea joins the ranks of the developed countries.

There are merits in both arguments. Basic research must be conducted, if only to monitor what is being done by other scholars throughout the world. In addition, doing basic research is one of the best means of training scientists and engineers seeking advanced degrees. Therefore, some of the brightest professors and graduate students should be engaged in it. But society's more immediate needs should also be addressed. A large fraction of the scientific personnel in universities should be involved in applied research for Korea to compete in the international arena with the industrial technologies that drive economic development.

The answer for Korea may lie in establishing time-phased plans to gradually shift emphasis toward basic research in universities as Korea's industries become more self-reliant in R&D activities. Unless one can produce research that can be published in internationally reputable journals, an individual's efforts would be better directed toward solving more immediate problems for industries or for the society at large.

Industrial Internship for Engineering Faculty

MOST instituted an internship program in 1993 to help science and engineering faculty members gain firsthand industrial experience. This attempt to close the gap between the scholar's traditional training in basic research and industry's need for technology development is proving successful. KOSEF initially received applications from both professors and industrial firms. Acting as matchmaker, it brought the parties together for the two-month summer and winter academic vacation periods. During the first trial in the winter of 1993, more than eighty such internship arrangements were made. The outcome has been most encouraging, and the program will be expanded greatly in the coming years.

We should conclude by stating that, unlike the developed nations, Korea has a very short history of research endeavors. It is a late starter, and it has yet to produce many accomplishments in original research. However, Korea could have a bright and innovative future. As the current trend of increasing collaboration between industries and universities continues—and it has every indication of doing so—the research results will begin to generate innovative technologies for Korea's industries. The most important first step is the reform of higher education, especially graduate education in science and engineering.

The tendency toward overemphasizing numerical growth of graduate enrollment, if not halted soon, will flood the market with underqualified scientists and engineers clamoring for jobs, while the universities will become an unbearable financial burden on the national R&D budget. Before Korea can accelerate its national R&D investment to reach 4 to 5 percent of GNP by the first decade of the next century—a goal advocated at the highest levels of government—the university research system must first be transformed.

The importance of educational reform must be impressed upon all those determined to create the national research enterprise needed to meet the challenges of the twenty-first century. The appropriate measures for reform must be decided at the highest councils of the nation, and they must be implemented soon.

NOTES

1. Rikard Stankiewicz, *Academic Entrepreneurs: Developing University–Industry Relations* (New York: St. Martin's Press, 1986).

2. World Bank, "Strategies for Rapid Accumulation," in *The East Asian Miracle*, A World Bank Policy Research Report (New York: Oxford University Press, 1993), 191–203.

3. Frederick E. Terman (Chairman), Donald L. Benedict, Kun M. Chung, Franklin A. Long, and Thomas L. Martin, *Survey Report on the Establishment of the Korea Advanced Institute of Science*, prepared for the U.S. Agency for International Development (1970), unpublished.

4. Young-Gul Kim, "An Experiment in Advanced Engineering Education—Korea's Approach," presented at the Conference on Training and Career Development for Engineers, Cambridge University, Cambridge, U.K., June 21–24, 1976.

5. As a working definition, a viable graduate program is one in which there are sufficient faculty members who can handle both classroom lectures and research supervision. For this purpose, a professor should not be required to teach more than two courses per semester and should not have to carry, on average, more than six or seven graduate students. The student to faculty ratio, including both undergraduate and graduate students, should be less than 20:1. In addition, professors should have a minimum of $30,000 in research funding at their disposal per annum, exclusive of the money to support most of their students.

6. Korea Science and Engineering Foundation, *Statistics of International Technical Cooperation* (Seoul: Korea Science and Engineering Foundation, 1995).

7. Joseph Ben-David, *Centers of Learning* (New Brunswick, N.J.: Transaction Publishers, 1977).

8. Roger L. Geiger, "The American University and Research," in *The Academic Research Enterprise within the Industrialized Nations: Comparative Perspectives,* The Government–Industry–University Roundtable (Washington, D.C.: National Academy Press, 1990), 15–35.

9. Morikazu Ushiogi, "Graduate Education and Research Organization in Japan," in *The Research Foundations of Graduate Education*, ed. Burton Clark (Los Angeles: University of California Press, 1993), 299–325.

10. Alan D. Beyerchen, "Trends in the Twentieth-Century German Research Enterprise," in *The Academic Research Enterprise within the Industrialized Nations: Comparative Perspectives*, The Government–Industry–University Roundtable (Washington, D.C.: National Academy Press, 1990), 79–92.

11. Sheldon Rothblatt, "Research and British Universities," in *The Academic Research Enterprise within the Industrialized Nations: Comparative Perspectives*, The Government–Industry–University Roundtable (Washington, D.C.: National Academy Press, 1990), 69–76.

12. Guy Neave, "Separation de Corps: The Training of Advanced Students and the Organization of Research in France," in *The Research Foundations of Graduate Education*, ed. Burton Clark (Los Angeles: University of California Press, 1993), 159–191.

13. John A. Armstrong, "An Industry Perspective on the Changing University," in *The Changing University*, ed. Dorothy S. Zinberg (Dordrecht, The Netherlands: Kluwer Academic Publishers, 1991), 17–23.

14. Young-Gul Kim, "Promotion of Science and Technology: Integrated Efforts between Industry and Academia," ST/ESCAP/833 Development Papers No. 8 (Bangkok: 1991).

15. Young-Gul Kim, "Sunday Essay—Rediscovering Korea after Twenty Years," *Chosun Weekly*, October 17, 1976, 3.

Chapter Eight

THE IMPORTANCE AND NEEDS OF PUBLIC LABORATORIES

Young-Hwan Choi and Boong-Kyu Lee

The Korean government has played a decisive role in the development of the country's technology and its institutional infrastructure, and public laboratories have been instrumental to Korea's achievements. During the 1960s, while initiating what Amsden describes as the "learning" process required for late industrialization, the Korean government recognized a need for institutions that could understand, master, and finally diffuse the technologies imported from abroad.[1] The legacy of that recognition is found in Korea's national network of public laboratories.

With the Korea Institute of Science and Technology (KIST) as its anchor, the public laboratories of Korea have played an important and, perhaps, crucial role in the technological development of the nation. But as the economy grew, so did the private sector, which gradually took over many of the functions that were formerly the sole domain of the public laboratories. Now that the chaebols possess their own R&D labs that equal or often surpass the research abilities of the public sector, the time has come for a reassessment of the role of Korea's public laboratories. This chapter provides that reassessment.

After a general discussion of the types and definitions of public laboratories in Korea, we focus on the group of publicly funded research laboratories that offer the greatest potential for science and technology (S&T) innovation, the government-funded laboratories (GFLs). In order to judge the GFLs and their relevance for the future, we explain their historical development.

Following this historical overview, we discuss issues such as the proper role, function, autonomy, and management of GFLs. We suggest ideas for reform and other policy recommendations throughout the final section.

PUBLIC LABORATORIES IN KOREA: A TYPOLOGY

Korea's Ministry of Science and Technology (MOST) classifies public laboratories into three major institutional types. In accordance with the original hangul names used in official MOST publications, these are (1) national and public testing laboratories (NPLs), (2) laboratories affiliated with public enterprises (LPEs), and (3) GFLs. Although somewhat confusing, MOST terminology is used throughout this chapter.

True to their name, NPLs primarily conduct testing on agriculture, fisheries, and public welfare rather than doing research. The LPEs include Korea's public enterprises, such as the Korea Railroad Corporation or Korea Electrical Power Corporation.

The focus of this chapter, the GFL, represents the most important type of laboratory because these labs are heavily funded and their mission is to improve S&T on a national basis. In 1992, 70 percent, or 742.5 billion won, of the total 1.0603 trillion won invested in the public laboratories was allocated for GFLs.[2]

GFL may be an unfortunate choice of term, since all the public laboratories are, whether directly or indirectly, "funded" by the government. GFLs are roughly analogous to the various U.S. National Laboratories. For instance, the Korea Standards Research Institute (KSRI), a GFL, is roughly the Korean equivalent to the National Institute of Science and Technology of the United States.

National and Public Testing Laboratories

NPLs refer to those institutions attached to national or regional administrative bodies and do work in primary sectors such as agriculture, welfare, and fisheries. As such, the staff members of these NPLs are government employees. As of 1992, 7,249 people were employed by the NPLs. Out of the total, 3,791, or 4.27 percent, of Korea's total research population (88,764), were classified as researchers.

These testing laboratories conduct any inspection, examination, analysis, appraisal, and technical assistance activities required by their supervisory administrative bodies. Therefore, with the exception of the limited R&D activities carried out by a few agricultural laboratories, most of these NPLs are really technical administrative bodies rather than actual research institutions.

The NPLs suffer from a multitude of problems. The first is that the compensation scale of the testing research staff is lower than that of LPEs or GFLs, to say nothing of the private sector, which makes the recruitment of top-level personnel difficult at best. Second, the budgetary items of the NPLs follow the composition format of their supervisory general administrative bodies, which discourages the initiation of independent or autonomous research. Third, the combination of insufficient funds, poor research environments, and rigid research management has led to constant morale problems, which contribute to the lackluster research output, quality, and efficiency of these institutions. It is not surprising, therefore, that there has been increasing criticism from various societal sectors over the mission and role of the NPLs.

Laboratories Affiliated with Public Enterprises

The general definition used for a public enterprise is any economic organization that is either owned or controlled through an ownership stake from a public institution. As of 1990, there were 120 such public enterprises controlled by the central government. At the local and provincial government level, there were 187 public enterprises. The 120 national public enterprises fall into four categories, grouped according to the degree of control exerted by their respective central government institutions: government corporations, government-invested institutions, government-financed institutions, and the subsidiaries of the government-invested institutions.[3]

Citing chronic inefficiencies in their management, the government has slated a large number of these public enterprises for privatization. However, their substantial influence, which accounted for 9.4 percent of the 1990 Korean gross domestic product, is expected to continue for some time to come.[4]

Laboratories affiliated with these public enterprises totaled 104 in 1992 and comprised 15.1 percent (159.5 billion won) of the total R&D budget for public laboratories. Of course, not all public enterprises have or operate LPEs, but there is a definite increasing trend. The increased budget allocation (77.0 billion won), more than double that of 1991, testifies to the growing importance of this sector.[5]

Government-Funded Laboratories

GFLs refer to those special nonprofit corporations that have been established through complete or partial governmental investment to support the nation's S&T needs. The staff members of these laboratories do not have civil servant status, but top-level personnel such as directors or auditors need to receive government approval of their appointment. As a result, staff members of these laboratories can be seen as quasi-government employees.

As of 1993, there were twenty-seven GFLs, of which twenty-one were under MOST jurisdiction. The Ministry of Trade, Industry, and Energy (MOTIE) controlled two GFLs; and there was one each in the Ministry of Agriculture, Forestry, and Fisheries; the Ministry of Communications; the Ministry of Construction and Transportation; and the Ministry of Finance.[6]

GFLs employed 12,900 people, of which 60.6 percent (7,822) were engaged in research (8.81% of the total Korean research population). R&D funds totaled 742.5 billion won, which amounted to 14.9 percent of the national expenditure on R&D. In 1992, 29.5 percent of research staff held Ph.D. degrees. Only 4.7 percent of researchers were female.

GFLs, an institutional type that may be unique to Korea, have three major characteristics that differentiate them from other public laboratories: (1) a higher pay scale than civil servants, (2) substantial research autonomy, and (3) a comfortable research environment. In the past, these selling points enabled the recruitment of quality research personnel and increased research productivity. Unfortunately, the growth of the private sector has largely negated these benefits, leaving GFLs with several serious issues to tackle.

These and other GFL issues comprise the remainder of this chapter. Immediately following is a historical overview of GFLs in Korea, starting with a discussion of the first and still perhaps most important GFL—KIST. As will be seen, KIST paved the way for the level of technology attained by the nation today and provided an example for less developed countries to follow.[7]

GOVERNMENT-FUNDED LABORATORIES: A HISTORICAL OVERVIEW

The original GFL was KIST, which was founded in 1966 as the first Korean multidisciplinary research institute in science and engineering. Funded by a special U.S. government grant extended in appreciation of Korea's military participation in the Vietnam War, the founding followed a year after the 1965 Summit Meeting between then-U.S. President Johnson and Korean President Park Chung-Hee in Washington, D.C. On the Memorial Tower at KIST is an inscription that explains the mission of the institute:

Recalling their agreement, in 1965, to cooperate in the establishment of a new institute to bring the benefits of applied S&T to the Korean economy and people, the two Presidents noted with pleasure the strong progress that had been made toward the establishment of the Korea Institute of Science and Technology, which is destined to make a fundamental contribution to the modernization of life and industry in the Republic of Korea.[8]

After analyzing the problems of the existing domestic research institutions as well as the key success factors of major foreign laboratories, the founding president, Dr. Choi Hyung-Sup defined KIST's basic philosophy with three tenets: autonomy from outside intervention and control, stability in long-term financial support, and the proper research ambiance to support morale and productivity.

Battelle Memorial Institute (United States), the National Research Council (Canada), the Commonwealth Scientific and Industrial Research Organization (CSIRO; Australia), the Max Planck Gesellschaft (West Germany), and the Research Institute for Physics and Chemistry (Japan) were among the major foreign institutions that served as examples for KIST. After a ten-month field survey, a task force decided upon mechanical engineering, chemistry and chemical engineering, material science and metal engineering, electronics, food, and industrial economics as KIST's six research areas.

Once the basic philosophy and structure were determined, KIST embarked on an ambitious recruiting program. To entice top-quality personnel working abroad, KIST, with the active backing from a supportive government, offered a compensation package that was exceptionally favorable, especially considering that Korea's per-capita gross national product at the time was less than $500. Besides free housing, KIST also promised a one-year sabbatical leave every three years. The attractive benefits, coupled with a patriotic appeal to contribute to the nation's development, succeeded in reversing the brain drain; and many Korean scientists and engineers gathered at the newly landscaped KIST campus. Soon, KIST emerged as the symbol of Korea's S&T effort as well as an object of envy for budding researchers.

Thus launched, KIST took a leading role in developing and upgrading Korea's industrial technology base throughout the 1960s and 1970s. KIST was not without its critics, however. The critics complained that the foreign-trained scientists were too academic and theoretical and did not meet the practical needs required by Korea's industrial sector. Moreover, because their working conditions were so superior to the other Korean institutions then, KIST researchers were pilloried as a "scientific aristocracy" who did not understand the realities of the domestic situation.

Nevertheless, at a time when Korean industrial technology was in its infancy, KIST was instrumental in the nation's efforts to assimilate and improve imported foreign technology. By reversing the brain drain abroad, KIST harnessed the ability of many top researchers. Many of the early leaders of Korea's budding technological infrastructure came from this labor pool.

A large part of the early success of KIST can be attributed to three factors. First was the personal interest of President Park Chung-Hee, who was, perhaps, most important to KIST's early success. In fact, one could say that President Park was the de facto founder of KIST. The political power, symbolized by the personal attention from the leader of an authoritarian military regime, made possible the seemingly impossible.

The next important factor was the legal framework embodied by the KIST Act, which guaranteed the "independence, autonomy, and stability" of KIST's administration. The law provided the institute's construction and operating funds as well as free lease to national assets. The government oversight inherent in prior approval and posterior audit requirements was precluded, at least for the early stages of KIST's existence.

The final factor responsible for KIST's early success was a comprehensive mixture of friendly U.S. assistance, financial backing from the Korean government, the visionary leadership of founding president Choi Hyung-Sup (who later served seven years as Minister of Science and Technology), the perception of an industrial need for S&T, and the active interest and support of the Korean people.

The Establishment of Specialized GFLs and the Forced-Merger Crisis

With the continued pursuit of Five-Year Economic Development Plans and the Heavy and Chemical Industry drive of the 1970s, demand for supportive technologies ballooned. This sparked the rapid formation of various new laboratories, including KIST spin-offs in specialized scientific and technical areas—from atomic energy to chemical research to shipbuilding and many others.

To nurture these new specialized laboratories in a manner consistent with KIST's mission, the Korean government enacted the Specialized Research Institute Law in 1973. This law became the legal foundation for government financial support and free lease to national assets. The government extended preferential participation rights in national research projects, eliminated customs duties on research equipment, and provided military draft exemptions for research staff. In addition, as part of its effort during the 1970s to create an S&T infrastructure, the government allowed the greatest possible autonomy to these new research laboratories.

As a result of these favorable policies, the specialized GFLs made significant contributions to the technology support required by the private sector. Rather than pursue actual innovative technology development, however, these laboratories concentrated on assimilating and improving upon foreign technologies. These efforts, along with countless reverse engineering projects, helped solve the technical problems of industry and strengthened the ability of local firms to digest and make use of new technologies.

In 1979, President Park was assassinated and, after a brief interim period, was succeeded by another former general, Chun Doo-Hwan. After several months in office, President Chun suddenly announced an abrupt abolition and amalgamation policy for the GFLs, citing duplicative research, insufficient cooperation, lagging research productivity, and an unnecessary abundance of administrative support. In fact, these valid concerns had been raised in the scientific community. The new military government merged the existing sixteen laboratories into nine and unified all administrative responsibility to MOST.

Although the forced-merger policy was much too drastic in its methodology and implementation, it had the positive effects of rationalizing the lax laboratory management and reducing unnecessary waste. But for the GFLs, which had created their own unique organizational cultures, the aftershocks of the draconian directive were serious and critical.

The forced merger between KIST and the Korea Advanced Institute of Science (KAIS) was especially troublesome. Although the justification was the purported synergy between research and educational functions, the result was cohabitation rather than marriage: irreconcilable differences between the societal norms of professors and researchers, constant conflict over the control of the merged entity, continued loyalty to one's "home" institution, and the flawed leadership of the two institutions' presidents.

After nine years of the forced cohabitation, KIST and KAIST (Korea Advanced Institute of Science and Technology, formerly KAIS) were again split into separate institutions. Nevertheless, they work cooperatively in Daeduk. The folly of the situation has been called "the lost decade" by many in the scientific community.

Identity Crisis of the GFLs and the Three-Pronged Challenge

An identity crisis resulted from the reorganization of GFLs. Three factors were responsible: improvements in research capabilities in industry and universities, squabbles within the government about who oversees which laboratories, and criticisms by the president's administration over poor management of the laboratories.

When these challenges emerged, it was clear that the GFLs had previously played a crucial role in implementing major national R&D projects and successfully pursuing joint research with private-sector R&D laboratories and universities. Successful national R&D projects during this period included the 1982 Special Research and Development Project (by MOST), the 1987 Alternative Energy Technology Development Project (by the Ministry of Energy and Resources), and the 1989 Industrial Base Technologies Development Project. In fact, the major technology areas in which Korea is now competitive, such as the memory element of semiconductors or the TDX-10 digital telephone exchange, were developed through these national projects.

However, this increased involvement in national R&D projects demanded boosts in financial support from the government. Increased government funding eventually diminished the autonomy of GFLs, thereby decreasing their effectiveness as research innovators. These cost and inefficiency problems grew more evident as industry and universities improved their innovation capacities, challenging the role of GFLs. Did GFLs carry out research that companies and universities could now perform (see Chapter 13)?

There was (and is) a squeeze on MOST and its GFLs by the Ministry of Trade and Industry, which has moved away from targeting industries and toward providing base technology support, previously the job of MOST. On the other hand, the Ministry of Education (MOE) has been criticized because Korea has so few research universities. In fact, the premier research university,

KAIST, is under MOST control, not MOE. All this further confuses and aggravates the functional challenge.

The second challenge to GFLs came from within the government as bureaucrats grew to recognize the importance of science and industry to national development. Ministries apart from MOST wanted a hand in overseeing the GFLs. This led to "jurisdiction battles" between MOST and contenders at the Ministry of Trade and Industry, the Ministry of Energy and Resources (which was merged into the Ministry of Commerce and Industry in 1993 to form MOTIE), and the Ministry of Communications. As a result, the Korea Telecommunications Research Institute (now renamed Electronics and Telecommunications Research Institute [ETRI]) moved to the Ministry of Communications; the Korea Ginseng and Tobacco Institute was transferred to the Ministry of Finance; and the Ministry of Trade and Industry created its own research institute, Korea Academy of Industrial Technology (KAITECH). During this uproar, the turf battles between rival ministries were so fierce that physical confrontations occasionally took place.

Amidst this reshuffling of GFLs, the Blue House criticized the management of the laboratories, claiming that the personnel, organization, and budget management were lax and inefficient. The president's administration claimed that research productivity was much lower than in private-sector laboratories. Furthermore, the technology developed in GFLs was said to be unsuitable and not focused for commercialization. Most of the latter criticism originated from the Ministry of Trade and Industry as part of its effort to wrest jurisdiction over the GFLs in the industrial area.

In response to these criticisms and challenges, in 1989, the government gave the Administrative Reform Investigation Committee the mandate to oversee the improved efficiency efforts of the GFLs. In 1990, the National Bureau of Audit and Inspection undertook a comprehensive evaluation. The following year, President Roh Tae-Woo ordered a complete reassessment of the operation of the GFLs.

These investigations led to the creation of the Combined Audit and Evaluation Committee (CAEC) of GFLs in the Science and Engineering Field, composed of private-sector experts and civil servants from the relevant ministries. After an eight-month evaluation, the CAEC came up with recommendations and decisions for changing functions, organization, and management of the GFLs.

In terms of function, those industrial research activities that were in competition with the private sector were privatized. Also, competing research activities among GFLs were unified; and research efforts were recommended for such new technology fields as environment studies, materials, and energy. In terms of organization, the quasi-independent Science and Technology Policy Institute (STEPI) was merged into KIST, as was the Basic Science Research Center into KSRI, both citing the lack of minimum-scale economies in personnel and resources.

The government reformed operation and management by classifying research areas into basic and public (common-use) technology, industrial technology, information and telecommunication technology, and resource and energy technology. For each area, a research planning body was created to exert overall operational control over the entire research activity spectrum—from the selection of appropriate research projects to the utilization and commercialization of the results. The system for using an international panel of experts to evaluate research output was expanded. Thus, a "carrot and stick" approach, in which operational autonomy was coupled with posterior evaluation and audits, was formalized.

In summary, the activities of the CAEC increased awareness of the issues surrounding research productivity and operational efficiency. But when considering the commotion and disruption caused by the eight-month audit, the actual results were minimal. GFL staff members were forced to undergo an eight-month period of unease and instability.

RECOMMENDATIONS FOR INCREASING INNOVATION FROM GOVERNMENT-FUNDED LABORATORIES

We suggest that GFLs suffer from three basic problems, for which we propose several solutions (see our model, Figure 8.1).

Figure 8.1
A Model of Technological Development

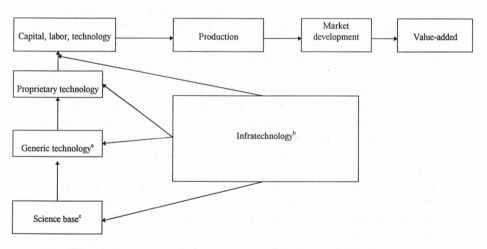

[a] Generic technology is the knowledge that is organized into the conceptual form of an eventual application.
[b] Infratechnology is technologies that facilitate R&D, production, and marketing in industries.
[c] The concept of science base is similar to that of fundamental research.

Clarify Roles and Functions of
Government-Funded Laboratories

First, the roles and functions of the GFLs must be defined more clearly. They have yet to develop a consensus on their exact mission, especially about the industrial and academic sectors. The most basic role of GFLs is to promote the creation and expansion of innovative technologies at the national level. This can be accomplished by filling the gap that exists between the roles assumed by industry and universities, which respectively play a leading role for and act as a source for technological innovation. At present, MOST is being squeezed by MOTIE, which has shifted from targeted industrial interventions to investments in base technology. GFLs should continue to provide support and assistance to corporations and universities in areas that present difficulties for them. Because this gap is being closed as universities and industry continue to enhance their research capabilities, the GFLs have to reexamine how much of this innovative work they will need to do in the future. They should play a greater role as an integrator and mediator for developing a comprehensive R&D system that synergistically involves industry, universities, and research institutes. In short, the GFLs should provide linkage across all institutions in the national system of innovation.

GFLs differ from one another in mission, in capability, and in relationship to their "clients." At the core are four multidisciplinary laboratories with strong basic research capabilities and links to higher education: KIST, KAITECH, KSRI, and the Korea Research Institute of Standards and Science (KRISS). Other GFLs may be grouped into industry-related (telecommunications, mechanical, chemical, bioengineering, and aerospace) sectors and technology-defined (energy, natural and marine resources, food, and environment) areas.

In their revised roles, all GFLs should do the following:

1. Continue to carry out R&D in their respective areas.
2. Develop human resources, especially in the multidisciplinary, education-related laboratories, independently or in cooperation with higher-education institutions.
3. Collect and analyze information on related technologies and by conducting technology forecasts, especially for industry-related and general research institutes.
4. Transfer best-practice technologies to small- and medium-size companies, especially by industry-related GFLs.
5. Spin off new high-technology enterprises. Already, ETRI, KAIST, KIST, and KRISS are making significant progress in this area.

The government must next decide how individual GFLs should focus their R&D efforts. Solving this problem entails classifying R&D and various technologies. According to the classical method, R&D is divided into three steps—

basic, applied, and development—with the responsibility for basic research going to universities, while development research is assigned to industry and applied research goes to the GFLs. However, this characterization is not appropriate because the trend toward an increasingly close relationship and interdependency between S&T have made it difficult to separate R&D activities into the three stages of basic, applied, and development.

An alternative method for assessing R&D roles divides the types of technology utilized in economic and industrial activities into science base, infratechnology, generic technology, and proprietary technology. Because they are broad and nonproprietary, the science base and infratechnology should be supported by the government and the public sector, as defined in Table 8.1. Since generic technologies are both proprietary and nonproprietary, they have a quasi-public characteristic. If confidentiality and exclusive usage are guaranteed, proprietary technology falls under the private domain.

Given this characterization of different kinds of R&D activities, how should responsibility be allocated across different types of institutions—universities, industry, and the three kinds of GFLs (multidisciplinary and education-related, technology-defined, and mission-related)? A suggested allocation is shown in Tables 8.2 and 8.3.

In determining what activities fall within each institutional type, three factors must be considered:

1. Responsibilities should be constantly adjusted in accordance with the socioeconomic changes and the resulting shifts in technological demands.

2. In order to ensure a healthy level of competition among the research institutes and effective diffusion of technical knowledge among them, some overlapping of activities should not only be accepted but also be planned.

3. Because the rewards of pathbreaking technology, along with basic research, are not quickly commercialized, they should be pursued through international cooperation.

Table 8.1
Domain-Based Characterization of Universities, Government-Funded Laboratories, and Industry

	Primary Domain	Secondary Domain
Universities	Science base	Generic technology
Government-Funded Laboratories	Generic technology Infratechnology	Infratechnology Science base
Industry	Proprietary technology	Infratechnology Generic technology

Table 8.2
Categorization of Technology or Technological Activities That Are Subject to Public Support

Criteria	Time Horizon	Risk/Rewards	Beneficiaries	Selection Criteria
Infrastructural Technologies Emphasizing productivity improvement and breadth of application	Continuous payoffs	Low risk: incremental improvement in productivity or quality	Many firms, many industries	Importance to productivity, technical quality
Strategic Technologies Emphasizing the criticality to the nation of industries to which the technology applies	About 5 years	Middle risk: high rewards through economic leverage	Defined group of firms	Competitive impacts
Pathbreaking Technologies Emphasizing technical challenge	Ten years or more	High risk: potential new industry	Unidentified in entirely new industries	Technical promise, entrepreneurial vision

Define the Degree of Autonomy Necessary for GFLs to Innovate Efficiently

The Korean government has always emphasized the harmony between autonomy and accountability for its funded laboratories. Nevertheless, the autonomy of the GFLs has yet to reach a desirable level.

The GFLs must be ensured a maximum of autonomy to enhance creativity. However, there is a need to audit them to confirm that the research funds, which are paid for by the taxpayers, are spent for appropriate research purposes. The key to ensuring autonomy for GFLs lies in harmonizing these two requirements. Eventually, when the GFLs achieve some level of financial independence, privatization of some of the GFLs as nonprofit companies should be the ultimate goal.[9]

How can the conflicting values of autonomy and accountability be harmonized? The research cycle can be divided into three stages: planning, operations, and audit and evaluation. With respect to planning, the government should present the basic objectives and key policies to be pursued by its funded laboratories on the basis of the national development plan. The power to make

Table 8.3
Role Classification for Universities, Government-Funded Laboratories, and Industry

	Primary Domain	Secondary Domain	Cooperative Institutions
Universities	Basic research	Strategic technology, pathbreaking technology	Government-funded laboratories, industry, international cooperation
Government-Funded Laboratories			
Basic research/education institutes	Basic research, pathbreaking technology	Strategic technology	Universities, international cooperation
General/central research institutes	Pathbreaking technology	Strategic technology, basic research	Universities, international cooperation
Industrial field-based research institutes	Strategic technology	Diffusion of best-practice technology to firms, infratechnology	Industry, universities
Public-use technology institutes	Infrastructural technology, strategic technology	Basic research, pathbreaking technology	Universities, international cooperation
Industry	Commercial product and process development	Infratechnology, strategic technology	Government-funded laboratories, universities

specific research plans for each laboratory should be fully delegated to the decision-making bodies, such as the boards of directors of each laboratory.

Many of the boards of directors of GFLs have been a mere formality, often operating as rubber-stamp approval bodies for previously made government decisions. Civil servants of related ministries serve as automatic members. Since this is an obstacle to the autonomous operation of the governing boards, it bears reevaluation. Only those crucial decisions, such as the appointment and removal of executives and adoption of long-range plans, should require ministerial approval. Other decisions should be reported on an information basis to the government.

In the future, the directors of the GFLs should be selected among experts, including people from industry and academia, who have a clear understanding of the roles and functions assumed by the particular institute. Each board must regain its right and responsibility to act as the ultimate decision-making authority for its GFL.

With respect to operations, the government should refrain from direct interference or control over research activities or operational management. It should not exert control over the internal budget allocations and other organizational activities. Institutional devices must be introduced to minimize direct government interference. Given the long bureaucratic tradition of Korean government ministries, the ministers must be vigilant in eliminating unnecessary bureaucratic oversight.

In terms of evaluation and audit, the government has the responsibility inherent in its financial and operational support to conduct fair analyses and audits of both the research outcomes and management aspects of the GFLs. The design for the research audit should be built into the laboratory's research planning function. Laboratory management audits must be adapted to the structure and management style appropriate to each research institute type. The audit activity should not be only control oriented but should focus on improving the laboratory in the future.

Maintaining stability of operations and continuity of research is just as important as guaranteeing autonomy. Staff researchers complain that the frequent reorganizations and mergers, abrupt changes in research topics and direction, and uncertainty about future funding continuity diminish morale and productivity. It must be admitted that the government too often "rocked the boat" of its funded laboratories. Therefore, the government must avoid damaging the stability of its funded laboratories. Research funding must be guaranteed to be continued; and, barring special circumstances, research topics should be maintained to their completion.

Reform the National Administrative System of Government-Funded Laboratories

The national administrative system of GFLs should be improved so that internal management innovation is promoted and research productivity and efficiency is maximized. As part of the reform, the national administrative system must make sure that the GFLs contribute to the technology-innovation needs of Korea, while maintaining their assigned role and place in the national R&D network. Reform of the system should focus on helping domestic firms compete internationally and ensuring the joint utilization of GFL capabilities by all relevant ministries. A national administrative system that is appropriate to the Korean situation must be created so that unnecessary duplication of effort and resources is avoided.

Several issues should be kept in mind before any new proposals are put forth. The following points include representative comments from the Korean scientific community:

1. The vertical bureaucratic tradition makes horizontal cooperation difficult. ("When jurisdictions differ among GFLs, the gulf dividing them widens.")
2. There is a long tradition of bureaucratic control and interference. ("The distance between GFLs and civil servants should not be too close.")

3. The size and scale of major foreign laboratories' personnel and budgets are discouraging when compared with those of Korean research institutes. ("Korea's competition is located outside its borders.")

4. As time passes from the point of formation, research organizations create idiosyncratic tendencies and unique cultures. ("Much time and effort are required for changing cultures.")

Given these realities, one can think of several alternative models, including the Max Plank Institute of Germany or the Organization for Applied Scientific Research of the Netherlands, as well as consortia of institutes under a parent or holding institute, such as CSIRO in Australia or the National Center for Scientific Research in France. But whatever option is examined, the stability of the GFLs should be maintained.

The most important reform would increase joint utilization of all GFLs among ministries. All GFLs in the science and engineering area should be combined into a federative body, not a single merged entity. The management of this federation should be undertaken by a "research consultative body," which can take the form of a committee secretariat or a holding or institute.

This consultative body would plan, select, and pursue research that meets both national requirements and industrial needs, exceeds a certain threshold, and requires multiparty cooperation. It could respond to the needs of all ministries requiring broad-based, cross-disciplinary research. In order for this proposal to work, the body would form research teams, raise and manage R&D funds, and oversee all other major activities involved in joint research projects. To enforce the decisions of this consultative body, some sort of legal framework should be created as a supportive measure.

We also recommend that any potential government interference into its funded laboratories be channeled through the federation for its prior approval. This guarantees that direct government meddling is minimized and research autonomy maximized.

To jointly distribute the research results of GFLs among ministries, all basic operating expenses should be provided through the consultative body of the federation. Thereby, the utilization of government research institutes would occur on a project–contract basis that ensures free and equal opportunity. When the cooperation of related GFLs is necessary, such requests would be submitted and pursued through the aforementioned consultative body. Perhaps a more fundamental solution would be full-cost allocation, favored by the Minister of Science and Technology in 1995, through a project management system.

It is not at all impractical to imagine a more decentralized structure in each laboratory, with a site manager in charge of all facilities management but separate and independent program managers in charge of functional units. Thus, it is possible to have parts of laboratories "belonging to" different agencies and operating under different statutory authority. The federation might also take over the institutional evaluation function discussed earlier. MOST policy is currently moving in this direction.

Besides accomplishing the aforementioned intralaboratory administrative reforms, the government should improve the internal management of GFLs. The solution must be found not only within the GFLs themselves but also through more active support and cooperation from the government. We recommend management changes in four areas: personnel, organization, budget, and research.

First, in terms of personnel management, the most urgent task is to improve the salary of staff researchers. The current salaries of GFL researchers are 68 to 78 percent of the salaries of researchers in the private sector and significantly lower than those of corresponding university researchers. It is also claimed that the salaries at GFLs in the science and engineering area are lower than those of funded laboratories in the social sciences. Naturally, this has an adverse effect upon researcher pride and morale.

The laboratories also need to upgrade and reform their policies to recruit higher-quality personnel. Strict personnel and research evaluation systems should be maintained. Seniority should be discouraged in favor of merit as the basis for advancement. Hiring researchers on a contract basis may also improve motivation. Sabbatical leaves and other opportunities for the replenishment of the research spirit would also be helpful.

To improve the relatively low social prestige of laboratory researchers, the proposal to bestow professor status on researchers that meet certain qualifications should be given serious consideration. This also dovetails with the previous call for increased education and training functionality from the GFLs.

Concerning organizational management, an often-mentioned proposal is to restructure the laboratories on a project basis. If this takes place, the resulting matrix organization must be led by principal investigators and be managed in a flexible manner.

The current organizational structure of GFLs is a hierarchical one, based on divisions and sections. Any changes in organizational form above the section level must receive both board and ministerial approval. This leads to rigid and inflexible organizational management, as well as poor horizontal cooperation among divisions and sections. The government must release its stifling interference and control so that its funded laboratories can structure themselves in a flexible manner—one that befits the rapidly changing external environment. Thus, the current management system in which power is centralized to each research institute president should be decentralized to the principal-investigator level.

The GFLs must quickly implement a multiyear budget system so that mid- to long-term research projects can receive continuous support. In order to foster financial independence as well as enlarge and diversify funding sources, contract research should be encouraged. Incentives should be provided to promote increased contract research from industry. Furthermore, assurances must be made that the increased funds can be used in an autonomous manner.

At present, when GFLs derive research income through contract research, the government subtracts this amount from its total budget allocation to the laboratories and thereby reduces its funding of the laboratories. Under this shortsighted policy, GFLs have no incentives to actively solicit contract research. This situation only aggravates their reliance on government financial support.

With respect to reforming research management, careful study must be conducted into whether the entire cycle encompassing research project planning, selection, evaluation, and posterior management is efficient and effective. A more systematic education and training program should be initiated for project managers of all levels.

Finally, the selection process for GFL directors needs to be reformed. As discussed, the ultimate goal may be the decentralization of the research management system. However, given Korea's long tradition of bureaucratic control and its so-called "vertical culture," the selection of its director is perhaps the most crucial determinant of laboratory success. Therefore, to provide for directors with vision and a strong sense of mission, each laboratory should be empowered to form an independent selection committee charged with the task of recommending multiple director candidates. Ideally, the board of directors, insulated from outside pressure, would then ultimately choose the most qualified candidate in an autonomous manner.

In conclusion, the GFLs of the future should be governed by an overriding principle of independence, which would entail independence of project selection, project funding, project oversight, and project management. Subject only to the minimum necessary oversight, GFLs may blossom into the optimal sources of creativity for improving the overall level of national innovation and expertise.

NOTES

1. Alice Amsden, *Asia's Next Giant—South Korea and Late Industrialization* (New York: Oxford University Press, 1989).

2. Ministry of Science and Technology (MOST), *Science and Technology Annual Report* (in Korean) (Seoul: MOST, 1993), 243–267.

3. The following section relies on the information and data included in, among other sources, Dae-Hee Song, *Public Enterprise Management Policies in Korea*, Research Volume 91-26 (in Korean) (Seoul: Korea Development Institute, 1991); Dae-Hee Song, "Korean Public Enterprise Performance" (in Korean), Working Paper 9115, Korea Development Institute, Seoul, August 1991.

4. The various issues surrounding public enterprises are discussed in Chapter 4.

5. Ministry of Science and Technology, *Science and Technology Annual Report.*

6. Korea Industrial Technology Association (KITA), *1993 White Paper on Industrial Technology* (in Korean) (Seoul: KITA, 1993), 76.

7. See, for instance, Hyung-Sup Choi, "Science and Technology Policies for Industrialization of Developing Countries," *Technological Forecasting and Social Change* 29 (1986): 225–239.

8. Ibid.

9. For a related discussion, see Lewis M. Branscomb, ed., *Empowering Technology: Implementing a U.S. Strategy* (Cambridge: MIT Press, 1993), where he makes similar recommendations for U.S. Department of Energy weapons labs.

Part Three

OTHER MODELS FOR INNOVATION-BASED DEVELOPMENT

Chapter Nine

JAPAN
Model, Mentor, and Competitor

Lewis M. Branscomb

What measures and models are available to Korea to evaluate alternative strategies for technology-based development? Through the last thirty years of Korea's continued rapid economic growth, change has been so rapid that its experience in each decade could scarcely be absorbed before it had to address the next one. As Korea faces yet another set of circumstances for which its recent history is only partly relevant, one is led to look for external experience that might illuminate the choices facing the nation. Part III explores the experiences of several selected countries against which Korean technology strategy may be tested.

Japan, which developed (like Korea) by leveraging technology from abroad, expanded and exploited its indigenous technical capability to the point where Japanese industry is roughly equal to that of the United States and Europe. The Japanese model is envied and emulated by all the rapidly developing economies in Asia. Indeed, Japan has been a reasonably explicit model for Korean science and technology (S&T) policy during the past three decades.

JAPAN AS MODEL, MENTOR, AND COMPETITOR

The development of Korean S&T institutions owes a joint debt to Japan and the United States. The American influence on Korean S&T policy began when Syngman Rhee created the Office of Atomic Energy in 1959. With funding from President Eisenhower through the U.S. Atoms for Peace program, plus continual investments from multilateral aid agencies, young Korean scientists were able to go abroad for advanced study, primarily to the United States, giving Korea a jump start on building its university system. (See also Chapter 7.) The formation of the Korea Institute of Science and Technology (KIST) ten years later was made possible by President Johnson, using two U.S. institutions, Battelle Memorial Institute and the National Bureau of Standards, as models and sources of assistance. However, many other Korean institutions are patterned after Japanese models, not American ones. Korea's autonomous ministries, along with their government-funded research laboratories and the assistance they provide to commercial firms, are much more Japanese than American. Korean technology policy is also patterned more closely on Japanese than American principles. President Park Chung-Hee saw Japanese modernization strategy as a model for Korea, since it validated a strong central role for government in promoting modernization.[1]

Korea's rapid industrial development also owes much to relationships with major Japanese firms, which made technology available in return for access to Korea's high-performance, low-cost labor market. Today, Korean labor costs no longer compensate for the high cost of technology licenses and imported machinery, components, and materials. Because Korea based its high-technology development primarily on the same industries that Japan dominates in foreign markets—automobiles and consumer electronics—Korea and Japan see each other as competitors. Thus, Japan is seen concurrently as a model, a mentor, and a competitor. We must ask how well the model fits Korean circumstances, how well Korea emulated Japanese strategies for success, and whether Japan's evolving policy is still an appropriate model for Korea.

The degree of influence of Japanese firms in Korean technology development can hardly be understated. Denis Fred Simon and Changrok Soh noted that, although the U.S. economy was roughly twice that of Japan in 1992, Japanese investments in Korea were double those of U.S. firms ($4.12 billion versus $2.71 billion).[2] Technical cooperation agreements, they note, show a similar pattern: 3,813 Japanese agreements by the end of 1992, compared with 1,991 U.S. agreements. Only in the value of payments for technology did the United States exceed Japan ($2.91 billion versus $1.91 billion). Japanese inventions continue to find protection in the Korean patent system in large numbers, reflecting the inadequacy of Korean invention rates. Of all the patents applied for in Korea, Japanese nationals generated 24.2 percent in 1975, while generating only 8.5 percent in the United States and 7.2 percent in Germany. In 1990, the Japanese applied for 70,000 patents in Korea, which constituted 23.4 percent of the patents applied for in Korea. The fraction of U.S. patents of Japanese origin had risen to 20.3 percent and in Germany to 14.9 percent.[3] Japan is the dominant source of Korea's trade deficit.

Japan's dedication to modernization has a much longer history than does Korea's. During the Meiji Era (1868–1911), the accelerated acquisition of technical knowledge from the West brought with it great emphasis on education and scientific and technical institution building. Thus, Japan's challenge was to build upon a cultural heritage of a well-developed industrial society and update it for contemporary needs. Korea faced the task of building a society that had not been allowed to develop during the colonial period.

Only a decade separates the contemporary initiation of forceful S&T development as an economic growth strategy in Japan and Korea. Ironically, it was the Korean War that led to a swift reversal of U.S. policy toward Japan, permitting the rebirth of Japanese civil industry. General Douglas MacArthur needed a strong Japan as a source of logistic support for the U.N. action in Korea. Thus, U.S. policy actively promoted the modernization of Japan after 1954. Korea's modernization began ten years later.

Why, then, did Japan pull ahead of Korea so far and so quickly? In the 1920s and 1930s, Japan pursued a major industrial expansion to support its vision of a dominant military and industrial power in Asia. A series of recent studies by leading Japanese R&D executives, now in their seventies and eighties, traces how each used his knowledge and training from the World War II defense industry for the rebirth and growth of the civil firms they led after the war.[4] Japanese engineers experienced in military aircraft led the automobile firms' technical development. Experts in military optics helped to build firms like Canon and other camera and optical instrument firms. This was possible because the level of education of scientists and engineers was quite high before the war.

The U.S.-led modernization of Japanese political institutions probably played an even larger role in fostering Japan's achievements. The end of military government, the development of democratic political processes, the enfranchisement of women, the development of labor unions, and the breakup of the giant family-owned (Zaibatsu) conglomerates contributed to a more open and energized society. The Japanese government that evolved was a unique combination of a market economy with democratic political processes and a more traditional society that looked to authority—in government, in industry, and in the family—to guide a national program of force-fed economic redevelopment.

Throughout the period when Japan most strongly influenced the pattern of technology-based industrial development in Korea, Japan continued to enjoy a special, if increasingly stressful, relationship with the United States. On the economic front, the United States was slow to recognize the depth and breadth of Japanese industrial competitiveness. Political recognition of this fact began in the early 1970s. During the 1970s and 1980s, most U.S. firms saw Japan as a low-cost manufacturer of increasingly impressive quality. It was not recognized that while U.S. firms continued to engage in joint ventures—sharing technology to get access to Japanese low-cost production—Japan was exceptionally skillful at internalizing, adapting, and extending these technologies.

As trade friction grew and Americans became increasingly nervous about losing their scientific and technical leadership to Japanese partners, the U.S. government continued its constrained industrial and trade policy. The strategic security alliance with Japan dominated (and still heavily influences) U.S. policy toward Japan. A critical element of this relationship is the Japanese constitutional constraint on strategic military development and deployment. Faced with a choice between a remilitarized Japan and a Japan that focuses all its national energies on economic dominance of foreign markets, the U.S. government prefers the latter, despite the political pressure from U.S. workers and firms losing market shares to Japanese competitors. Given Korea's much smaller economy and more immediate security threat from the North, it is unlikely that Korea's resistance to U.S. pressure to open markets will go as far as to threaten the security alliance.

EXPORT-ORIENTED INDUSTRIAL POLICY

In the early stages of their postwar industrialization, both Korea and Japan based their industrial policies heavily on exports for many of the same reasons: need for much larger markets than those available domestically, desire to access to foreign exchange to finance technology acquisitions, an impetus for quality and prices that meet world standards, and a desire for relationships with foreign firms to gain access to markets and complementary assets. The fraction of manufactured goods that were exported was high for both countries. Korean exports in 1990 still represented 16.6 percent of gross domestic product, while the growth of the Japanese economy has brought the Japanese export percentage down to 9.8 percent.[5]

The Japanese internal market has always been a competitive battleground for Japanese manufacturers, based not on prices (which tend to be higher than export prices in many cases) but on product function and appeal. Today, that domestic Japanese market is seven times the size of that of Korea. While the Japanese can afford to accommodate to U.S. political pressures to expand domestic consumption (to mitigate Japan's manufacturing trade surplus), Koreans feel that their industrial policy must continue to have a strong export thrust.

TECHNOLOGY POLICY FOR
INTERNAL DEVELOPMENT

To maximize the acquisition of technological capability, both nations have controlled direct foreign investment, technology license agreements, access to foreign exchange, and market access by foreign firms. U.S. firms complained of these pressures when Japan's Ministry of International Trade and Industry (MITI) was severely controlling foreign investment. Today, Koreans complain that Japanese firms are attempting to marginalize the competitive advantage of Korean firms. A survey of 110 Korean electronics, electrical, and machinery firms reported that 70 percent were unhappy with their Japanese partners. The surveyed firms reported that 90 percent of the technology they had acquired was either outdated or already popularized in the West, Simon and Soh reported. While the Japanese government insists that Korea is still the largest recipient of Japanese know-how in the Pacific basin, Simon and Soh quote a 1991 survey of Japanese firms complaining about "Korea's excessive zeal for technology transfers."

Both nations have pursued a policy of technology investment to support import substitution, to build industrial infrastructure, and to give export-based industry a captive domestic market in which to develop. Both countries, with a time shift of about one decade, have gradually adjusted these protections as Korean firms became more competitive in export markets and pressures grew from other nations with open markets. While constraints remain in selected markets (primarily in agriculture and financial services), this strategy has run its course in both nations.

SOME DIFFERENCES BETWEEN JAPAN AND KOREA

Government Science and Technology Structure

Both Japan and Korea integrated technology policy into their policies for economic development early in their postwar recovery. In this respect, both differ from the United States, which began the process in the 1980s and reversed it with the new Republican Congress in 1994. However, Korea and Japan approached the development of S&T policy quite differently. In Japan, MITI led the technology policy from the start. A science policy had been in place since 1933, when the Japan Science Council was created. Funded from both public and private sources, it aimed at encouraging research and cooperation among universities and industry. The Ministry of Education (MOE) in Japan, like the MOE in Korea, has played a relatively weak role in technology promotion. Japan's Science and Technology Agency's operating role has been largely confined to energy and space technology and, more recently, has expanded into policy development. The agency with the influence in technology policy is MITI. It not only seeks consensus strategies with leaders of the private sector but also operates the key agencies, such as the Agency for Industrial Science and Technology (AIST).

MITI was born from a reorganization of the Ministry of Commerce and Industry in May 1949. The Industrial Technology Agency was the technology policy arm of MITI from the beginning, evolving into AIST in 1952. Its first *White Paper* on industrial technology was issued in February 1951. One of AIST's first acts, in 1949, was the promotion of quality control in Japanese industry. In July 1950, the private-sector Japan Science and Technology Association invited W. Edwards Deming from the United States to Japan to teach Japanese firms the practice of statistical quality control. Few U.S. firms were paying Deming serious attention at the time. Royalties from the Japanese publication of his lectures created the fund from which the prestigious Deming Award has been given each year.

The effective collaboration of government agencies with private institutions in the promotion of technology-based development is a hallmark of the Japanese system of innovation, and it should be emulated by Korea. Historically, the privatization of some Japanese government institutes was accelerated by the U.S. occupation. The Research Institute of Physics and Chemistry (Riken), founded in 1917, was privatized under the Zaibatsu dissolution directive of 1948. The Japanese Society for the Promotion of Science, founded in 1931, is another nongovernmental institution through which public funds are channelled in support of higher education and research in science and engineering. It serves today as another nongovernmental mechanism, both for domestic consensus building and for bridges to foreign independent-sector institutions, such as the U.S. National Research Council.

The Japanese Council for Science and Technology was established in February 1959, comprising the prime minister as chairman and ministers from finance and education, the director-generals of the Economic Planning Agency and the Science and Technology Agency (STA), the chairman of the Science Council of Japan, and three "men of learning and experience." Thus, MITI integrates technology policy with industrial policy, while the Prime Minister's Council and the STA integrate science policy with technology policy.

In Korea, the Ministry of Science and Technology (MOST), created in 1967, had to build a research infrastructure at the same time it sought to create the linkages between technical research and economic development. It was initially established as an arm of the Economic Planning Board (EPB) to formulate and coordinate S&T policies. Its aim was to foster human resource development, set up an R&D system, promote international linkages, support industrial-technology development, and create an environment conducive to S&T development. The Ministry of Trade, Industry, and Energy (MOTIE) has only recently begun to complement MOST with substantial investments in the commercial technology base. The relationships between MOST and MOTIE are competitive to some degree. With the removal of MOST from the EPB, and the EPB's absorption into the Ministry of Finance and the Economy, it is unclear how the linkages from industrial policy to technology policy and to science policy can be managed, and how the whole can be structured into the heart of economic policy.

Government Science and Technology Research Institutions

In Japan, the creation of publicly supported research laboratories began with Riken in 1917. Thus, Japan has benefited from fifty more years of experience at independent research in support of industry than Korea. The development of government-sponsored research institutions began in Korea in 1966 when KIST was founded. MOST was formed the following year, creating the mechanism for building additional research institutes.

As is seen from the tables that follow, Korea made up for lost time with the creation of many institutes. Some were formed by MOST, while others were made by MOTIE. By 1976, Japan had developed its industry and its universities to the point where it was performing only 5.4 percent of its national R&D in such institutes, in contrast to Korea's 38.3 percent. Japan's reliance on such institutes in 1995 was at the level of 4.4 percent, while Korea still (according to 1992 figures) performed 12.6 percent of its R&D in government-sponsored research institutes.

Table 9.1 compares Korea, Japan, and Taiwan in this respect. These data show that Korea has made much heavier use of government-sponsored, nonprofit research institutes than either Japan or Taiwan. Korea has made correspondingly less use of universities as performers of R&D and thus as places to nurture scientific and engineering talent.

Government as a Source of Science and Technology Research

In Japan, because of the prewar institutional infrastructure, public investments in R&D were a significant fraction of the national investment from 1960 to 1980. However, the private-sector share of national R&D has grown rapidly with the economy (see Table 9.2).

In Korea, the government financed 90 percent of the total in 1965, which was reduced to 52 percent in 1980 and to 16 percent in 1989 (see Table 9.3).

Table 9.1
R&D by Performer: Korea, Japan, and Taiwan

	Year	Korea	Japan	Taiwan
Universities	1976	3.2	19.9	NA
	1980	12.2	18.0	21.6
	1985	10.3	14.2	16.9
	1990	7.6	12.2	13.2
Research Institutes	1976	38.3	5.3	NA
	1980	26.8	4.0	10.5
	1985	20.0	4.2	20.5
	1990	14.8	4.4	17.4
Industry	1976	24.9	61.6	NA
	1980	38.4	65.1	54.6
	1985	65.0	71.8	50.1
	1990	74.0	75.5	52.4

Source: Jean M. Johnson, *Human Resources for Science and Technology: The Asian Region,* NSF 93-303 (Washington, D.C.: National Science Foundation, 1993), Table A-18.
NA, Not available.

Table 9.2
Japanese Public and Private R&D Expenditures as a Percentage of GNP

Year	1960	1970	1980	1990
Private R&D/ GNP	0.83	1.19	1.41	2.32
Gov't R&D/ GNP	0.28	0.40	0.49	0.46
Govt/ Private	33.70	33.60	34.80	19.8

Source: Science and Technology Agency, Prime Minister's Office, *Japan White Paper on Science and Technology—1995,* (Tokyo: Science and Technology Agency, 1995).

Table 9.3
Government as a Source of R&D Expenditures

	1965	1970	1975	1980	1985	1989
R&D expenditures	2.1	10.5	42.7	211.7	1,155.2	27,051
Gov/Private	90/10	71/29	67/23	52/48	19/81	16/84
Percentage of GNP	0.26	0.38	0.42	0.57	1.59	1.92

Source: Tae-Sup Lee, "The Role of Government in Science and Technology Development in Korea," Lecture at John F. Kennedy School of Government, Harvard University, May 4, 1993. (Mr. Lee is former Minister of S&T in Korea.)

Importing Technology

Japan based its early postwar strategy on importation of technology, as has Korea. However, as Japan became an international competitor, it realized that the cost of technology imports would rise rapidly with economic success. As early as the 1960s, the government initiated policies to promote domestic R&D. Japanese policy has consistently understood the importance of building industrial infrastructure to enhance the capacity for technology absorption and independent development. The government has given significant attention to encouraging local suppliers by controlling capital goods—including scientific instruments, production tools, process equipment, and information systems—for different industrial sectors. This emphasis on internal technological infrastructure is perhaps the most important difference between Japanese and Korean policy.

Korea took a different approach, fostering imports of modern tooling as the quickest way to accelerate the capability to compete in international markets with high-technology goods (see Chapter 13). This approach was successful; but the result, discussed in Chapters 2, 3, and 4, has led to major drawbacks:

a serious negative impact on the balance of trade, a shallow economy from the technological point of view, and an uncomfortably high degree of vulnerability to Japanese and U.S. companies.

Building the Human Resources and Knowledge Infrastructure

Both nations have a long tradition of honoring formal education and of providing universal access to it. Korea and Japan have the highest ratio of university enrollments in the twenty- to twenty-four-year-old population in all of Asia, and Korea surpassed Japan in 1984. By 1990, 37 percent of Koreans in this age group were enrolled in universities, compared to 30 percent in Japan and 28 percent in Taiwan.[6]

Important differences exist, however, in the way that Koreans and Japanese have gone about improving their personnel. Furthermore, the level of development is quite different in the two countries, with greatest differences found in science and engineering in the domestic universities. The majority of Taiwan's doctoral degrees are from the United States. About one-half of Korea's doctorates are obtained in U.S. universities, while only a tiny fraction of Japanese doctoral degrees are obtained abroad (Table 9.4).

Thus, although even more Koreans attend universities in their own country than in Japan, Korea pursues a deliberate policy of encouraging higher levels of training, especially the doctorate, at U.S. universities.[7] This decision reflects the appreciation Korea has for the more practical, hands-on training that students receive in the United States, in contrast to the more theoretical approach characteristic of the Confucian tradition.

This policy, combined with incentives for Korean graduates of U.S. universities, seems to be quite successful for Korea. Koreans are more willing to return to Korea after completing their degrees than are other Asians who re-

Table 9.4
Doctoral Degrees Earned by Asian Nationals within the Country and in the United States in 1990

Country	Within Country		In U.S. Universities	
	Natural Science	Engineering	Natural Science	Engineering
S. Korea	399	439	343 (46.2 %)	350 (44.4 %)
Taiwan	104	165	446 (81.1 %)	460 (73.6 %)
Japan	937	948	56 (5.6 %)	17 (1.8 %)

Source: Organization for Economic Cooperation and Development, *OECD Economic Surveys: Korea 1994* (Paris: OECD, 1995), Table 5, P. 10.

ceive doctoral degrees from U.S. universities. In 1991, only 25.3 percent of Korean degree recipients had firm plans to stay in the United States, compared to 57.5 percent of Indians, 51.2 percent of Chinese, 31.9 percent of Taiwanese, and 31.5 percent of Japanese. However, the Japanese have had more resources and considerably more time than Korea to develop the quality of science and engineering in higher education. In addition, until recently, the Japanese have given much less emphasis to the doctorate, preferring a terminal baccalaureate or master's degree, supplemented by training provided by the employer.

In Korea, the chaebols have been much more inclined to sponsor the development of private universities than have the large Japanese firms. An example would be the Pohang University for Science and Technology, sponsored by Pohang Iron and Steel Corporation (see Chapter 7). The creation in 1971 of the Korean Advanced Institute of Science and Technology (KAIST), a very impressive and promising institution, was an important step toward developing a postgraduate institution for science and engineering. It has the character of the best institutes of technology in the United States. In the period dating from its founding until 1992, KAIST has produced 1,308 Ph.D.'s and 6,939 M.S.'s.

There are two other striking differences between the structure of higher education in science and engineering in Japan and in Korea. First, when compared to Japan, Korean universities stress natural science much more than engineering. Of the 51,266 bachelor's degrees awarded in natural science and engineering by Korean universities in 1990, 23,195 were in natural science (45.2%) and 28,071 were awarded in engineering (54.8%). In Japan, which traditionally focuses much more strongly on engineering, only 23.6 percent of the degrees were in natural science and 76.4 percent were in engineering. These figures suggest an underemphasis on engineering in Korea and a systemic problem facing Japanese intentions to strengthen basic research and technical creativity. The United States stands in contrast to both Korea and Japan; 61.9 percent of U.S. science and engineering degrees were in science.

Another difference between Korea and Japan lies in Korea's greater opportunities for women to study science and engineering. While Japan awarded twice as many bachelor's degrees in science and engineering than did Korea in 1990, more Korean women (8,550) earned those degrees than did Japanese women (7,582). If Korea continues to offer expanded opportunities for women, it can overcome some of the handicaps of having only one-third of Japan's population. Neither country comes close to the United States, however, in offering opportunities to women to study science and engineering.

Technology Executives in Senior Management Positions

While we have no data on the percentage of senior corporate executives who have R&D or technology responsibilities in Korea, it seems that chaebols function more like holding companies or conglomerates and financial responsibilities are paramount at the top levels. Japan is unusual in its concentration of engineers and others with technical management experience in senior management, at least in comparison with U.S. firms.[8] MITI has produced an empirical analysis showing that the fraction of technical executives at the top level correlates well with the business performance of the firm.[9] Measuring performance by profitability and sales growth, MITI found that firms where 45 percent of the people in the top level of management were technical had a performance of 5.32 on their scale, while firms with less than 25 percent enjoyed a performance of only 4.7. More surprising, among all the firms surveyed, 35.9 percent of Japanese chief executive officers in 1990 were promoted from technology executive positions.

Lessons in Policy Research and Analysis

An important lesson that Korea might learn from Japan is the importance of a strong analytical base for S&T policy analysis and design. In 1986, the STA organized the National Institute for Science and Technology Policy, serving as an analytical arm for the Prime Minister's Science and Technology Council. In Japan technological data are collected in a methodical way through "foresight" projections of S&T trends. International trends are documented, competitive intelligence is collected from around the world, and policy alternatives are examined. These impressive activities engage large numbers of scientists and engineers inside and outside government. During this process bureaucratic views are informed by a much larger community of experts, and the groundwork is laid for consensus on scientific and technological opportunities and priorities. This consensus eventually emerges in public policy.

In Korea, MOST and the Science and Technology Policy Institute serve a similar role but with fewer resources and weaker linkages to decision making at the highest levels of government. As an essential part of the innovation-based strategy for Korean development, this capability to forecast and reach consensus must be strengthened, both in capability and in policy influence.

In conclusion, we note that Korea has followed a developmental path strongly modeled after Japan's, despite substantial differences in the conditions the two countries faced after 1960. Japan's growth has slowed, as one might expect for an industrial superpower that has focused its energies on raising the quality of life of the people, improving its infrastructure, and meeting the demands of global responsibilities. Japan's industry, which is highly competitive in most markets, is finding it necessary to invest abroad to retain full access to world markets. Japan must now strengthen its basic research to generate more innovations internally. It must establish the kinds of international cooperative relationships in S&T that are common among European and North American countries.

To compensate for high wages and an expensive infrastructure, Japan is now moving production to low-wage, rapidly industrializing countries, leveraging its strengths in capital, technology, and management. Japan has excelled with production efficiencies, product quality, and rapid incremental improvements. Now it must master the complex systems approach to combining hardware, software, and service offerings for the current demands of leading markets.

Korea, still on a rapid "catch-up" path, must establish the infrastructure required to support a highly industrialized economy. Korea is experiencing many of the trade policy pressures that Japan encountered a decade ago. These pressures call for the intensified development of indigenous technological capability to gain sweeping advantages in the marketplace.

With the exception of KAIST, Korea (unlike Japan) has not generated a system of higher education in technology and engineering to reduce dependence on foreign universities. MOST should be given a stronger hand in postgraduate S&T education. The rapid growth of Korea's small- and medium-size industry was sacrificed for the sake of the capital needs of the chaebols in the 1970s and 1980s. This policy created serious deficiencies in the nation's technological enterprise. In this respect, Taiwan has important advantages over Korea, as discussed in Chapter 10. In responding to the globalization of markets, Korean firms will need to establish relationships abroad in end-product markets to become brand-named producers of quality products and to tap all the technology resources available to them around the world. However, these relationships will not form unless Korea boosts its capacity to innovate domestically and accelerates its generation of indigenous technology.

NOTES

1. Alice Amsden, *Asia's Next Giant—South Korea and Late Industrialization* (New York: Oxford University Press, 1989), 52.

2. Denis Fred Simon and Changrok Soh, "Korea's Technological Development," *Pacific Review* 7, no. 1 (1994): 93.

3. Science and Technology Agency, Government of Japan, *White Paper on Science and Technology, 1992* (Tokyo: Japan Information Center of Science and Technology, 1992), 160.

4. Hiroshi Inose, "A Farewell to Arms" *Look Japan* (March 1993): 28; Ryoichi Nakagawa, "Planes—Trained for Automobiles," *Look Japan* (April 1993): 34; Shigeru Nakajima, "It's Electronic," *Look Japan* (May 1993): 32; Takeo Tsurugaya, "Eyes to the Bottom of the Ocean," *Look Japan* (June 1993): 32; Masao Kinoshita, "Pushing the Boat Out," *Look Japan* (July 1993): 34; Kihachiro Matsuyama, "The Dawn of Japanese TV," *Look Japan* (August 1993): 34; Tadashi Matsudaira, "From Fighter Planes to Bullet Trains," *Look Japan* (September 1993): 34; Hirotoshi Torikata, "Bombs Away," *Look Japan* (October 1993): 32; Mankichi Tateo, "From Canons to Rotor Shafts," *Look Japan* (November 1993): 30; Tatsuo Hasegawa, "In the Driving Seat," *Look Japan* (January 1994): 32; Kazuo Horikawa, "Steel for Action," *Look Japan* (February 1994): 34.

5. Organization for Economic Cooperation and Development (OECD), *OECD Economic Surveys: Korea 1994* (Paris: OECD, 1995), 196.

6. Jean M. Johnson, *Human Resources for Science and Technology: The Asian Region*, NSF 93-303 (Washington, D.C.: National Science Foundation, 1993), Figure 2, p. 7, and Table A-2, p. 62.

7. It is striking that in July 1995 every member of President Kim Young-Sam's Advisory Council on Science and Technology—except one official, whose advanced degree was from Kyoto University in Japan—had earned his Ph.D. degree from a U.S. university.

8. Edward Roberts, of PA Associates and the MIT Liaison Program, found that in Japanese firms, 90 percent of the technical executives held positions on the board of directors; in the United States, the comparable figure was 20 percent. The growing number of outside directors and the diminishing number of employee executives in U.S. firms explains only a part of this dramatic difference.

9. Ministry of International Trade and Industry, Government of Japan, *Comprehensive Management Performance Indices—Manufacturing, 1983* (Tokyo: MITI, 1984).

Chapter Ten

TAIWAN
Innovation in Small and Medium Enterprises

Lewis M. Branscomb

KOREA AND TAIWAN: SIMILAR CIRCUMSTANCES

Since the early 1960s, the Republic of Korea and Taiwan have demonstrated extraordinary records of economic growth. From 1970 to 1990, their real growth rates averaged in double digits. In many respects, this exceptional economic performance in both countries had its roots in similar histories, similar size, and with cultures strongly based on Confucian traditions.[1] Both countries were occupied by Japan, and both were liberated from Japanese control during World War II.[2] Koreans and Taiwanese faced severely depressed living conditions in the aftermath of the war (1962 income per capita was U.S.$87 in Korea and U.S.$162 in Taiwan).[3] In both countries, the governments and their people gave highest priority to two issues: the security of the state and rapid economic development, with development acting as the prerequisite to security.

As a result of threats to the security of Taiwan and Korea, military concerns often dominated both regimes for twenty to thirty years after liberation. After Park Chung-Hee's military regime toppled a democratic government paralyzed by student unrest, the military took control of the Korean government.

In Taiwan, military concerns greatly influenced the nationalist regime's development strategy. Even today, with democratic structures in both countries, strong centrist elements exist in national politics and policy.

Both nations have pursued economic strategies in which scientific and technological developments have played a major role. Also, both began their reforms with import-substitution strategies. Korea was persuaded by its planners to adopt an outward-looking strategy, while Taiwan followed its U.S. advisors and the international financing community, adopting a package of economic policies that rationalized prices while liberalizing trade and foreign investments in the 1960s.

Many leaders of the Kuomintang (KMT) turned away from the defeated Japanese and chose to follow the U.S. model of development. At the same time, native Taiwanese tended to have favorable views of Japan (and many citizens spoke Japanese). Once the Japanese industrial resurgence became evident, both Korea and Taiwan quickly recognized Japan as a dramatic model for rapid, export-oriented development. Today, both Taiwan and Korea compete and collaborate with Japan; both seek to exploit the large market in the United States.

HUMAN RESOURCE DEVELOPMENT
IN KOREA AND TAIWAN

In both Taiwan and Korea, education is highly valued, students work very hard to earn a place in higher education, and education is available to all (like in Japan) through rigorous academic competition. Families in both Taiwan and Korea send very large numbers of their best science students abroad—especially to the United States. Many have returned home to participate in the accelerated development of their nation's industry. Chi-Ming Hou and San Gee, when analyzing the sources of technological advances in Taiwan, stressed how education and training improved the capability of the workforce.[4] They report that even as late as 1952, 42.1 percent of the population age six and older was illiterate. By 1988 this percentage had dropped to 8.8 percent, by which time more than 10 percent of the population had received higher education. While capital investment contributed to labor productivity's growth from 1953 to 1980, the capital/labor investment ratio increased at only 2.8 percent per year. Nevertheless, labor productivity grew at an average rate of 6.77 percent a year from 1953 to 1981.

Education policy did not neglect the teaching of technical skills in Taiwan. Vocational schools specializing in technical skills were created at a higher rate than general secondary schools, and they enroll twice as many students. Taiwan and Korea's higher-education sectors both experienced a serious "brain drain" in the 1970s, and both countries have adopted policies to provide incentives for students educated abroad to return. Korea has been more successful with this policy than Taiwan. However, Taiwan could take advantage of many business relationships with overseas Chinese-owned businesses, particularly in the United States. By the mid-1980s, the robust private sectors in both nations offered good opportunities for highly skilled expatriates, reducing the severity of the brain drain substantially.

Such factors helped these two countries enter the 1990s with real income per capita approaching many industrialized states with well-established market economies. Both nations are motivated by expectations for continued growth at rates still dramatically higher than those enjoyed by Japan, the United States, or Europe (see Table 10.1).

MAJOR DIFFERENCES: ECONOMIC POLICY, POLITICS, AND INSTITUTIONAL DEVELOPMENT

Economic growth rates in both Korea and Taiwan are beginning to plateau. Each faces somewhat different problems in making the transition that Japan successfully made in the 1980s. It is instructive to explore how differences in circumstance or policy between the two countries might explain this widening gap. The most striking difference in their technology development strategies can be found in how the industrial structure has evolved and in how government influences private decisions.

The Korean government has played a strong hand in its extraordinarily rapid economic growth, relying on the huge chaebol conglomerates to capitalize on imported technology. The smaller firms in the private sector are largely devoted to satisfying the domestic market with conventional products. Taiwan's KMT government, on the other hand, controlled large segments of the economy through wholly state-owned corporations. In addition, they used parastatals, organizations controlled jointly by state agencies such as the armed forces pension fund and the KMT (itself one of the largest shareholders on the island). However, this state domination did not preclude the development of a dynamic group of small- to medium-size enterprises (SMEs). The government's tolerant administration of its myriad regulations, together with conservative economic and fiscal policies, were instrumental in the success of SMEs in the 1960s and 1970s.

Scholars seeking an explanation for the growth of SMEs in Taiwan often point to Confucianism, "which posits patriarchy both as a macro-concept, viewing the state as an extended family headed by a patriarch/emperor, and as a micro-concept at the cellular level of the family."[5] Creating a family firm is a way to extend the family; but when the firm grows too large, creating a new firm offers an alternative to service in a large, impersonal, and autocratic enterprise. A second explanation is that the rigid political and bureaucratic control of state functions and enterprises by KMT authorities and their mainlander constituents provided incentive for Taiwanese entrepreneurs to seek

Table 10.1
Comparisons of Republic of Korea with Taiwan

Characteristic	Korea 1987	Korea 1990	Taiwan 1987	Taiwan 1990
Total population	41,591	42,797	19,598	20,313
GNP (constant 1987 U.S. dollars PPP billions)	210	271	121	146
Per capita GDP	$5,050	$6,330	$6,170	$7,190
GNP growth rate percentage	12.8	8.6	11.9	5.3
Gross savings, percentage of GDP	36.2	36.0	38.5	29.2
Gross Investment, percentage of GDP	37.1	36.2	20.1	21.9
Current account U.S. dollars millions (current prices)	3,854	-8,728		
S&E as percentage of labor force	30.1	37.2	28.7	38.1
Doctoral degrees earned in U.S. universities		673		906
National R&D in constant 1987 dollars PPP millions			1,381	2,476
National R&D / GDP	1.95 %	2.12 % (1989)	1.12 %	1.38 % (1989)
Industry share of R&D funding	79.6 %	84.1 % (1989)	73.5 %	77.9 % (1989)
Share of R&D performed in government institutes	3.7 %	3.7 % (1989)	10.2 %	17.0 % (1989)

Data from William Reinfeld, "Infrastructure and Its Relation to Economic Development: The Cases of Korea and Taiwan," in *East Asian Infrastructure Strategies,* ed. Ashoka Mody and Hirofumi Uzawa, (Washington, D.C.: World Bank, 1995), Table 1; and from Council for Economic Planning and Development, Republic of China, *Taiwan Statistical Data Book,* Vol. 80 (Taipei: Republic of China, 1991), 51–107.
PPP, purchase price parity. This is a system applied by economists at OECD to alter exchange rates so the same amount of money in every currency has the same purchasing power in the domestic economy.

their own patriarchal authority in the independent business sector. These effects are present in Korea as well, but apparently with much less impact. The most striking differences between the Korean and Taiwanese approaches to technological development lie in three spheres: political, institutional, and economic.[6]

Contrasting Political Histories

The KMT consolidated its political power in Taiwan quite early after World War II. Consistent with the ideology of Sun Yat Sen, the ruling Chinese from the mainland created a popular political system, centrally controlled but reaching down to the village level and to every business and civic organization. The older Taiwanese elites, who often enjoyed good relations with the Japanese, were excluded from power in the KMT government. Moreover, the rebellion against KMT rule in 1948 was brutally crushed, resulting in large numbers of Taiwanese casualties. However, the KMT's land-reform program was quite successful, helping to establish the KMT as a legitimate government in the eyes of the people. Land reform provided the population with a stake in preserving the political status quo. As a result, with the exception of disturbances in 1948 and 1967, the KMT never faced the level of popular political opposition found in Korea, which drove a series of military governments to force-feed rapid economic development through intrusive economic strategies.[7] In the early postwar years, the KMT strategy kept Taiwanese entrepreneurs at bay, while focusing public investment on state institutions. However, this strategy set the stage for more dynamic Taiwanese growth, with less government micromanagement in recent years compared to Korea.

Contrasting Institutional Patterns

In terms of government structure, Taiwan, unlike Korea, does not have a Ministry of Science and Technology. The National Science Council serves this role. A unique institution in the Taiwan structure is the Science and Technology Advisory Group, which advises the Executive Yuan independently of the Science Council. For years, many distinguished, industrially experienced scientists and engineers from the United States and elsewhere have given Taiwan much practical advice on applying technology strategies to develop industry. For example, the board of the Industrial Technology Research Institute (ITRI), designed by the government to support the information industry, appointed a committee of three very distinguished industrial scientists—Pierre Aigrain from France and Ian Ross and Bob O. Evans from the United States—to make recommendations on how ITRI could be made more effective.[8] These three advisors were among the Science and Technology Advisory Group and had long experience with helping the Taiwan government formulate technology policy. Each chaired a team of technical experts to review the ITRI divisions.

At the institutional level, Korea relied on the chaebols for the acquisition of technology, while debt financing came from foreign sources. Foreign direct investment (FDI) was held to minimal levels as domestic markets were protected from foreign competition. Taiwan, by contrast, pursued a conservative economic strategy. Holding interest rates high even through the first oil shock, they almost always generated a budgetary surplus. These high interest rates drove domestic savings, which financed expansion with less dependence on foreign capital than in Korea. In the 1960s and 1970s, the government of Taiwan tightly controlled a large government-owned and parastatal industrial sector while working well with large, privately owned firms like Formosa Plastics and Tatung. At the same time, the government paid little attention to small- to medium-size firms even as they were growing in importance.

Taiwan depended far more heavily than did Korea on FDI, even as it retained monopolistic control in the public industrial sector. Inflation was tightly controlled, enabling foreign investors to better estimate their risks.

Thus, conditions were right in Taiwan for a vigorous private sector composed of small- to medium-size firms oriented to export markets. They were not only less tightly controlled than were firms in Korea; they were less constrained by the government regulations than their Korean counterparts. Related factors greatly contributed to how SMEs developed in Taiwan. These factors included the tolerance of informal and illegal channels of credit, trade, and exchange, as well as a persistent, stable macroeconomic environment with stable prices and currency.

Contrasting Economic Policies

The Korean government has consistently taken a much more expansionist view of economic management than Taiwan. It has opted for detailed control over the strategy for industrial development. The Korean government held to low interest rates, even in periods of rapid inflation, as the necessary price for rapid accumulation of capital for economic expansion. Thus, the public sector was frequently in deficit. The Korean regime never enjoyed the level of political control that the KMT was able to establish, both nationally and locally. As a result, the Korean government repeatedly sought the collaboration of industrial leaders to ensure sufficient growth to maintain popular control. Business leaders, including those of the great chaebols, enjoyed a collaborative relationship with the Blue House, at least after the arrival of the Yushin constitution and the subsequent election of Park Chung-Hee in 1973 (see Chapter 2). Political relations between business and government were not always as close or as relatively tranquil as in Japan. Nevertheless, the Korean government stayed very close to business leadership and exercised a great deal of sector-specific control over industrial development strategy.

The KMT government and the banks under its influence were very reluctant to assume investment risks for private firms, let alone in targeted sectors. This very conservative banking system was successful in largely eliminating bank failures, creating a safe storehouse of value that permitted savings to accumulate. The failure of Taiwan banks to act as an efficient vehicle for recycling savings into productive investment resulted in the creation of a large, informal (and illegal) financial market known as the "curb" market. This informal market filled the gaps for private small- to medium-size firms. Thus, a major difference between the Korean pattern and that of Taiwan lies in the source of entrepreneurial risk capital, which Taiwan used to promote the health and growth of the SMEs.

The economic strategy difference between the two countries can also be seen in the debt/equity ratios typical of industrial firms. In Korea throughout the 1970s, this ratio was in the range of 350 to 450 percent. Heavy dependence on short-term debt first made Koreans extremely sensitive to interest rates, forcing the government to keep rates low. In Taiwan, on the other hand, most banks imposed strict ceilings on debt/equity ratios. In the 1970s, corporate-sector debt/equity ratios in Taiwan stood between 160 and 180 percent.[9] In the United States, with a strong stock market providing equity capital, a ratio of 30 to 50 percent is more typical.

Both Korea and Taiwan launched major capital industry development schemes just before the 1973 OPEC (Organization of Petroleum Exporting Countries) oil embargo. They reacted quite differently to this crisis. In Taiwan, the Central Bank of China raised the discount rate three times—from 8.5 percent to 14 percent—and the supply of real domestic credit was reduced by 14 percent. Domestic oil prices shot up by 88.4 percent, and electricity rose by 78.7 percent.[10] The big industrial expansion in heavy industry was extended. By 1975, Taiwan had kept inflation under control.

In Korea, the government pressed on in spite of the inflationary pressures. Interest rates remained unchanged in 1974–1975, and the money supply continued to grow at 30 percent per annum. The Korean won was devalued. With foreign financing, the chaebols continued to press ahead. After the second oil shock, exports fell and unemployment rose. The military took control of the government again, and in 1980 Korea had a -5.7 percent growth rate, with inflation still running at 28.7 percent.

Korea paid a high price in political and social terms for its unrelenting growth policies in the 1970s, but the policies paid off in Korea's penetration of world markets. This also brought very heavy concentration in Korea's industrial economy.[11] In 1987, the ten largest firms in Korea produced 63.5 percent of gross domestic product (GDP); in Taiwan the ten largest produced only 14.3 percent of GDP.[12] Thus, "under the mighty chaebol lies a substratum of very weak small and medium-sized companies that are starved for capital and are technologically backward."[13]

ENCOURAGING SMALL- AND MEDIUM-SIZE ENTERPRISES IN TAIWAN

The pattern of export growth in Taiwan was centered in the SMEs. In 1983, SMEs (300 employees or less) in Taiwan contributed 65 percent of Taiwan's exports and 70 percent of total employment.[14] By 1985, more than 100,000 firms, each with paid-in capital of less than U.S.$1 million, contributed 28.9 percent of total domestic sales and 71.1 percent of exports.[15] In 1993, the 900,000 small- and medium-size businesses accounted for 97 percent of Taiwan's firms. They still provided 70 percent of the island's jobs but then produced 50 percent of manufacturing output and 55 percent of export income.[16] This more diversified and decentralized economy has also provided political benefits in Taiwan, since a new class of entrepreneurs has arisen with a stake in the system. However, in fields like electronics, where labor-intensive segments are gradually declining in favor of capital-intensive segments and where industry depends on access to many growing-scale economies, small firms face serious challenges to retaining their technological competitiveness.

Taiwan initiated its industrial technology upgrading effort in 1959 with a "Plan of National Long-Term Development of Science." A council was formed to support indigenous basic research, which, in 1967, became the National Science Council. Two key government institutions were created to support SMEs in the information industry, where much of Taiwan's investment was concentrated. The first, and best known, is ITRI, established in 1973, and the Institute for the Information Industry (III), formed in 1979. ITRI is an R&D institution covering a range of industrial technologies. Its Electronics Research and Service Organization (ERSO) supports the hardware side of the information industry. As ITRI has come under budget pressure, it has started expecting the firms it assists to raise the percentage of their cost sharing from 30 percent to 50 percent. The III complements ERSO by focusing on software and applications development, market information, and training in support of both public and private enterprises. Both ITRI and III have responsibility for diffusion of technology to the firms that need it, as well as for developing new technology. Technology developed in ERSO can be licensed, or new firms can be created ("spun off") to exploit it. These spin-off firms are financed with a majority of private capital. Six microelectronic chip companies were founded by this mechanism in the 1980s.

Although ITRI has been criticized for management problems, it would appear that ITRI and III are more effective than their Korean counterparts in providing useful assistance to SMEs and in initiating new high-technology firms. However, the Taiwanese also recognize that in an industry like microelectronics, economies of scale are very significant for competition. In 1989, ITRI initiated a consortium of chip makers to form a "technology-development alliance" that would develop sixteen-megabit dynamic random access memory chips. Using this mechanism, ITRI hopes to gain the benefits of scale in new technology acquisition while retaining the agility and competitive entrepreneurship of small- to medium-size firms.

Taiwan is also concerned that SMEs may neither perform enough R&D on their own nor take advantage of ITRI and other government activities in support of innovation. The government has tried to provide strong incentives for firms to invest in internal R&D, while strictly enforcing the conditions that must be met to receive the incentives. A third concern is that government R&D programs are scattered, inconsistent, and poorly coordinated. Furthermore, they are part of a national technology strategy that fails to look to commercial and defense development needs in a coherent fashion.[17]

Taiwan has been consistently more receptive toward FDI than Korea; but in the 1970s, FDI was viewed cautiously and was regulated. In 1980, this attitude began to change. The Taiwan government initiated a high-technology industrial park development (*Hsinchu*), then reached out to overseas Chinese entrepreneurs who had been successful in California's Silicon Valley and elsewhere. By December 1988, there were ninety-six firms in this park doing NT$48.3 billion in sales. The government in 1988 altered the regulatory process for approval of FDI by shifting to the "negative list" approach; that is, all FDI was allowed except in those activities precluded in the government's list.

Chinese businesspersons living overseas have also been a very important source of capital for FDI. As noted in Chapter 3, overseas Chinese from such places as Hong Kong, Indonesia, the Philippines, Singapore, Taiwan, and western countries have been a major source of capital inflow, all directed to China. This has made China the second-largest recipient of FDIs in the world after the United States.

Taiwan's Response to Globalization

Taiwan is responding to globalization by seeking mergers and alliances with firms in overseas markets.[18] The need for technology, concern over the limited scale and scope of SMEs, and the need for market access all suggest mergers and alliances as a supplement to exports. Strong foreign-exchange reserves and the appreciation of the Taiwan currency make this possible. Taiwan's FDI enterprises are effective at generating and acquiring technology. For example, when compared to spending patterns of domestic firms, the FDI firms invest more in R&D per employee and spend more on R&D in relation to sales.[19]

Since the opening up of markets in the People's Republic of China, Taiwanese firms are turning in increasing numbers to the mainland for investment, driven by a labor shortage and yuan (NT$) appreciation. The ethnic and cultural ties between Taiwan and China offer a unique opportunity for Taiwan, which the small- and medium-size firms are exploiting.[20]

For both Korea and Taiwan, the policies that led to their achievements no longer assure their success. Both countries are reevaluating their strategies. Korea can best learn from Taiwan about two assets: the value of a diversified, independent, and entrepreneurial SME business sector, and how a set of policies can support the technological infrastructure that SME firms require for success. This support comes, in part, from government institutions such as

ITRI, which is largely funded by the Ministry of Economic Affairs. Technical support is accompanied by incentives to SMEs to engage in technology development internally.

Today, these firms are actively seeking alliances with foreign firms, either through FDI or by mergers and alliances in foreign markets. This should ensure a continued flow of innovation into the Taiwanese economy. Both Taiwan and Korea must examine the strength of the domestic technical infrastructure and the human resources needed to keep local firms strong and competitive.

NOTES

The author is extremely grateful to Dr. Danny Lam, Fellow at the Center for Science and International Affairs, John F. Kennedy School of Government, Harvard University, for valuable insights and much research material for this chapter.

1. A significant difference, however, is that Korea is ethnically rather homogeneous, although in religious terms the population is divided between Confucians, Christians, and Buddhists. Taiwan is dominated by officials and others who fled the communist revolution on the mainland, and speak predominantly Mandarin. They live together with the Taiwanese, ethnic Chinese from the South who came to Taiwan between the sixteenth and twentieth centuries. They speak a southern dialect now known as Taiwanese. Strong social distinctions exist between the Taiwanese and the mainlanders—resentment by the former and condescension by the latter. See Emily Martin Ahern and Hill Gates, eds., *The Anthropology of Taiwanese Society* (Taipei: Caves Books, 1981), 266–281.

2. Japan's rapid recovery after the end of the U.S. occupation was assisted by large numbers of experienced engineers from pre-war defense companies who became leaders in the automobile industry and other commercial firms. Taiwan's human resources were augmented by about two million mainland Chinese, among whom were many experienced professionals and managers. Korea enjoyed neither of these benefits as it went about staffing the new enterprises.

3. For Korea: William Reinfeld, "Infrastructure and Its Relation to Economic Development: The Cases of Korea and Taiwan," in *East Asian Infrastructure Strategies*, ed. Ashoka Mody and Hirofumi Uzawa (Washington, D.C.: World Bank, 1995), Table 1; for Taiwan: Council for Economic Planning and Development, Republic of China, *Taiwan Statistical Data Book* (Taipei: Republic of China, 1991), 29.

4. Chi-Ming Hou and San Gee, "National Systems Supporting Technical Advances in Industry: The Case of Taiwan," in *National Systems of Innovation: A Comparative Analysis*, ed. Richard R. Nelson (New York: Oxford University Press, 1993), 393.

5. Danny Lam and Cal Clark, "Beyond the Developmental State: The Cultural Roots of 'Guerrilla Capitalism' in Taiwan," *Governance: An International Journal of Policy and Administration* 7, no. 4 (July 1994): 412–430.

6. Much of the following discussion is drawn from Yuan-Han Chu, "Comparative Political Economy of Economic Adjustment: The Case of South Korea and Taiwan," Chapter 4 in *Authoritarian Regimes under Stress: The Political Economy of Adjustment in the East Asian Newly Industrialized Countries*, Ph.D. diss., University of

Minnesota, 1987 (Minneapolis: University Microfilms International No. 8727407, 1990), 57–124.

7. Thomas B. Gold, *State and Society in the Taiwan Miracle* (New York: M. E. Sharpe, 1986), 64, 100.

8. Aigrain is a former Minister of Science and Technology in France and a senior executive in the huge Thomson electronics conglomerate. Ross is the former head of the renowned Bell Telephone Laboratories. Evans is a former vice president of International Business Machines (IBM) in charge of the corporate engineering staff, and former president of the Systems Development Division and the Federal Systems Division.

9. Chu, "Comparative Political Economy," 76–77.

10. Ibid., 84.

11. In 1973, the top forty-six chaebols' value added contributed 9.8 percent of Korea's value added. By 1982, it only took thirty chaebols to produce 32 percent of Korean value added. Even more striking, by 1983, the five largest chaebols produced 40 percent of the entire Korean gross national product. Ibid., 106–107.

12. Lam and Clark, "Beyond the Developmental State," Table 1, p. 414, quoting data from Gol-Hong Sung, "Paths of Glory: Semiconductor Leapfrogging in Taiwan and South Korea," *Pacific Focus* 7 (spring 1992): 63.

13. Lam and Clark, "Beyond the Developmental State," 108.

14. Ibid., 110.

15. Hou and Gee, "National Systems Supporting Technical Advances," 388.

16. Republic of China President Lee Teng-Hui, quoted in *The Free China Journal*, August 5, 1994, p. 3.

17. Danny Lam, private communication, August 1994.

18. Hou and Gee, "National Systems Supporting Technical Advances," 403–405.

19. Ibid., 408. Dr. Yeo Lin (private communication) believes that, while this may have been true in the early 1980s, it is no longer true.

20. The Economic Affairs Ministry's Statistics Department reports that 60 percent of the Taiwan firms with mainland projects are SMEs. Deborah Shen, *The Free China Journal*, August 5, 1994, p. 3.

Chapter Eleven

CONTRASTING MODELS
Brazil and Small European Countries

Lewis M. Branscomb and Henry Ergas

As Korea looks outside of Asia to examine models for its innovation policy, it can turn in two directions. First, Korea can examine a rapidly industrializing nation with a tradition of strong industrial policies. Brazil, which is such a country, shares with Korea a determination to join the ranks of the wealthy. Like Korea, it must find ways to add value to its natural resources and to technologies it can acquire from abroad, through foreign direct investment (FDI) or purchase. On the other hand, Brazil is a much larger nation, has a larger economy, and is more plentifully endowed with natural resources than Korea. Would not Korea do better to choose for its model a nation whose size and population are smaller than Korea, no longer natural resource rich, yet with a very high standard of living and a mature and sophisticated industrial base? Such nations are to be found in Europe, and both Sweden and Switzerland provide interesting examples. A study by the Korea Institute for Industrial Economics and Trade (KIET) in mid-1994, which compared the competitiveness of industrial economies, ranked Korea fifteenth out of eighteen nations studied.[1] Sweden and Switzerland ranked among the top four, along with Hong Kong and Singapore. In this chapter, we examine the value of the Brazilian and European models for charting Korea's future.

INDUSTRIAL POLICY IN BRAZIL

Brazil boasts the largest and most sophisticated system of research and development (R&D) institutions in Latin America, although it only invested 0.72 percent of its gross domestic product (GDP) in national R&D in 1990. Furthermore, as Carl J. Dahlman and Claudio R. Frischtak have noted in their studies of Brazilian innovation, during the 1960s and 1970s, Brazil's economy grew very rapidly. Richly endowed with natural resources, having the sixth-largest population and the fifth-largest land area in the world, Brazil amassed an economy that even today is the ninth or tenth largest in the world.

On inspection, the Brazilian economy does not look at all like that of Korea or Taiwan. Table 11.1 shows the weakness of manufactured exports in the Brazilian economy while pointing out Korea's excessive reliance on exports. The current weakness in GDP per capita and low growth has occurred despite the fact that Brazil enjoys some advantages in its recent history, at least when compared with Korea and Taiwan. Brazil was spared serious security threats during this period and participated in World War II on the side of the Allied nations. It emerged peacefully from its colonial period beginning in 1822, and its industrial development traces back to the late nineteenth century.

Brazil's relatively poor economic performance in the past twenty years has important roots in political instability, as well as the tensions between the industrialized south, centered on Sao Paulo, and the underdeveloped and largely impoverished Amazon basin. But public policy has been an important contributor to their situation. The most dramatic contrast between Brazil and both Korea and Taiwan lies in the dominance of the Brazilian government in its nation's scientific and technological enterprise. Up to 90 percent of its national R&D is funded by the government and conducted in government institutions, compared to only 15 percent in Korea. These Brazilian institutions tend to be more self-contained and less service oriented than their counterparts in

Table 11.1
Manufactured Exports from Brazil, Korea, and Japan

Country	GDP per capita 1988 (U.S. dollars)	GDP growth, 1980-1988 (percentage)	Manufacturing output, 1980-88 (percentage)	Manufacturing exports, 1980-1988 (percentage)	Manufacturing export as share of output, 1987 (percentage)
Brazil	$ 2,241	2.9	2.2	6.2	11.8
Korea	$ 4,079	9.9	13.5	14.7	103.1
Japan	$23,195	3.9	6.7	5.3	32.4

Source: Carl J. Dahlman and Claudio R. Frischtak, "National Systems Supporting Technical Advance in Industry: The Brazilian Experience," in *National Innovation Systems: A Comparative Analysis,* ed. Richard R. Nelson, (New York: Oxford University Press, 1993), Table 13.1, p. 415.

Taiwan (such as the Industrial Technology Research Institute [ITRI]) and less focused on attempting to assist the small- and medium-size enterprises (SMEs). In general, Brazilian science and technology (S&T) policy is more mission oriented and less diffusion oriented than in Taiwan.[2] Furthermore, Brazil has not made the kinds of educational investments at the vocational level that Taiwan has made, nor has it approached Korea's level of university and overseas training.

While Brazil's policy in the recent past has included severe constraints on FDI and import protection for local industry—not so different from Korea's policy—Brazil did not match that protection with economic policies and services that encourage rapid growth of domestic firms.

Brazil was not always inhospitable to FDI. Brazil developed so extensively through open FDI in the period immediately after the war that by 1960, half of the capital goods were produced by subsidiaries of foreign firms. This strategy, combined with the failure of domestic firms to develop competitive capabilities, led to a strong overreaction in the twenty-one years of military rule after 1964, when a strongly protectionist policy was bolstered by militaristic nationalism.

Brazil's reaction to the oil shock in 1973 is, like the cases of Korea and Taiwan, illustrative of its policies. Brazil failed to respond with economic reforms; its debt spiraled out of control, leading to a radical reduction in investment and an outflow of capital. Unlike Korea, which invested aggressively in imported machinery and technology, Brazil restricted imports to encourage import substitution. This strategy imposed a further burden on the domestic industry's technological capability. Long after both Korea and Taiwan had shifted their economic growth strategies from import substitution to export promotion, Brazil was still seeking autarchy, largely for political reasons.

In short, the Brazilian government's interference in its industrial economy was perhaps no greater than the Korean government's. However, it was often counterproductive, leading to structural rigidities that exacted a high price in competitive performance. Korea, Taiwan, and, even more impressively, Japan have steadily and carefully increased the exposure of their domestic firms to foreign competition while monitoring the effects. This liberalization has come very late in Brazil.

The Brazilian economy still relies heavily on access to domestic raw materials and a low wage base. Its industrial technology has poor underpinnings in R&D. Dahlman and Frischtak report that in 1982 state enterprises accounted for 62.6 percent of industrial R&D, with eight producers responsible for more than half of it. The same concentration of technical capability within the government sector is reflected in the distribution (in 1986) of R&D workers, shown in Table 11.2.

Many Brazilians are fully aware of this concentration of technical capability in institutions other than the productive sector. In fact, the paucity of R&D

Table 11.2
Distribution of Researchers According to Place of Activity

Brazilian Institution	Number	Percentage
Universities	36,112	68.3
S&T Institutions	10,856	11.8
Government Agencies	3,203	0.7
State Enterprises	1,811	0.3
Private Institutions	727	0.5
Private Firms	295	0.1
Other	111	---

Source: Carl J. Dahlman and Claudio R. Frischtak, "National Systems Supporting Technical Advance in Industry: The Brazilian Experience," in *National Innovation Systems: A Comparative Analysis,* ed. Richard R. Nelson, (New York: Oxford University Press, 1993), Table 13.7, p. 426.

workers in private firms is similar to conditions in Mexico. Brazilians observe that their technology policy in recent years has vacillated between the extremes of laissez-faire and state centrism. They see too much investment in projects of high prestige but low commercialization potential, actions imbedded in economic policies that never developed the technical infrastructure required for a modern industrial state.

A recent study for the Ministry of Science and Technology documents these issues and puts forth recommendations for policy changes.[3] Almost all the recommendations stress the need to build technical capability in the private sector while linking the intellectual resources in the universities and other S&T institutions more effectively to industry. Many of these recommendations are similar to those being stressed in the United States and are worthy of consideration by Korea as well. They are very seriously needed in Brazil. As Schwartzman and his colleagues observe, after 1980 "the science and technology sector entered a period of great instability and uncertainty, characterized by institutional turmoil, bureaucratization, and budgetary uncertainty." Thus, it is not sufficient for a nation to follow well-designed policies; it must enjoy the trust and exhibit the efficiency to implement them effectively.

SMALLER EUROPEAN ECONOMIES

Compared to the United States, Japan, and Germany, Korea is a small country, which it perceives as a disadvantage. How do the smaller European nations such as Switzerland, Sweden, the Netherlands, and Belgium (each smaller than Korea) compete in world markets for high-technology manufactured goods? None of the gross expeditures on R&D (GERD) of these European countries exceeds 1.3 percent of the OECD's (Organization for Economic Cooperation and Development) GERD. Yet their wage rates are among the highest in the world. Taking hourly labor rates in electrical and electronic manufacturing (wages and nonwage compensation) in different countries as an example, Switzerland is highest at $25, with Germany, Sweden, and Belgium close behind. The United States is at $15, along with France, Japan, and the United Kingdom, with Spain close behind. Mexico trails at $2 per hour. How do the smaller countries compete with Germany, France, and the United Kingdom? How might Korea emulate their success?

The weaknesses and strengths in Korea's social capital lie at the heart of the answer, defining the ability to create and reproduce human and physical capital.[4] The concept covers not only institutional arrangements but also tacit norms of obligation, conduct, and reciprocity, which guide the myriad transactions. Thus, social capital is reflected in low transaction costs and thus in efficient utilization of both physical and human capital.

The concept of social capital includes the broad range of factors that affect transaction costs in a society. When James Coleman studied Sicily to find why this small region remained so poor, he found a low-trust environment, which leads to high economic costs. The behavior patterns associated with low trust, once established, become self-reinforcing. The outcomes will legitimate the behavior itself.

Economists take the view that where there is a coordination problem, decentralized processes are relatively ineffective. People do not band together to create a public good. Rather, they are tempted to a free ride or "cheap ride." Thus, there is a need for some kind of coercive process to supply the public goods—government regulations or subsidies. In *Experimental Economics*, Douglas D. Davis and Charles A. Holt found an overwhelming tendency not to free ride when the subjects knew each other.[5] Social norms of reciprocity came into play. Thus, with sufficient social cohesion and trust, people do not limit themselves to short-term, self-oriented behavior in life.

The salient feature of the smaller European countries is the pervasiveness of formal structures with clearly identified functions for dealing with S&T systems. Often they are exclusively based on delegation of quasi-official functions, with some content of representation of national interest. Examples include setting standards, allocating resources to the S&T system, and organizing human capital.

One striking feature of these countries is strong industry associations, with compulsory membership, for organizing industrial technology. The Netherlands and Austria require approval of the relevant industry association before a firm can begin to operate. In the extreme case of Austria, industry associations operate as an arm of the legislature. The small size of the country in relation to world markets keeps this structure from functioning as a cartel.

INDUSTRY STRUCTURE

These smaller but sophisticated European countries typically have dual industry structures. Each has a core of large, export-oriented firms, surrounded by a nebula of SMEs. These firms are often highly specialized suppliers and also serve export markets.

Four of the smaller nations—Sweden, the Netherlands, Finland, and Switzerland—are home to 45 of the *Fortune* World 500 companies, with revenues of $580 billion. There are 31 in Sweden, 22 in Switzerland, and 29 in the Netherlands.[6] Germany, with a GDP of $1.152 trillion, has only 30. The United States, with a GDP of $5 trillion, has 164.

One would expect small countries to have more concentrated industrial structures than larger countries, because their relatively small scale economies may not be large enough to be efficient and thus competitive. One might expect that large countries, since they would be more able to focus on domestic markets, would have a larger percentage of smaller firms in their economies. This is not the case. In the United States, 50 percent of workers work in firms with fewer than 500 employees. In Switzerland, a much higher percentage of workers—close to 80 percent—work in small firms. Austria would be similar. Thus, the typical industrial structure in these small countries includes a few large, powerful multinational firms (such as Nestlé, Hoffmann La Roche, and Brown Bovari in Switzerland, or Ericsson, SKF, and ASEA in Sweden) with a large number of quite sophisticated smaller enterprises.

There are important synergies between the multinationals and the SMEs. The larger enterprises invest in R&D, but they also create structured associations that provide a broad range of services to the SMEs that provide innovative support. The preservation of the SMEs is viewed as a major policy priority. Contrast this situation with Korea, where the chaebols undertake almost all the industrially financed R&D but are regarded as predatory by many of the SMEs.

In the smaller European countries mentioned previously, industry associations serve four purposes: (1) worker training; (2) industrial extension services, problem solving, and cooperative research; (3) standards setting and conformance testing; and (4) export promotion and marketing.

These activities result in formalized restrictions on competition through labor markets, capital markets, and in product markets. However, they also provide informal social networks—social capital that enhances their productivity to levels that allow them to compete with larger but less efficient economies.

It is important to note that these governments achieve a high level of strategic coherence in their economies but do not rely on government authority to direct it. The power of their system lies in its reliance on consensus, with strong social pressure to ensure conformity to expectations. The Swiss say that their government is built on the model of their unique militia system—not a standing army but a mobilizable military system with required participation by all male citizens. The federal government is very reluctant to expand the central government's role. Committees are created and associations formed to address new problems.

R&D INVESTMENTS

In addition to their focus on technology diffusion and low transaction costs, the smaller European nations are serious investors in R&D. Sweden and Switzerland—like the United States, Germany, and Japan—invest between 2.7 and 3.0 percent of their GDP in GERD. What is more impressive is the distribution of the uses of R&D assets.

Table 11.3 shows that Sweden's R&D intensity in its high-technology industry is much higher than its big-country competitors—the United States, Germany, and Japan.[7] In 1992, Sweden's communications industry invested 35 percent of production costs in R&D, compared to 9 percent for the twelve main OECD countries.[8] The Swedish pharmaceutical industry spent 30.4 percent of its production on R&D in that year, compared to an OECD average of 11.9 percent.

THE APPRENTICESHIP SYSTEM

If you examine Swiss workers, who are screened for ability from age 8, the key career discriminations are made at middle school. From this point on, 60 percent of the students go to apprenticeship programs. These programs are co-managed by labor–business–government organizations. The industry associations define the skills that will be needed in the future and define the curricular requirements. Close to 70 percent of Swiss-born employees in industry have completed an apprenticeship.

In Germany, 50 percent of firms have less than 100 employees, but 29 percent of employees are apprentice trained. Germany's apprenticeship training is very expensive. A rigorous economic study in Germany showed that only 10 percent of apprenticeships produced revenues associated with apprenticeships in excess of cost. For this low level of appropriability to be sustained, there must be effective control (or acceptance) of free riding. Studies have

Table 11.3
R&D Intensity (Business Expenditures on R&D/Total Production), 1992

Technical Level of Industry	Number of OECD countries	U.S.	Germany	Japan	Sweden
High-technology	8.1	10.5	6.6	5.8	15.8
Medium-technology	2.5	2.5	2.7	2.6	3.9
Low-technology	0.5	0.5	0.4	0.8	0.5

Source: Organization for Economic Cooperation and Development (OECD), *Industry and Technology: Scoreboard of Indicators 1995,* Annex Table 8.5, (Paris: OECD, 1995), p. 162

shown that such apprenticeship programs result in a workforce that is more productive and more adaptable, and the workers produce better-quality products. Thus, over their working lives, high wages can be sustained and the small business scale found in small countries can be overcome.

The high levels of skill certification translate into high transparency in the labor market. But the smaller European nations also enjoy advantages in higher, professional education.

THE HIGHER EDUCATION SYSTEM

University R&D in Switzerland is financed through a National Science Fund, established as a private institution. Directors are appointed by the Swiss Confederation in agreement with the Organization of Employers (Vorort) and in agreement with labor unions. They, plus a few Nobel Laureates, comprise the directors. The Vorort also sits on appointment boards for the key universities. Large firms also provide staff to university research centers and supply both direct and collaborative, or "mandate," funding. Mandate funding results when several key firms in an industry (e.g., Ciba Geigy, Sandoz, and Hoffmann La Roche in pharmaceuticals) collectively decide that a technical process is important enough to pool funding for a project at a university, run by the university. In Switzerland, private firms provide 15 to 20 percent of funding for university research—high by world standards. (In the United States, only about 10 percent of university research funding is provided by private firms.)

The focus of public investment in Swiss and Swedish universities is captured in Table 11.4, which shows government R&D expenditures on universities to be far higher than for government laboratories. The same pattern is found with respect to total R&D expenditures, public and private.

In addition to research collaboration, standardization is another area where collaborative decisions promote specialization in the economy, while promoting exchanges of information about future directions. Indeed, these structures lead to toleration of high levels of collusive behavior in nations such as Austria, Switzerland, the Netherlands, Sweden, and Norway. In Switzerland, a cartel agreement has contractual status. There are 500 industry associations officially engaged in fixing prices.

What are the hallmarks of success in these countries? First is the effectiveness of the development and diffusion of skills. Next are the productivity and transaction cost effects associated with the strong social capital that these countries enjoy. Finally, these societies achieve high levels of social equity and low levels of poverty, compared to countries like the United States.

What lessons should Korea learn from the experience of these countries? First, the European nations have had experience over many decades, even centuries, in developing the balance between public goods and social oligopoly

Table 11.4
Sectoral Performance of Total and Government-Funded R&D

	European Union (1992)	Sweden (1991)	Switzerland (1992)
Total R&D by sector of performance			
Business	63.3	68.2	70.1
Government	16.4	4.1	3.7
Universities	18.9	27.6	25.0
Gov't-funded GERD by performer			
Business	19.4	22.2	4.3
Government	37.7	10.9	13.2
Universities	41.8	66.8	80.6

Source: Organization for Economic Cooperation and Development (OECD), *Industry and Technology: Scoreboard of Indicators 1995,* Annex Tables 6.5 and 6.7, pp. 148 and 150. (Remainders from 100% totals are private, nonprofit institutions.)

and in defining the lines between collusion, cooperation, and competition. Korea is struggling with much the same issue, but at a much less subtle level of adjustment. Political scandals testing the acceptable relationships between big business and politics in Korea are far from the levels of maturity these countries enjoy.

Second, Korea can learn from a policy that supports a strong multinational industry system to enable a small country to reach global markets, then sustains this success through a very strong network of SMEs. Korea must strive to find this balance for itself and decide how to make its large conglomerates more cooperative and less predatory.

Third, Korea could also learn from how the small European economies show strong inertia in the key industries that are regarded as national hallmarks. These countries are extremely competent at preserving or rejuvenating historic strengths. The revival of the Swiss watch industry is an impressive example. But how much flexibility can a highly structured society have? Can such a country respond to entirely new areas?

Fourth, Korea can learn from how the small European countries concentrate R&D in their universities and their industries, not in government laboratories. Also, Korea could emulate how the most competitive high-technology industries in these countries are supported by very high levels of R&D intensity.

Fifth, human resource development is a key priority in these countries, both at the levels of professional education and in providing apprenticeships for workers. These nations offer a mechanism for the efficient diffusion of technical and organizational knowledge and provide a source of value added in their mature, high-wage, resource-poor countries. Korea would do well to emulate their traditions in this area.

Finally, the social capital that these countries have accumulated is the true key to their successes. It is also the one area that will be difficult and time consuming for Korea to emulate.

Trust is the key to acceptable risk taking in industry. It is the key to low transaction costs, which are at the heart of high productivity. Trust allows all elements of the society to function together. As Christopher Freeman has observed, "The main cost advantages enjoyed by enterprises in the technologically leading countries relate . . . to externalities, to the availability of infrastructure, and to learning by interacting."[9] Korea enjoys a degree of ethnic and cultural homogeneity that allows the accumulation of the required level of trust. But its social, political, economic, educational, and research institutions are so young that patience will be required before European levels of trust are achieved. Offsetting that European advantage is the economic cost of the levels of redistribution of wealth to reduce the stress of market-driven change. In Europe there is more optimism that society, through government, can manage change successfully with better social outcomes.[10]

Koreans do bring one great advantage to their economic competition—they are in a hurry. Will Korea's resolve to catch up quickly with the wealthiest industrial nations allow them to patiently invest in the necessary social capital? This is a crucial question that only the future can answer.

NOTES

1. Denis Fred Simon and Changrok Soh, "U.S.–Korean Industrial and Technological Cooperation in the Context of Globalization and Regionalization," October 15, 1995, unpublished paper for the sixth U.S.–Korea Academic Symposium on Economic and Regional Cooperation in Northeast Asia, Chicago, September 6–8, 1995.

2. Henry Ergas, "Does Technology Policy Matter?" in *Technology and Global Industry: Companies and Nations in the World Economy*, ed. Bruce Guile and Harvey Brooks (Washington, D.C.: National Academy Press, 1987), 191–245.

3. Simon Schwartzman, *Science and Technology in Brazil: A New Policy for a Global World* (Rio de Janeiro: Fundacao Getulio Vargas Press, 1995). Study was performed by the Sao Paulo School of Business Administration, Getulo Vargas Foundation.

4. This discussion draws on lectures by Henry Ergas on comparative S&T systems at Harvard University in spring 1995.

5. Douglas D. Davis and Charles A. Holt, *Experimental Economics* (Princeton: Princeton University Press, 1994).

6. Charles Edquist and Bengt-Ake Lundvall, "Comparing the Danish and Swedish Systems of Innovation," in *National Systems of Innovation: A Comparative Analysis*, ed. Richard R. Nelson (New York: Oxford University Press, 1993), 289.

7. Japan places relatively higher R&D investment in low-technology industry, falling below (in 1992) the OECD average in R&D intensity in their high-technology industry. This is consistent with Japan's emphasis on efficient production processes rather than product development.

8. The twelve are the United States, Canada, Japan, Australia, Denmark, Finland, France, Germany, Italy, the Netherlands, Sweden, and the United Kingdom.

9. Christopher Freeman, "Technology Gaps and International Trade," in *Small Countries Facing the Technological Revolution*, ed. Christopher Freeman and Bengt-Ake Lundvall (London: Pinter Publishers, 1988), 81.

10. Henry Ergas, "Why Do Some Countries Innovate More Than Others?" Center for European Policy Studies, 1984.

Part Four

STRATEGIC POSITIONING FOR KOREA'S FUTURE ECONOMY

Chapter Twelve

A NEW TECHNOLOGY-BASED INNOVATION MODEL
The Role of Government and National Strategy

Young-Hwan Choi and Lewis M. Branscomb

A technology-based innovation model describes the economic processes and conditions that enable technology-based innovations (TBIs) to be generated, applied, adapted, and diffused to appropriate industries. It shows how institutional actions, environments, policies, processes, and outcomes effectively interact. It thus provides a comprehensive perspective and a framework of analysis to help implement policy decisions. The TBI model we present here is prescriptive, normative, and optimizing, since it "allows" TBIs to be generated, applied, adapted, and diffused. It is a design that fits in with South Korea's special circumstances. Finally, it lays the foundations for the promotion and execution of the most effective strategies for TBIs.

Let us begin by defining TBIs. The modern definition of *innovation* is based on the classical concept developed by Joseph Schumpeter in the 1930s. More recently, Christopher Freeman has suggested that social innovations in the field of technology policies had to be included in the definition of an innovation. Using Schumpeter and Freeman, we may thus define a TBI as "the use of new or established science (including social science) and technology-based ideas, methods, or concepts to create new products, source materials, processes, and services that improve cost, quality, performance, or efficiency."

Before we propose a specific TBI macro-model, let us examine accepted alternative types of models of innovation. These can be grouped into the traditional linear model (also known as the "pipeline" or "ladder" model following Ralph Gomory), and the interactive or recursive model, also known as the "chain-linked model" (Stephen Kline), "system forms model" (M. Lansiti), and "cyclic development model" (Ralph Gomory).

The models belonging to the linear type assume, from a supply-oriented point of view, that innovations arise in the research laboratory or in the inventor's shop. They are then brought to the market after proceeding sequentially through applied research, development, design, and production. The interactive-type models, taking a demand-oriented perspective, underpin and reinforce the importance of technological integration, the concurrent adaptation of new technology, product design, manufacturing process, and quality assurance. The models of the latter type are better suited to the kind of industrial innovations that most influence economic competitiveness. However, models of both types fail to take into account the dynamic response to an innovation by suppliers, distributors, customers, and governments.

Henry Ergas has proposed an innovation model that overcomes some of these limitations, defining innovation at the level of the economy rather than the firm.[1] It consists of four parts:

1. *Generation*: all events from technology and market concept to introduction into manufacturing (an area which encompasses the entire innovation process as conceived by the linear model).

2. *Application*: the commercialization phase, including the early development of manufacturing know-how, introduction of a full product line, and customer acceptance.

3. *Verticalization*: the responses of suppliers of parts, materials, and services to the innovation; also, the reactions of distributors and of suppliers with complementary assets. In short, the recognition that every innovation changes the immediate environment within which it is introduced.

4. *Diffusion*: the responses of the rest of the social environment, especially to the ways the innovation changes the practices of the end user. This phase reflects the changes in education and training as well as resulting government policies and regulations. Diffusion encompasses all the feedback to the future evolution of the innovation from the larger economic, political, and cultural environment.

Ergas's point, and the point of this chapter, is that innovation is a dynamic process—influenced by an environment that includes changes induced by the presence of the innovation itself. Any public policy environment that gives high priority to enhancing TBIs will have to take these dynamic relationships into account. A macro-model that represents TBIs, and which can incorporate such a viewpoint, is suggested in Table 12.1.

Table 12.1
Inside the TBI Model

Major Institutional Factors	Demands	Technology Factors
Research Institutes	International Environments	R&D
Corporations	Government Policies	Manufacturing Technologies
Universities	Market Demands	Quality Improvements

A technological revolution, which Christopher Freeman and Carlota Perez call the "change in a techno-economic paradigm," has an especially important impact on domestic and international environments.[2] For example, the development of electronic information technologies has resulted in an "information revolution" that has widely affected industrial organization, employment patterns, productivity of labor, and quality of working life. Technological revolutions of this kind are also taking place in the fields of biotechnology, and new materials may emerge in new process approaches to environmental and energy management.

All TBIs, whether individual events or changes on the scale of technological "revolutions," are driven by forces and sources of demand that are both international and domestic in origin. Since the international environment in most cases lies beyond the sphere of national control, it is assumed as a "given condition," what Michael Porter calls "chance events." In contrast, the domestic environment can be controlled and influenced to a certain degree by means of public-policy instruments and the nation-level responses they invoke. Therefore, once TBIs are regarded as the top priority for the development of industries and the national economy, the government should formulate and implement innovation-based policies aimed at constructive change in many areas of the national life: politics, economics, defense, environment, education, and culture.

From this perspective, Korean science and technology (S&T) policy should be far more than a simple directive for promoting S&T. It must be an efficient policy of innovation and diffusion, one that ultimately becomes a comprehensive structural policy. Therefore, Korea needs to replace a mere sequential approach (which treats S&T policy as an input, in the tradition of the linear model) with an "interrelated innovation model" that integrates S&T policy with all areas of national policy.

NATIONAL GOALS, TECHNOLOGY-BASED INNOVATIONS, AND RELATED POLICIES

A technology-based innovation strategy should be considered only as a means to pursue national development on the macro level and industrial growth on the micro level. As Eugene B. Skolnikoff of the Massachusetts Institute of Technology (MIT) argues:

Government policies necessarily have an influence on the nature of technology that emerges within each country. Policies for science and technology, as all policies, are intended to serve the objectives of the state, which can mean many things: contributing to the overriding goal of survival; advancing the economic interests of the state, whether in competition or cooperation within other states; maximizing its citizens' welfare, defined either narrowly in economic terms or more broadly to include personal security, political freedom, and cultural attainment; or serving other values, such as preserving a particular form of government, advancing the spread of ideology, or promoting acceptance of a religion. Or it can, and usually does, mean a mixture of many purposes—often in conflict with one another—that requires compromises and trade-offs among the various objectives.[3]

What are the national objectives for South Korea? Although there are many state-supported research institutes (including the Twenty-First Century Committee) in a variety of fields, it is difficult to say that South Korea has developed clearly defined national objectives for the next ten or twenty years. Achievable national objectives should be determined that account for likely changes in domestic and international environments, the peculiarities of domestic conditions, and the limitations of available resources. These values must be based on the assessments of professionals as well as the consensus of citizens.

Our task in this chapter is simply to concentrate on how to achieve national objectives through "strengthening competitiveness," the focus of much attention both in South Korea and abroad. Of course, the strengthening of competitiveness only has meaning insofar as it can make South Korea economically powerful, improve the quality of the citizens' living standards, realize the political goal of institutionalizing a liberal democratic political system, and eventually enabling South Korea to join the ranks of developed nations.

Michael Porter suggests that six items determine the "national competitive advantages" of nations:

1. *Factor Conditions*: the nation's position regarding factors of production, such as human and financial capital, physical material and energy resources, the stock of knowledge, and the infrastructure necessary to compete in a given industry

2. *Demand Conditions*: the size, quality, nature, structure, and growth rate of domestic demand for the industry's products or services

3. *Related and Supporting Conditions*: the presence of internationally competitive domestic suppliers and supporting industries providing complementary assets

4. *Firm Strategies, Structures, and Rivalries*: the conditions in the nation governing how companies are created, organized, and managed, and the nature of domestic rivalry

5. *Chance Events*: developments outside the control of companies (and usually the nation's government), such as inventions, breakthroughs in basic technologies, wars, external political developments, and major shifts in foreign market demands

6. *Government*: government activities at all levels that can help or hinder the nation's competitive advantages through antitrust policy, regulation, investment in education, government purchases, and other policies

In order to realize competitive advantage, government strategy must address these six factors. The fifth factor calls for both a system of information that allows Koreans to monitor and assess significant events abroad and the international relationships that may help in managing change in the international political and economic environment.

THE CONSTITUTIVE VARIABLES WITHIN TECHNOLOGY-BASED INNOVATIONS

The major institutional factors for creating technology are industry, universities, government-funded research institutes, and national and corporate research institutes. Industry, continually motivated by its pursuit of profit, is the main actor. The desirable division of labor among these actors is shown in Table 12.2.

A national strategy based on TBI must take into account a number of changes in the paradigm of industrial innovation in the advanced countries. The new elements of the industrial innovation paradigm are usually production centered, not research driven. They must be described by an interactive innovation model, not by the pipeline from science to the market. They have changed the level of performance that is required to be competitive in the world markets. Following are some examples:

- Production processes and systems (rather than product R&D) are emerging as the primary elements of the technological strategy for low-cost and high-quality products.
- Incremental product improvements are being led by manufacturing and process engineers supported by design and R&D personnel, a radical departure from the traditional processes of sequential development and production.

Table 12.2
Suggested Division of Labor among Sources of S&T Activity

	Proprietary Technologies	Generic Technologies	Infrastructural Technologies	Scientific Knowledge
Manufacturing Industry	x			
Commercial S&T Services	x		x	
Government-Funded research Institutes		x	x	x
Universities		x		x

- Quality is increasingly controlled through accurate characterization and precise control of industrial processes, rather than postproduction tests.

These new patterns of the production-centered innovation paradigm have two significant implications. First, science enters the innovation stream at many points—"upstream" in the research laboratory and "downstream" in the factory. Second, downstream activities (e.g., refining process technologies, creating production systems, and supporting existing technologies through field services) become as important as the upstream activities centered on R&D.

THE CONSTITUTIVE ELEMENTS OF RELATED POLICIES FOR TECHNOLOGY-BASED INNOVATIONS

Central and local governments and nongovernment organizations may take several different kinds of actions as they seek to implement a technology-based strategy:

- *Technology-Creating Actions*: Governments may provide direct or indirect support for the development of new technologies or the modification of existing technologies. One extreme encompasses the basic research undertaken to support the creation of knowledge. The other extreme includes programs that involve direct government expenditures for the development of a product that will be placed into immediate use. Between these extremes, there are demonstration programs, mission-oriented R&D programs leading to prototypes, and so on.
- *Actions Affecting Product Characteristics*: Government regulatory actions can include anything from relatively weak persuasion (jawboning or administrative guidance) to controlling specific technologies or products in great detail through regulation. The government may regulate the gamut of standards involving the product, its performance, and its technological basis.
- *Market Stimulation*: Innovations may be induced by market incentives generated through changes in price controls, the indirect effects of regulation in related industries, modifications in the market structure (e.g., antitrust policy), or direct government purchases.
- *Capability-Enhancing Actions*: Investments to enhance information infrastructure, education and training, establishment of S&T centers, provision of subsidies, tax exemptions and patents to encourage technological innovations, and so on.

How should the aforementioned policy actions be implemented? How they are combined depends on the type of TBI. As we can observe in Figure 12.1, indirect policies should be taken up for incremental innovation while direct, indirect, and overt policies should be properly combined to maximize their effects for radical innovation.

Using our broadened understanding of the elements governments can use to develop TBI policies, let us now examine Henry Ergas's model of the innovation processes in contemporary economies in greater detail. The government's

Figure 12.1
Policy Actions for the TBI

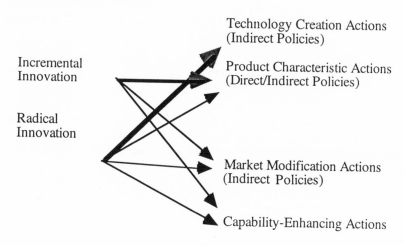

role in the generation phase involves training of R&D personnel, encouragement of innovators, and investment in R&D and in the infrastructure necessary for ideas to flow and for research to be applied and commercialized. Accessible, active markets for innovative products are the best source of stimulation for innovations.

During the application phase, sophisticated process technology and manufacturing systems are most important. Firms able to do concurrent engineering can shorten the time required; the speed of developing manufacturing know-how is critical to bringing down the initially high cost of an innovative product using new technology. The application phase includes all the activities believed to constitute innovation by many entrepreneurs of small firms. In fact, first market entry does not ensure the success of an innovation. The responses of customers and competitors often—perhaps usually—demand some level of redesign, repricing, or repositioning of the product in the market.

Verticalization reflects short- to medium-term dynamic effects of the introduction of an innovative product or service and tests the responsiveness of the economic system. This phase best displays the strength and adaptability of the independent suppliers of components and technology, and most rewards agile manufacturing. The strength and flexibility of small- and medium-size enterprises (SMEs) are particularly important at this stage. The primary attributes of a growing economy here include responsiveness and a depth of technical capability throughout the industrial "food chain."

The diffusion aspect of economic innovation reflects the broadest level of influence by public policy on innovation outcomes (although governments have an increasing impact on each of the four stages). Here, all the issues of technology assessment and public policy come into play. When the innovation has been successfully introduced, who ensures that higher education picks up the new ideas and incorporates them into the curriculum? Who looks after the training that workers may need in the new processes? What regulatory structures must change in response to innovation, either to allow the new innovation to develop without inappropriate constraints or to protect the public from harmful side effects? What kinds of trade policies or industrial structure policies might be needed to ensure the health of the innovation? The third and fourth stages of innovation, as defined by Ergas, describe what people hope to achieve through "agile manufacturing" and other forms of business alliances.

The Ergas model also describes the hoped-for benefits of government attempts to improve the infrastructure—especially information infrastructure and related elements, such as enterprise integration, computer-aided acquisition and logistics systems (CALS), and its associated commercial product definition standards (PDES). If this infrastructure is strong and responsive and decision makers have access to good information, the dynamic attributes of innovation are more likely to be successful.

The Ergas model suggests that government and private firms often work concurrently and benefit the economy most effectively when dedicated to common goals. According to the model, this is especially true in areas such as environmental regulation, establishing standards, and government procurement.

With respect to other forms of cooperation, the model explicitly shows the importance of relationships forged between primary manufacturers and their specialized suppliers, technology-defined firms that are crucial to the success of high-technology industrial economies. In the United States, such firms tend to be ignored by technology policymakers in government.[4] An exception is SEMATECH, a major government-sponsored effort to focus primarily on small high-technology firms supplying manufacturing tools to integrated circuit producers, and secondarily on the interface between the suppliers and the producers.

THE GOVERNMENT'S ROLE IN ENCOURAGING TECHNOLOGY-BASED INNOVATIONS

Based on the premise of the TBI model suggested previously, the role of the government is to suggest the objectives and visions of national development, build upon the national consensus, and establish the basic directions and paradigm for TBIs. Japan offers a good example for this, where the visions of industrial and technological innovation are expressed and led by the Ministry of International Trade and Industry (MITI). These visions are formulated by the government in conjunction with industry advisory councils representing industrial and financial institutions, as well as academics, journalists, labor, small business, consumers, and local public entities. This vision-forming interaction is crucial to the government–business interface and constitutes an important role for the Japanese government (especially MITI). Such consensus visions reduce uncertainty about the future as well as promoting brisk market activities and favorable competitive conditions (see Chapter 9).

After establishing the initial goals and strategies, the government should construct a national system of innovation that best suits the conditions of Korea. This has several options, including the following:

- Create as many "opportunities to innovate" as possible by generating, expanding, and developing market demand, taking advantage of changes in domestic and international environments.

- Strengthen "capacities to innovate" by motivating major institutional actors, industry, universities, and research institutes through the provision of a variety of incentives and support.

- Form an "environment for innovation," an economic environment and sociocultural foundation conducive to TBIs, based on the principles of free competition and cooperation.

Pursuing all these activities should produce a chain reaction of TBIs in all industrial areas and other spheres of economic activity.

In this century, Milton Friedman has argued for "small government," maintaining that the functions of government should be limited to the roles of judge, coordinator of monopolies, and controller of externalities. Likewise, John Maynard Keynes argued for a theory of the "minimum intervention of the government," claiming that the government should be confined to the spheres beyond the private control and those activities which would not be done by any one else but the government. In similar fashion, Michael Porter has advised the Korean government that

Moving to the next stage requires that economic decision making be decentralized into a growing number of private sector hands. The prime role of government must shift from direct intervention to providing the resource foundations for upgrading and creating a more challenging environment in which firms compete. Rule setting and signaling need to replace a direct role in decisions. Efforts to stimulate investment in advanced and specialized factors, upgrade home demand, institute world-class product and environmental standards, de-concentrate economic power, and preserve rivalry are prime government roles in moving to the innovation-driven stage.[5]

In reality, most countries have intervened in private industrial and economic activities, each nation in its own way and with varying degrees of intensity. The practical question, therefore, is how much and what type of intervention government should undertake. The historical grounds for intervention in R&D can be summarized as follows:

- The government should support the R&D activities when the social rate of return is higher than the private one, that is, when individual firms will underinvest because of lack of appropriability of the R&D outcome. The government ought to intervene to correct the "market failure."

- The most generally accepted example of a public good in R&D is basic research, since it is often devoid of immediate economic value to an individual firm and thus prone to underinvestment.

- The government, in pursuit of its legal responsibilities, should actively support public activities such as public health, national defense, and environmental protection. Governments must also ensure fair business practices and competitive industrial structures.

Arguments against government intervention claim that it does not ensure the correction of the market failure, and it may even result in "government failure." We must thus ask how government can correct the market failures while avoiding failures of its own? In this connection, Charles Wolf argues that since the market and the government are defective in their own ways, the choice is not one over another. One must find a way to combine the two options in the context of concrete situations, admitting that the market often functions more effectively than the government. His argument is, in practice, convincing, although it is theoretically unsatisfactory.

Using Charles Wolf's argument as a premise, we believe that it is appropriate for the government to effectively combine indirect and direct policies according to the way technological innovation takes place.

THE GOVERNMENT'S ROLE IN ESTABLISHING BASIC STRATEGIES FOR TECHNOLOGY-BASED INNOVATIONS

Henry Ergas, in his comparative study of technology policies in OECD countries, describes three generalized patterns that characterize most western industrial countries.[6] The first is a "mission-oriented" strategy, characterized by focusing on a small number of technologies of particular strategic importance, combined with centralized decision making and the commitment of resources to achieve these technologies. By elevating the level of sophistication of the most advanced technologies, the government hopes to lift all other technologies to higher levels. The United States, the United Kingdom, and France tend to share this strategy, driven largely by a primary commitment to defense R&D. These countries attempt to exploit radical innovation, that is, technical "breakthroughs" such as the transistor or the laser, which promise to remove previously existing physical limitations on improved performance of some function or make possible a qualitatively new function or service. Their ideal is to create entirely new industries based on new technologies— the Xeroxes, the Polaroids, the Digitals, the breeder reactor programs, the supersonic air transports.

The second pattern is a "diffusion-oriented" strategy, characterized by decentralized policies and reliance on diffuse decision making to keep up with and take advantage of radical innovations occurring elsewhere. By seeking to lift the average level of technical performance, the government hopes to support the highest levels of achievement indirectly. Germany, Sweden, and Switzerland are primarily diffusion oriented in their S&T policies (see Chapter 11). These countries focus on rapidly assimilating new technologies into existing industries to add more value to their existing products in a continuous, evolutionary way. They place secondary value on the types of technical breakthroughs that create the basis for new industries that would move their economy away from dominant technological paradigms.

The third pattern is exemplified by Japan, which, Ergas argues, combines both of the other strategies into a unique hybrid. Japan has mounted significant centralized programs to advance specific technological goals. It has also devoted important resources toward improving the diffusion of new technologies that are largely imported from mission-oriented countries. Ergas characterizes this third strategy as a producer's strategy, combining a strong emphasis on diffusion and workforce training with highly selective targeting in selected areas that are very complementary to upstream or downstream industry sectors (e.g., integrated circuits, specialty materials, or computerized machine tools).

Both the diffusion and hybrid strategies depend primarily on high returns from incremental improvement. With the exception of the United States in the early period following World War II, the countries that have followed diffusion-oriented strategies seem to be more successful than those that have used the radical breakthrough strategies. Germany and Switzerland, in particular, have been very successful in upgrading their mature capital-goods industries. They have continuously introduced improved process technologies, while using their highly skilled workers to integrate their design with manufacturing. This has enabled them to introduce high-performance process or manipulating equipment as well as other types of capital goods into world markets.

As noted in *Empowering Technology*, government strategies for improving the performance of the economy can take two forms: prescriptive and enabling.[7] Prescriptive, or targeted, approaches aim at short-term effects in specific areas of industry. Sometimes attacked as an intrusive "industrial policy," they are nevertheless more popular politically because intended beneficiaries are usually explicitly identified. Enabling strategies have their focus on infrastructure and public goods, are often capital intensive, and may have structural side effects that might be ignored in planning. They offer great long-range value but are less popular than other strategies, since their results are hard to quantify.[8]

In contrast to prescriptive strategies, capability-enhancing policies are designed to prepare workers for an increasingly sophisticated work environment. They focus on developing workers' problem-solving abilities to accelerate the commercialization of innovative ideas, increase productivity while lowering costs through infrastructural R&D, and build a core of basic research knowledge and competence. Capability-enhancing policies diffuse economic benefits and increase competition by increasing overall innovation capacity, not by "picking winners."

Christopher Freeman offers another way of looking at technological innovation strategies, classifying six strategies as (1) offensive, (2) defensive, (3) imitative, (4) dependent, (5) traditional, and (6) opportunist. Offensive strategies could be undertaken by the firms in the superpowers of S&T. They depend on occupying positions of proprietary uniqueness, returning large rents from their innovative technology. Some other developed countries are inclined to pursue defensive strategies. Smaller, agile economies, such as Singapore, might be called opportunistic. Most of the developing nations by and large rely on imitative, dependent, or traditional strategies. Which strategy a country or a firm adopts depends on the level and capability of the country's firms and their internal and external situations.

Among these choices, Korea's unique situation requires a "dualistic policy" because the level of its S&T is divided into two areas: the relatively undeveloped and the advanced sectors. In order to help Korea's lagging SMEs as they struggle against the effects of the chaebol, Korea must adopt a "capability-enhancing policy." Such a policy would be diffusion oriented, emphasizing access to technical and market relationships and information, sources of technical assistance, and support for meeting quality and performance and design standards required of a supplier to the global economy. Such a policy toward the lagging SME sector of the economy must be harmonized with the more advanced sectors, which require a more aggressive, prescriptive approach. The policy for the advanced sector should be more mission oriented, aimed at breaking into leadership positions through discontinuous technological change. The interrelationships between dualistic policy and hybrid strategy are summarized in Table 12.3.

Since the available resources for technological development are very limited in Korea, policies for the advanced industrial sectors will have to be supported by so-called "specialization" policies. Even if Korea's science and technological investment goal of 5 percent of the gross national product should be realized by the early twenty-first century, this could amount to no more than that of Japan or West Germany in the mid-1980s. Korea, therefore, has to strategically concentrate its R&D resources and energies into some specialized areas with the greatest potential. We argue that such a specialization strategy should be incorporated into the basic philosophy of the Highly Advanced National Project.

Most of the developed countries that are poor in natural resources are pursuing specialization strategies (see Chapter 11). For instance, Switzerland has been specializing in such industries as fine chemicals, pharmaceuticals, fine

Table 12.3
Dualistic Policy and Hybrid Strategy for South Korea

	For the Advanced Sector	For the Backward Sector
Mission-Oriented Program Aggressive, Prescriptive Policy	Good Starter Strategy Upstream Strategy Radical Innovations Discontinous Technology	
Diffusion-Oriented Program Enabling, Capability-Enhancing Policy		Good Finisher Strategy Downstream Strategy Follow-Through Strategy Discontinuous Technology

machinery, banking, and chocolate. Likewise, Sweden has been concentrating on heavy electric plants and machinery (i.e., heavy trucks, automobiles, mining equipment, robotics, and steel). The Netherlands specializes in petrochemicals and plastics, while Italy focuses on the ceramic tile, footwear, furniture, lighting, woolen fabrics, textiles, and jewelry industries. Japan enjoys particular strength in consumer electronics, robotics, semiconductors, automobiles, machine tools, and other areas. In this light, how should Korea specialize?

One useful set of guidelines comes from general proposals made by Kristensen and Levinsen for small countries. They claim that relatively large R&D programs might be established in areas under the following conditions: (1) where it is important for the small country to pursue an indigenous R&D effort to meet its social and economic objectives; (2) where current R&D makes it natural to establish "axes of penetration"; and (3) where cost, personnel, type of activity, and fields of S&T are appropriate for the small country's R&D capability.

In addition, areas should be considered where industries with large added value already exist, even though they may not be based on cutting-edge technologies. According to Hollis B. Chenery, Korea is a large country in terms of its population and the size of its economy but is like a small country when its available resources for technological innovation are compared to the resource-rich developed countries. Since Korea cannot engage in full-scale competition worldwide, it must concentrate its efforts on specialized areas of industry, choosing sectors where it has established clear comparative advantages and demonstrated the potential for accelerated growth.

NOTES

1. Henry Ergas, "Global Technology and National Politics," unpublished paper for the Council on Foreign Relations, New York, June 26, 1989, 1–21.

2. Carlota Perez, "New Technologies and Development," in *Small Countries Facing the Technological Revolution*, ed. Christopher Freeman and Bengt-Ake Lundvall (London: Pinter Publishers, 1988), 92.

3. Eugene B. Skolnikoff, *The Elusive Transformation: Science, Technology and the Evolution of International Politics* (Princeton, N.J.: Princeton University Press, 1993), 26.

4. The concept of "national competitiveness" has been criticized by those who note that competitiveness is defined economically at the firm level. Firms are not confined to nations; nations, save those with fully socialized economies, do not compete in world markets. The term is taken as shorthand for the ability of a nation's economy to sustain the standard of living of its citizens in an open global market. Thus, policies to promote competitiveness that rely on reducing real wages would not fit this definition, even though firms enjoying this increased labor productivity would, in theory, increase their shares in world markets.

5. Michael E. Porter, *The Competitive Advantage of Nations* (New York: The Free Press, 1990), 11.

6. Henry Ergas, "Does Technology Policy Matter?" in *Technology and Global Industry: Companies and Nations in the World Economy,* ed. Bruce Guile and Harvey Brooks (Washington, D.C.: National Academy Press, 1987), 191–245.

7. Lewis M. Branscomb, ed., *Empowering Technology: Implementing a U.S. Policy* (Cambridge: MIT Press, 1994), 10–26.

8. Such a trend could be clearly seen in Congressional actions between 1984 and 1994, when the Clinton administration began the vigorous implementation of a new technology policy, based on the 1988 Trade and Competitiveness Act. However, the election of 1994 brought control of Congress by conservative Republicans, who have rejected the idea of direct government intervention in industrial technology. They have radically reduced government action, even to the point of using Congressional resolutions to express an intent to abolish the U.S. Department of Commerce. These policies reflect a reversion to the linear model and are highly controversial.

Chapter Thirteen

TECHNOLOGY TRANSFER AND INTERNATIONAL COOPERATION

Sung-Chul Chung and Lewis M. Branscomb

"Globalization" of the Korean economy is currently receiving great attention in Korea as opportunities increase for establishing alliances and economic relationships abroad. The government and businesses are trying to adapt to international norms and practices to face the new challenges and opportunities. More important, Korean relationships with five key trading partners—which have complex and sometimes tense interrelationships—have become increasingly important and complex.[1] The future of Korean technological development will continue to be intertwined with the fate of its partners. While a strong commitment to export trade has dominated the entire history of Korea's supercharged development, it has been managed through inward-looking public policies (see Chapters 2 and 3). These policies must now turn outward if Korea is to grasp the opportunities that lie ahead.

Acquisition of advanced technology from foreign sources has been one of the main concerns of Korea's science and technology (S&T) policy for over thirty years. The industrialization of Korea has been a process of learning how to absorb and improve upon borrowed foreign technologies for industrial development. From a policy perspective, this was based on a managed policy of technology transfers. Even within this limited perspective, however, the Korean government did not pay sufficient policy attention to technology-transfer issues. While the Korean government created an enormous demand for new technologies by implementing ambitious industrial development projects, it actually blocked the inflow of technologies by implementing a very restrictive policy toward direct foreign investment (DFI) and foreign licensing (FL), the primary mechanisms for international technology transfer. Thus, Korean industries had to rely more on informal modes of technology transfer for much of their technology acquisition.

The strong export orientation of Korean industries fostered rapid acquisition of technological capability. It exposed domestic producers to international competition, and it gave them opportunities to work with foreign firms with advanced technologies through relationships such as original equipment manufacturer (OEM) production arrangements. In short, a strong export orientation not only generated demand for new technologies but also facilitated the acquisition of technologies through informal channels. In this way, Korea had already laid the foundation for a change that is sweeping over all advanced countries, including increasing reliance on joint ventures, business alliances, and other forms of collaboration that involve technology sharing.

Three trends in Korea's external economic environment support this conclusion: (1) intensifying international competition based on the principles of free trade, free movement of capital, and stronger protection of intellectual property rights; (2) globalization of economic activities by dispersing sources of technology and production, by-products of business alliances; and (3) shifting patterns of opportunity for Korean access to markets and sources of technology. Denis Fred Simon and Changrok Soh identify five of the key shifts:[2]

1. The market in the People's Republic of China offers an opportunity for Korea to be an alternative to the United States and Japan as China's technology supplier.
2. Russia's vast and underfunded scientific establishment offers the opportunity to commercialize Russia's research.
3. There is a growing trade deficit with Japan and weakening access to Japanese advanced tools and technology, which suggests shifts to more collaborative relationships with Japanese firms and diversification of relationships.
4. The growing competitiveness of the U.S. market is a challenge, but U.S. globalization of sourcing of components offers new business relationships.
5. The rising economies of ASEAN (Association of Southeast Asian Nations) countries provide Korea with its own offshore production alternatives, which can help it regain cost advantages.

This chapter reviews the past S&T policy of Korea within a simple framework of supply and demand, and discusses policy options lying ahead under the new environment.

INTERNATIONAL TECHNOLOGY-TRANSFER POLICIES: 1960s–1980s

The 1960s

In 1962, Korea launched its First Five-Year Economic Development Plan. This plan and its successor initiated an outward-looking development strategy. It had two major aims: developing light consumer-goods industries for import substitution and expanding exports of industrial goods to obtain the foreign exchanges needed for industrialization. The plan targeted some additional important objectives. For example, it aimed to build the basic industrial infrastructure, including electricity and transportation, and sought to develop several key materials-supplying industries such as fertilizers, cement, petroleum refineries, and chemical fibers.

Since Korea lacked technological capability at the outset, it had to rely almost completely on foreign technologies for industrialization. The government adopted quite open policies toward foreign technology and capital, as expressed in the Foreign Capital Inducement Act of 1962. However, since the start of the Second Five-Year Development Plan (1966–1971), Korea opted for a restrictive technology-transfer policy. This policy especially applied to DFIs and FLs. The government turned to this rather contradictory policy because Korea faced a serious shortage of foreign exchanges in the early stage of its industrialization drive.[3] The expansion of its industrial production base resulted in massive imports of foreign capital goods, which became a major source of learning through reverse engineering by Korean firms.[4] Government policy preferred long-term foreign loans to DFI for industrial investment, allocating large-scale foreign loans to selected big firms to secure the economies of scale in mature, strategic industries.

The 1970s and Early 1980s (1972–1981)

Beginning with the Third Five-Year Development Plan, the Korean government turned its eyes to more capital- and technology-intensive heavy machinery and chemical industries. The world experienced two oil shocks, and the general prospects for maintaining a stable supply of raw materials from the international markets deteriorated. This posed a serious problem for Korea, which lacks a large supply of natural resources. In addition, the "Nixon Doctrine" led to a partial withdrawal of U.S. forces from Korea, increasing Korea's defense burden.

These factors turned government priorities toward developing heavy machinery and chemical industries under the Third and Fourth Five-Year Development Plan periods. This policy was considered by many experts to be premature at that stage of development. To facilitate industrial development, import protection was reinforced for the strategic industries, decreasing the import liberalization ratio from 61.7 percent in 1968 to 50.5 percent in 1976. In the case of the strategic industries (i.e., industrial machinery, electronics, automobiles, shipbuilding, and metals), the import-liberalization ratio declined even more—from 55.9 percent to 35.4 percent during the same period.

The drive for heavy industries created enormous demand for technologies that were not available from domestic sources. In response, the government eased its restrictive legal measures. New government policies—"The Guidelines on Direct Foreign Investment" and the "Principles on Foreign Ownership"—streamlined DFI approval procedures on the one hand; but at the same time, the government tightened its regulations on the operation of DFI firms.

Toward the end of the 1970s, the demand for foreign technologies increased in response to the massive investment in heavy machinery and chemical industries, and the foreign exchange situation improved. The government thus took a series of measures to gradually liberalize DFI and technology imports. (These steps are discussed in Chapter 2.) However, these liberalization measures failed to induce significant foreign investments for two reasons: the general economic slowdown in Korea and around the world, and the bad publicity about the investment climate in Korea.[5]

Private Firms' Responses to the Policy in the 1960s and 1970s

The modes of technology acquisition by individual Korean firms in the 1960s and 1970s varied widely. In the case of shipbuilding and machinery industries that make differentiated products, they relied more on formal transfer of technology, mostly in the form of FL and consultancies. Thus, these industries accounted for a major share of FL through the 1970s. In contrast, small firms had to resort to imitative reverse engineering of foreign products and processes.

In contrast, the chemical, cement, paper, and steel industries, which employ highly capital-intensive continuous processes for production, acquired technologies through technical training and assistance provided by suppliers of turnkey plants. In this case, informal modes of technology transfer were much more important than formal ones.

The electronics and automobile industries, which use assembly systems for mass production of standardized products, acquired technologies through a mixture of formal and informal channels. They depended on FL for technology acquisition but to a lesser extent than the first group of industries. At the same time, they obtained technologies through technical-assistance agreements with foreign suppliers of "packaged" technology, including assembly processes, product specification, production know-how, component parts, and other items.[6]

The 1980s and Early 1990s (1982–1990)

Entering the 1980s, the government gradually reduced its involvement in industrial development, promoting the role of markets for efficient allocation of resources while liberalizing economic policies. As industrial development continued, the technological requirements of Korean industries became more complex and sophisticated. Although domestic regulations were removed, technology inflow did not increase significantly. Thus, beginning at the end of the 1980s, Korean firms started to shift their efforts from the quest for low production and marketing costs to technology acquisition.

Unfortunately, the government's excessive protection of and assistance to strategic industries resulted in imbalances and distortions in the economy toward the end of the the the 1970s. Government allocations of credit for industrial development led to an oversupply of money, which, in turn, caused inflation and wage hikes. Excessive government involvement also created a concentration of credit in heavy and chemical industries, leaving many plants with severe problems of overcapacity.

To overcome the extremely adverse internal and external environments, the Korean government reexamined its role in economic development. It then undertook a series of institutional reforms to promote the role of market forces and reduce government intervention. These reforms included further liberalization of trade and DFI, which contributed to the creation of a more competitive environment and more efficient allocation of resources. Consequently, the import-liberalization ratio rose from 50.5 percent in 1976 to 84.8 percent in 1984.

In the field of DFI, the government substantially loosened its regulations to improve the foreign investment environment in Korea. The Foreign Capital Inducement Act was revised in this vein in 1983. In 1984, a new "Guidelines for Direct Foreign Investment in Korea" contained two important changes. One was the introduction of a "negative list system," which excluded 71 of 520 manufacturing industries from access to DFI.[7] Liberalization continued, and by the end of the 1980s, the foreign investment liberalization ratio rose to 92.5 percent.

Along with DFI, FL was also liberalized substantially during this decade. In 1984, the approval system was converted into a notification system, under which government approval was not required for technology import. In 1986, the government allowed the importation of trademarks while reducing tax deductions on royalty payments. Thus, in a technical sense, Korea completely liberalized technology imports through a series of measures taken during the 1980s.

TECHNOLOGY TRANSFER: TRENDS AND STRUCTURE

Trends and Structure of Technology Transfer: 1962–1990

During the period of 1962 to 1990, Korea obtained 6,944 licenses for imported technologies, but 83.1 percent were for technologies purchased during the latter half of the 1980s (1984–1990). This reflected increased technology imports as a result of the policy liberalization. It also increased the price of technology because of the shift of demand toward high technologies. In 1978, when the first of the liberalization measures was taken, technology imports increased by 26.8 percent; since then, technology imports have increased at an annual rate of about 20 percent.

Technology imports by Korea during the past three decades were concentrated in a few industries: machinery (25.8%), electronics and electrical equipment (23.6%), and chemicals (17.2%) accounted for more than 66 percent of the total cases of technology imported. For royalty payments, these three industries' share exceeded 70 percent of total payments.

A very similar trend can be found in the origins of technology imports. Of the total value of technology imported during the period of 1962 to 1990 (a total of U.S.$4.93 billion), 3,536 cases (59.9%) came from Japan and 1,826 cases (26.3%) were from the United States. This shows how heavily Korea depends on Japan and the United States for technology.

Direct Foreign Investment

DFI has not been active in Korea because of government restrictions. Especially during the 1970s, the government's reinforcement of DFI regulation decreased the inflow of DFI, even though the economy grew very rapidly during the period. In contrast, foreign loans grew significantly. The total outstanding foreign debt grew, from 1970 to 1982, from U.S.$20.3 million to U.S.$37.1 billion. This trend was caused by the Korean government's distinctive foreign investment policy that preferred loans to direct investment.

From 1962 to 1986, the cumulative total of long-term foreign capital reached U.S.$49 billion. Commercial loans accounted for 64.5 percent, and borrowings from development agencies yielded 13.8 percent, but DFI stood at 3.9 percent. In the 1970s, DFI's share of the total foreign capital in Korea was much lower than the average share of all developing countries, estimated at 10 to 20 percent.[8] DFI stock, as a percentage of Korean gross domestic product (GDP), was also significantly lower than those of other Newly Industrialized Economies. For the years 1984 to 1986, DFI stock as a percentage of GDP in Korea stood at 2.8 percent, which was far lower than Taiwan (8.1%), Hong Kong (20% to 26%), Singapore (58.2%), and Brazil (13.6%).[9]

With the liberalization of DFI in the 1980s, DFI inflow into Korea increased rapidly. However, its contribution to technology transfer still remained insignificant relative to FL and capital-goods importation. This is largely because Korea, which was poor in natural resources and an increasingly costly site for production (high wages, labor disputes, etc.), did not offer an attractive climate for DFI. Foreign firms continued to complain about bureaucratic obstacles placed in their way.

Nevertheless, some argue that Korea's approach had been more cost-efficient, enabling Korea to remain economically independent.[10] Politically, the government faced a general sentiment against foreign capital that prevailed in the 1960s and 1970s. In return for the policy, however, Korean firms had to give up an important channel for technology transfer that DFI firms would have provided.

The New International Environment and Korea's Options

Korea's dependence on Japan and the United States for both trade and technology has made its economy vulnerable to the shifts in markets and trade relationships that are now emerging. The United States and Japan have been the largest markets for Korean exports, importing more than 50 percent of their total exports. Korean industries have also been the major base for U.S. and Japanese firms' OEM production. In addition, the two countries have been the main sources of Korean FDI. Even minor changes in these countries affect the performance of Korean industries. This is evidence of a serious structural weakness of the Korean economy. In the late 1970s, the government began to encourage geographical diversification of exports and imports, and technology imports from European countries began to rise gradually. By 1990, the Japanese share was still 45.1 percent, but the European Community countries' share had only risen to about 15 percent.

Overseas factories now account for 10 percent of the overall production of Samsung, LG (formerly Lucky Goldstar), and Daewoo. The goal is to reach 30 percent by the year 2000. In one year—from 1993 to 1994—Korean overseas investments grew by an astonishing 88.3 percent.[11] Half of this $2.39 billion investment, in dollar value, was in Asia. Of 1,442 projects, 1,209 were invested there, largely in China.

Today, as noted by Simon and Soh, large Korean firms are establishing alliances of many different kinds in many regions of the world—most important, in Asia.[12] These alliances, made possible by the increasing sophistication of Korean technology, are replacing arm's-length technology-transfer mechanisms, such as licensing and FDI, which formed an important dimension of Korea's past protectionist policies. A recent example, cited by Simon and Soh, is the alliance between Samsung and Hewlett Packard to build a high-end computer workstation in Korea. As of 1995, they note that Samsung is ninth in the world in the number of key technology alliances in semiconductors (Table 13.1).

The drive toward alliance relationships with foreign firms comes from several sources. Product cycles have shortened, economies of scale are increasingly important, and R&D intensity continues to rise in many of Korea's strategic industries. With the growing sophistication of their own technology, Korean firms can now trade on somewhat more equal terms to address the

Table 13.1
Technology Alliances among Global Chip Makers

Company	Number of Alliances	Major Project and Partner
IBM	31	256 MB DRAM (Siemens and Toshiba)
AT&T	24	0.25 micron circuits (NEC)
Hewlett-Packard	17	0.35 micron circuits (AND)
Siemens	17	256 MB DRAM (IBM and Toshiba)
Motorola	15	Microprocessors (IBM)
Toshiba	13	256 MB DRAM (IBM/Siemens)
Matsushita	13	IC's (National Semiconductor)
Texas Instruments	12	PC's (Acer [Taiwan] and Samsung)
Samsung	10	256 MB DRAM (NEC), RISC computers (ARM)

Source: Adapted by Denis Fred Simon and Changrok Soh, *Korea Economic Weekly,* April 3, 1995, 7.
MB, megabytes; DRAM, dynamic random access memory; IC, integrated circuits; PC, personal computer; RISC, reduced instruction set computer.

accelerating pace of competition through alliances. Korea's research establishment is now maturing to the point where it can begin to commercialize research of other nations whose economies are less agile.

This point is particularly interesting and encouraging for Korea's technical future. An example, cited as illustrating the Minister of Science and Technology's mid-entry technology strategy, involves a three-way collaboration between Russian scientists, a Korean government-funded laboratory, and an industrial company. A process for a super-hard, diamondlike carbon coating for videocassette recorder heads has been commercialized by Daewoo, based on applied research at the Korea Institute of Science and Technology. This research had resulted from collaborating with a laboratory of the Russian Academy of Sciences, which had made the basic scientific discovery.[13]

THE NEW INTERNATIONAL ORDER: ITS IMPACT ON KOREA

The aggressive globalization efforts of the Korean chaebols signify a major shift in Korean economic policy. Korea began with a government-guided, defensively protected and managed assault on foreign markets using imported machinery and technology. Now it is headed toward success in world markets, using all the tools and relationships practiced by the world's great multinational corporations. Korea must, therefore, join the international institutions and embrace the new regulations that are opening markets everywhere, regardless of whether it feels it is fully ready to compete.

Korea has initiated the processes that are expected to lead to its admission to the Organization for Economic Cooperation and Development (OECD) in late 1996 or 1997. In anticipation, the government is moving its policies and structures, slowly but steadily, into line with those of the OECD nations. With or without OECD membership (there are those opposed to opening financial markets to the extent required by OECD), Korea will face much more intense competition in its own markets in the future.

Much of this pressure comes from the Uruguay Round of GATT (General Agreement on Tariffs and Trade) negotiations. This was the top political issue in Korea near the end of 1993, when the multilateral negotiation had nearly concluded. The issue was centered on vulnerable sectors such as agriculture and small and medium industries, areas where Korea does not command comparative advantages. As a political issue, the adverse effects of the new rules had been much more emphasized than the potential opportunities for Korea.

The GATT agreement is based on the principles of free trade and national treatment. It includes new rules on market access, antidumping actions, industrial subsidies, technological barriers, government purchases, trade-related investment, opening of services in wholesale and retail markets, import restrictions, and intellectual property rights. In the new international economic environment based on this multilateral agreement, only those firms that are internationally competitive can expect to survive.

GATT also has important implications for S&T development in Korea. Government intervention in S&T development by means such as subsidies or protection will be substantially limited by the GATT agreement. Korea will have to abandon its heavy reliance on government subsidies, protection, and support. It must look to incentives for private investment, encouraging cross-sectoral and international cooperation in R&D and promoting stronger basic and academic science.

Some major studies have been conducted on how the new rules would affect Korean industries. As a result, many argue that the opening of domestic agricultural goods market may eventually destabilize the whole domestic agricultural base. The Korea Institute of International Economic Policy (KIEP) predicts that reduction of industrial subsidies will certainly affect small- and medium-size industries.[14] Financial and distribution industries are expected to be seriously affected by the new rules of the game. In the case of service industries, however, foreign access to domestic markets will not be widened in a massive way. Thus, the impacts in this area will not be as great as those in agriculture and finance.

On the contrary, the new order offers Korean exporters freer access to international markets. The Korea Institute for Industrial Economics and Trade (KIET) concluded that the new rules would have positive effects on Korea's exports by expanding access to international markets and lowering trade barriers (Table 13.2).[15] KIET estimated that the net increase in exports will reach $4.5 billion from 1995 to 1999. According to a KIEP study, the electronics,

Table 13.2
Effects of the World Trade Organization System on Korean Industries

Industry	Market Access	Subsidies	Techno- logical. Barriers	Govt. Purchases	Trade- Related Invest.	Intell. Property Rights	Overall
Autos	+ +	+ +	+ +	n	+	n	+ +
Electronics	+ +	n	+	+	+	-	+ +
Machines	- -	- -	- -	- -	- -	- -	-
Fiber	+ + +	- -	n	n	+ +	- -	+
Steel	+ +	- -	+ +	n	+ +	n	+ +
Chemical	+ +	- -	+	n	- -	- - -	+ +
Shipbuilding	+ +	+ +	n	n	n	n	- - -
Electric	n	- -	- -	n	n	n	- -

Source: N. Choi, *UR Chegyuli KuKnae Sanupe Michinun Younghyang Bunsuk (An Analysis of the Impacts of the Uruguay Round on Domestic Industries)* (Seoul: KIET, 1994).
Note: Overall effect includes factors not tabulated here and is not an average of prior columns.
+++, highly positive; n, neutral; − − −, highly negative.

automobile, fiber, steel, and chemical industries will be the major beneficiaries of the new system, while negative effects are inevitable in the shipbuilding, machinery, and electric industries. Overall, the OECD predicts that the Korean economy will grow an additional 2.3 percent from 1995 to 2002. This would be caused by expanding free trade in manufactured goods under the World Trade Organization system.[16]

In terms of S&T development in developing countries, the impacts of the new rules are not so evident. Here are a few of the possible outcomes:

• The race among nations of the world for technological supremacy will be intensified.

• Access to technology will become more difficult and costly for nations that do not enjoy strong internal R&D capability.

• International cooperation in S&T will be concentrated among the limited number of technologically developed countries.

• Government roles in S&T development will have to be limited to a greater extent for nations with interventionist policies.

• Private enterprises, especially multinationals, will play the leading role in scientific and technological advances, leading to globalization of S&T within their control.

These trends lead to a conclusion that the conventional developing country strategy, based on learning through imitation and reverse engineering, will no longer be effective. Latecomers will face greater difficulties in catching up. With the liberalization of trade and investment, the globalization of economic and R&D activities will proceed so quickly that the developing economies must eventually abandon their current economic development and technology acquisition strategies. These trends pose a serious challenge to those developing economies that still lag far behind advanced economies in S&T.

Korea must decide where it stands between the developing and the industrialized world. Can it commit itself to the open competition implied by their aspiration to be a G-7 (Group of Seven) country?

POLICY RESPONSES

Many in Korea believe that the post–Uruguay Round international order hinges upon interdependence and globalization. This is well reflected in the Five-Year Plan for a "New Economy," which is the basic framework of economic policy of the present government. The international economic policy contained in the plan pursues greater opening of markets; it also strives for further internationalization of Korea's economic institutions and practices. In November 1994, President Kim Young-Sam reconfirmed the policy by announcing that his administration would place top policy priority on globalizing the national economy; encouraging DFI; liberalizing financial markets; opening up domestic markets; and expanding global sourcing of technologies, resources, and information. Thus, the policy shift that Korea has adopted conforms with the current changes in international environments: the globalization of markets; the emergence of a new, knowledge-based competitive order; competitive cooperation; and economic convergence.

R&D and innovation are becoming a critical source of comparative advantage, while R&D is becoming more costly and complex. Therefore, public and private research institutions of all sizes are reviewing new strategies to optimize their existing technological strengths, using these resources to create new opportunities for wealth. Alliances and partnerships are becoming an essential way of accessing key resources, personnel, know-how, and markets, and of keeping up to date on current trends.

It is now widely accepted that globalization is a process of positive sum benefits. However, it is also important to recognize that globalization challenges many areas of policy. A nation can no longer have its own policy, independent of others. National strategies should, therefore, be built on cooperation and agreed-upon paradigms for the exercise of national power within an international context. Globalization raises the possibility of a divergence between global strategies of firms and national interests.

The Korean government has to reorient its policies and reduce the disparities that exist between the domestic policy system and the international rules of the game. According to a report by the Switzerland-based Institute of Management Development, Korea not only ranked twenty-fourth out of forty-one nations in liberalization of its economy; it also ranked poorly in the degree of internationalization of its economy.[17] The study reported that Korea is most inward oriented in trade, industry, DFI, and other related policies. It also concluded that Koreans and Korean companies have not been exposed sufficiently to international business practices.

One particularly sensitive area concerns the protection of intellectual property. Korea has been under heavy pressure, primarily from the United States, to strengthen its intellectual property protection regime. These complaints are mirrored in Korean criticisms of Japanese firms for "almost explicit efforts to forestall technology transfer."[18] A survey of 110 electronics, electrical, and machinery companies conducted by the Korea–Japan Economic Association reflected the judgment that "over 90 percent of the technology Japan sells to Korea is either outdated or already popularized in the West."[19] Of the firms surveyed, 85.5 percent said that they had received only part of what they asked for and could not complete their projects as a result. For their part, the Japanese firms complain about "Korea's excessive zeal for technology transfers."[20]

In the face of these changing environments, it seems that Korea does not have many policy options. To survive the intensifying competition in the global market, Korea's products have to be better but cheaper, which only the best in technology can achieve. However, considering the complex and global nature of modern technology, one cannot be the best without joining forces with others. Furthermore, to be an active part in the global network of cooperation, Korea should be able to complement its partners scientifically and technologically, abiding by the rules of the game set by the international community.

How can Korea achieve the parity needed for partnerships and alliances? Globalization of S&T can be accomplished only when it is pursued in an internationally accepted, rational manner. It must be based on internal scientific and technological capability, employing a system that facilitates competition in R&D among individual scientists as well as among research organizations.

More specific, Korea must gain comparative advantage over others in certain areas of technology, which will form the basis to compete and cooperate with other countries. It must strengthen its implementation of key national R&D programs, which will develop emerging technologies to spark industrial development over the coming century. Korea's policies must also give priority to public welfare and social infrastructure, which constitute the foundation for sustainable development.

Second, Korea must build the foundation for raising creative scientists and engineers to lead scientific advancement and industrial development in the era of global competition. To participate in the world technical community at a sufficiently high level to attract collaborations with scientists and engineers in advanced countries, Korea must markedly upgrade its internal capabilities in S&T. The universities should be special targets for improvement. By the Ministry of Science and Technology's assessment, Korea ranks thirteenth or fourteenth overall in S&T among the market economies but is only twenty-fourth or twenty-fifth in basic science.[21] The task of upgrading Korean science is no less daunting than the task of creating an indigenous base for technological innovation.

Third, Korea should play an active part in international cooperation in S&T under the principles of reciprocity and mutual benefits. Considering the complex nature of modern technologies and the enormous costs of R&D, no single nation can attain supremacy in each technology. Therefore, Korea should seek to expand and participate in multilateral or bilateral cooperative schemes through which the nations can complement each other technologically. Through such an arrangement, Korea will be able to harvest its share of the benefits.

To facilitate active international cooperation in S&T, the Korean government must revise its domestic laws and practices into those that are internationally accepted. It must liberalize DFI and FL of technology. Furthermore, it must widely deregulate to enhance international mobility of R&D resources. A key requirement is to develop both the regulations and the trust in protection of intellectual property.

It is also very important for Korea to pay more policy attention to creating global networks of R&D laboratories. It should seek places to conduct overseas research in cooperation with local scientists, using local facilities and resources. For this effort, the government must encourage domestic R&D institutes, both government and private, to establish laboratories at the sites of major technological activities around the world. For this purpose, the large numbers of Korean scientists and engineers with advanced training and language skills from foreign study can be a big asset. Simultaneously, Korea should create a domestic environment that can attract foreign research organizations. This is very important because Korean research organizations' exposure to international competition and the presence of foreign research organizations in Korea will help create a climate that catalyzes competitive R&D at home.

Fourth, Korea needs to change its historical role as a latecomer in S&T by becoming a catalyst for international cooperation. In return for the benefits it has received from the world science community, the Korean government should be known for formulating and sponsoring an international joint research program addressing a major issue of global concern. For the balanced development of the world, Korea needs to play the role of a leader in linking the developed and developing countries in the field of S&T. Through these efforts, Korea should actively participate in the global networks of S&T cooperation, contributing to the advancement of S&T and keeping abreast of new developments.

Korea must compete in the world market on the basis of innovation and quality. Government protection, subsidies, and regulation can no longer be relied on for the next stage in its development. The new plan, therefore, includes concrete measures for greater liberalization and to strengthen the protection of intellectual property rights. This has been further reinforced by the recent policy announcement by President Kim Young-Sam emphasizing globalization.

The policy changes are well tuned to the internal and external changes, but Korea's overall policy is too short-term oriented; the leading role of S&T in the nation's future is still not fully recognized in the new plan. As Simon and Soh remark, "As the world has shifted away from emphasis on a unidirectional pattern of technology transfer to bidirectional patterns of technology transfer, to get technology you must possess some form of technological asset or advantage. Nations with strong domestic infrastructure in terms of technological assets and capabilities can play the game of global competition."[22]

NOTES

1. Denis Fred Simon and Changrok Soh, "Orbital Mechanics of South Korea's Technological Development: An Examination of the 'Gravitational' Pushes and Pulls," *Technology Analysis and Strategic Management* 6, no. 4 (1994).

2. Ibid.

3. Korean Development Bank (KDB), *Kisul Doipui Hyoukwa Boonsuk (An Analysis of the Effects of Technology Transfer)* (Seoul: KDB, 1991); Linsu Kim, "The Evolution of Public Policies and Private Sector Responses in Science and Technology in Korea," unpublished paper for the STEPI International Symposium on Changing Technological Environment and Policy Responses, Seoul, October 30–31, 1991.

4. Linsu Kim and Young-Bae Kim, "Innovation in a Newly Industrializing Country: A Multiple Discriminant Analysis," *Management Science* 31 (1985), 312–322.

5. Bohn-Young Koo, "Role of Government in Korea's Industrial Development," in *Industrial Development Policies and Issues*, ed. K. Lee (Seoul: KDI, 1986).

6. Linsu Kim and Jinjoo Lee, "Korea's Entry into the Computer Industry and Its Acquisition of Technological Capability," *Technovation* (September 1987): 277–293.

7. Under the old positive list system, direct foreign investment was allowed only in those industries listed in the law. See Chapter 5.

8. Choong-Yong Ahn, "Technology Transfer and Economic Development: The Case of South Korea," in *Pacific Cooperation in Science and Technology*, ed. K. Minden (Honolulu: East–West Center, 1991).

9. Sanjaya Lall, "Technological Capabilities and Industrialization," *World Development* 20 (1992), 165–186.

10. Linsu Kim and Carl Dahlman, "Technology Policy for Industrialization: An Integrative Framework and Korea's Experience," *Research Policy* 21 (1992): 437–452.

11. "Korea's Big Rush Abroad," *Business Korea*, December 1994, 31.

12. This discussion benefited from a paper by Denis Fred Simon and Changrok Soh, "U.S.–Korean Industrial and Technological Cooperation in the Context of Globalization and Regionalization," October 15, unpublished paper for the sixth U.S.–Korea Academic Symposium on Economic and Regional Cooperation in Northeast Asia, Chicago, September 6–8, 1995.

13. Described at the workshop on Mid-Entry Strategy for S&T Innovation in Korea, at the Science and Technology Policy Institute, Seoul, July 19, 1995.

14. Korea Institute of International Economic Policy (KIEP), *UR Chong Jum Gurn: An Overall Assessment of the UR's Impacts on Korea* (Seoul: KIEP, 1993). UR refers to the Uruguay Round of the GATT.

15. N. Choi, *UR Chegyuli Kuknae Sanupe Michinun Younghyang Bunsuk (An Analysis of the Impacts of the Uraguay Round on Domestic Industries)* (Seoul: KIET, 1994).

16. Organization for Economic Cooperation and Development (OECD), *Assessing the Effects of the Uruguay Round* (Paris: OECD, 1993).

17. Institute of Management and Development (IMD), *The World Competitiveness Report 1994* (Lausanne: IMD, 1994). See also "Korea's International Competitiveness Plunges," *Business Korea*, October 1994, 26–42.

18. Simon and Soh, "U.S.–Korean Cooperation."

19. Quote from Simon and Soh, "U.S.–Korean Cooperation." They refer to a study reported in the International Business Council (IBC) International Country Risk Guide, August 1992.

20. *Japan Economic Journal*, February 2, 1991, 5.

21. Ministry of Science and Technology, "Uri Naraui Gwahak Kisul Sujun" ("The Scientific and Technological Level of Korea"), unpublished internal document, Seoul, 1993. The ranking was measured on the basis of such statistics as R&D expenditures, number of scientists and engineers, number of patents registered, citation index references to Korean publications, and the number of those publications.

22. Simon and Soh, "U.S.–Korean Cooperation."

Chapter Fourteen

KOREAN INFORMATION TECHNOLOGY
Status and Policy Implications

Yong-Teh Lee and Lewis M. Branscomb

The Korean information industry is thriving. With a compound growth rate that averaged 24.6 percent from 1991 to 1995 (Table 14.1) and a rate of growth from 1994 to 1995 of 45.6 percent, the industry will play a key role in determining how Korea can join the ranks of advanced countries in the twenty-first century. Its economic merits include the industry's ability to create a systematic and well-structured economy, to develop high-technology export opportunities, and to foster advanced educational vehicles that will generate a strong multiplier effect on the economy in general. Its social benefits, industrial productivity effects, and high profile in the international marketplace will enhance Korean society immensely. With these factors in mind, we outline the current and future status of the industry. Finally, we show how government policies can foster innovation through targeted support of the information industry.

The information industry in Korea and the rest of the world consists of three subsectors: hardware, telecommunications services, and computing services. The hardware subsector focuses on computers, integrated circuit (IC) chips, peripherals, and communications devices, along with television sets and telephones. The telecommunications group includes telephony, video broadcast and cable, data transmission, and networking technologies. Computing services covers data processing, networking, software, and information services.

Table 14.1
Korea Information Industry Output, 1991–1995

Classification	1991	1992	1993	1994	1995	Growth Rate (1995/1994)
Computers and Peripherals	3,499	3,646	4,233	4,947	6,795	37.4
Communications Equipment and Devices	2,648	2,681	2,967	3,491	4,693	34.4
Semiconductors	6,394	7,754	8,724	13,788	24,797	79.8
Computing Devices	1,048	1,212	1,596	2,180	3,312	51.9
Communications Services	7,413	8,313	9,303	10,411	11,100	6.6
Total	21,002	23,606	26,823	34,817	50,697	45.6

Source: Federation of Korean Information Industries (FKII), White Paper (Seoul: FKII, February 1996).
Notes: The output of broadcasting is estimated at $1.6 billion in 1994. This figure is not included in the communications services. The production of TV sets in 1994 amounts to about $2.7 billion. This figure is not included in the communications equipment and devices. The telephony is included in the communications services.

The Computer and Communication Promotion Association of Korea classifies the industry as follows: telecommunication services, enhanced communication services, broadcasting services, and equipment for enhanced communications. The National Computerization Agency divides the industry into four broader categories: hardware, software, computing services, and enhanced communications. The Federation of the Korean Information Industry differs, sorting the industry into computers and peripherals, communication equipment, semiconductors, computing services, and enhanced communications. In reality, the scope, definition, and classification of the industry must be constantly redrawn.

GROWTH OF THE INDUSTRY IN KOREA

In 1991, the annual output of the Korean Information Industry amounted to U.S.$21 billion. In 1995, this had grown to around U.S.$45.6 billion—a compounded annual growth rate averaging 24.6 percent over this period. The latest figure of 45.6 percent in 1995 signals a strong continued upward trend. The industry owes this high level of growth to the continually increasing demand for computer systems, databases, networks, on-line services, and other innovations.

The 1995 exports for the information industry amounted to over U.S.$24.7 billion, accounting for 19.8 percent of Korea's entire export economy. Since 1991, the average annual growth rate has been 28.1 percent. Semiconductors led the export market in 1995 with U.S.$17.6 billion, followed by computers and peripherals, communication equipment, and computing services. Despite its humble beginning, the Korean semiconductor segment has excelled in export and production, making Korea a world leader in the semiconductor industry (see Tables 14.1 and 14.2).

OVERVIEW OF THE INFORMATION INDUSTRY SECTORS

PC Manufacturing

The first eight-bit personal computer (PC) of Korean manufacture was produced in 1980 by TriGem Computer Corporation; the first sixteen-bit IBM (International Business Machines) XT clone was produced by the same company in 1983. Since then, Korean PC manufacturing has grown at an unprecedented rate.

There are now three groups of PC manufacturers in Korea: five large leading companies; a few medium-size companies; and a range of small, merchant-assembly companies. TriGem, Samsung, Daewoo, LG (formerly Lucky Goldstar), and Hyundai are the five largest producers. Qnix, New Tech, Union, Jeil Jeongmil (First Precision), and others make up the medium scale. The small, merchant-assembly companies are primarily retailers, but they also pursue production and value-added activities. More than 1,000 such small operations are estimated to be in Korea.

Until 1992, the Korean PC market stagnated for a couple of years; but since 1993 it has been revived by a large demand for 386 or 486 models. In 1995, the size of the Korean PC market exploded to 1.5 million units for U.S.$2.5

Table 14.2
Korea Information Industry Exports, 1991–1995

Classification	1991	1992	1993	1994	1995	Growth Rate (1995/1994)
Computers and Peripherals	2,471	2,705	3,086	2,978	4,664	56.6
Communications Equipment and Devices	1,089	1,173	1,502	1,816	2,393	31.8
Semiconductors	5,603	6,773	6,982	9,909	17,627	77.9
Computing Devices	14	16	12	14	21	50.0
Communications Services	--	--	--	--	--	--
Total	9,177	10,677	11,582	14,717	24,705	67.9

Source: Federation of Korean Information Industries (FKII), White Paper (Seoul: FKII, February 1996).
Note: Units: U.S. $ millions.

billion. About 43.3 percent of the machines sold were Pentium models, with multimedia PCs with sound cards and CD-ROMs rapidly gaining their shares. In 1995, the market share of multimedia PCs comprised more than half the total PC market in Korea.

The five major PC manufacturers captured more than 60 percent of the Korean market in 1994—a 10 percent increase from 1993. In contrast, the market share of small assembly companies dropped from 35 percent in 1993 to 20 percent the following year. The Pentium PC's market share in 1994 was a disappointing 2.9 percent, but about half the new PCs sold in 1995 were Pentium based.

Despite the rapid growth of Korean PC manufacturing, 50 percent of Korea's total computer sales in foreign markets were made under foreign companies' brand names. Original equipment manufacturer (OEM) agreements between Korean and overseas firms have prevailed as the dominant mode of Korean PC export because of the lack of name recognition for Korean companies outside of Korea.

The export of finished computer products under Korean brands was highest in the late 1980s, peaking in 1989 with the export of 1.5 million systems (U.S.$802 million). Korean PC manufacturers, however, failed to capitalize on this success. Overly optimistic, they focused on low-price distribution networks, particularly in the U.S. market, which did not work. In a few years, they had to return to the OEM model.

Limited sales of Korean PCs overseas have been due, in part, to the perception that they are more expensive than their Taiwanese counterparts. The Korean industry has recently succeeded in changing this impression. Now price compatibility of Korean PCs is enhanced, and the overall quality is believed to be superior to that of competing products, leading recently to an increase in OEM orders for Korean manufacturers.

All in all, the past fifteen years has brought exceptional growth to the Korean PC industry. Advancement of technology, export contribution, and expansion of business have been substantial. The industry's continued expansion requires that it improve cost competitiveness, enhance aftersales services, and improve user satisfaction with solutions.

High-demand innovations and near-future products, such as portable PCs, handwriting and voice recognition, and wireless and video communications, all point to the need for acquiring or developing new technologies. New approaches must be devised to cooperate with foreign developers and create advanced research-and-development (R&D) centers in Korea (Tables 14.3 and 14.4).

The Korean Semiconductor Industry

Korean semiconductors have become increasingly visible in recent years. In the 1990s, Korea grew tremendously in both quality and quantity, especially in the memory field. The major accomplishments of the year 1993 were the successful development of 4-megabit static random access memories (SRAMs) and 64-megabit dynamic random access memories (DRAMs) by

Table 14.3
Domestic PC Sales Volumes

Model	1993	1994	1995	Growth Rate, percentage (1995/1994)
386	260,000	60,000		
486	465,000	964,248	720,000	-25.3
Pentium	--	34,758	650,000	1,870.1
Notebook	37,000	46,884	90,000	191.9
Others	38,000	32,000	40,000	125.0
Total	800,000	1,137,890	1,500,000	132.0

Source: Federation of Korean Information Industries (FKII), White Paper (Seoul: FKII. February 1996).
Note: Figures for 1995 are estimated.

Table 14.4
PC Exports: Quantity Sold and Value

	1993		1994		1995		Growth Rate, 1995/1994	
Model	Quantity	Amount	Quantity	Amount	Quantity	Amount	Quantity	Amount
Desktop	546,000	281	501,000	213	360,000	147	-28.1	-30.0
Portable	108,000	88	119,000	91	130,000	93	9.2	2.1
Total	654,000	369	620,000	304	490,000	240	-20.9	-21.1

Source: Federation of Korean Information Industries (FKII), White Paper (Seoul: FKII. February 1996).
Note: Value units: U.S. $ millions.

the semiconductor companies. In 1994, the development of 256-megabit DRAM was under way.

In 1994, Korean semiconductor production increased by 62.5 percent, with output of U.S.$14.2 billion, which is 14.2 percent of the total global market. The U.S.$6.2 billion revenues from DRAM production captured 27.9 percent of the world market.

Focused R&D and market research must be conducted to further develop the industry. Logic integrated circuits and application-specific integrated circuits (ASICs) are underdeveloped sectors, but Korean manufacturers are enhancing their R&D activities on these parts. To remain on the cutting edge, the industry has to meet the challenges of further innovation, particularly the challenges of demand, noting the current and cyclical shortages in ICs of every kind (Table 14.5).

The Korean Computing Service Industry

Computing services include database services, systems integration (SI), and software products. In the United States and Europe, this sector has already proven to be the leading industry of the near future; and this will eventually be true in Korea.

Table 14.5
Semiconductor Production and Export (1994)

	Production	Export
Electronic IC	1,079	743
Ultramicro Assembly Circuit		
Analog IC	600	380
MOS Logic	293	207
Others	186	156
MOS Memory	6,925	6,800
SRAM	463	420
4 MB DRAM	3,925	3,900
16 MB DRAM	1,900	1,920
Mask ROM	275	245
Others	362	315
Other Ics	5,163	4,580
Magnetodiode	1,063	715
Transistor	471	253
Diode	178	150
Photo Diode	154	106
Others	260	206
Total	14,230	12,838

Source: National Computerization Agency, 1995 National Informatization White Paper (Seoul: National Computerization Agency, 1995).

In 1993, a survey conducted with 811 Korean computing service (CS) companies, revealed that 61 percent of these companies had less than 30 employees, while only 13 percent had more than 100 employees. In addition, 78 percent of the firms had less than U.S.$0.5 million paid-in capital, while only 124 companies had more than U.S.$1 million. This shows that most Korean CS companies are small and weak. Medium-size companies are negligible in number; and the large companies, while strong, belong to the conglomerates. Most of these large companies are young in the market and are outgrowths of the conglomerates' internal divisions.

Korean packaged software, except for Hangul (Korean alphabet) word processing, has been unable to progress significantly. Much of the packaged software used in Korea today has been imported.

SI services, especially customized application software development, once comprised the major business lines of the CS sector. Customized software development is currently limited by several key factors:

- Bid-based pricing, as an inherent and standard feature, causes excessive price competition and highlights low pricing over quality and functionality.
- Low levels of true computerization in both public and private sectors deter the industry's growth.

- Since most customized products focus on nonstandard, extremely specific business operations, they are costly to develop and maintain.
- CS providers tend to simply superimpose western or other existing models on Korean installations rather than building models appropriate to their clients.
- Up until very recently, the price of computerization was generally higher than most local users could afford.

Many of these problems are now being solved. Sweeping reforms in the public and private sectors have begun creating new environments for all spheres of economy and society. Transparency instead of secrecy, self-regulation instead of strict codes, and respect for consumer satisfaction and competitiveness instead of monopolistic policies are all providing a more open foundation for the information industry and an information-based society. To cater to these new needs, new concepts such as SI, client–server, and open-systems architecture are evolving rapidly.

The Enhanced Communication Services Industry

The enhanced communication services sector of the information industry includes packet switching, networking services such as Integrated Services Digital Networks (ISDNs) and Circuit-Switched Digital Networks (CSDNs), and other basic transmission services using voice and video.

Packet switching is the dominant mode internationally for distant data communications of low traffic volume. It is used primarily for electronic mail and information retrieval. There are currently eight packet-switching networks operating in Korea: DACOM, Korea Telecom, POS-Data, Hyundai Electronics, Ssangyong Computer, Stock Exchange Computer Service, Daishin Information and Communication, and SDS. In addition, a fair number of new entries to the market is anticipated.

Two of the major carriers, DACOM and Korea Telecom, have grown in ways that reflect the overall increasing demand for packet-switching services. DACOM began service in January 1984 with three switches in three major cities. By the end of 1993, it had 9,401 digital network service subscribers; by 1994, the figure grew to 11,166. To meet increasing overseas needs, DACOM expanded its service to 150 public networks in fifty countries. Korea Telecom's HINET-P service, which began in September 1991, has 216 nodes serving over 7,500 subscribers.

The remaining private networks mainly serve parent companies and a small number of electronic data interchange users. In 1992, the government opened the entire market to the private sector. The explosive increase in the number of Internet users has led to a rapid expansion of Internet service providers. The Internet has apparently led to extensive growth among the leading data communications carriers as well as to the newcomers.

Korea Telecom has also been involved with developing ISDN (Integrated Services Digital Network) and CSDN (Circuit Switched Digital Network) services. It serves eleven cities with 2B+D ISDN (two 64-Kbps [Kilobits per second] B channels and one 16-Kbps D channel); there are some 5,800 available circuits. CSDN is provided by Korea Telecom for data transmission at 56 Kbps; the service is available in five major cities. CSDN covers high-speed facsimile and image and voice information exchange transmissions.

Korea Telecom also provides local area network (CO-LAN) services utilizing a Voice Data Multiplexor for voice and data exchange facilities on existing telephony circuits. By 1993, this service was available in thirty-three districts, providing ninety-one telephone exchanges. It includes data compression and digitalization of high quality at low costs with variable functions.

Cable television (CATV) is a new and important entry in Korea, where service began in March 1995. Currently, fifty-three system operators are providing services to 365,000 households. The CATV industry expects to have 500,000 households connected to the service network by the end of 1995. As CATV progresses into interactive services and two-way communication, the national information superhighway should support this large increase in traffic.

The growing needs for business communication, including the use of mass data transmissions on existing facilities and the new use of CATV, assure that the entire industry will expand. Healthy growth will require an influx of the open competitive spirit and a balance between pure competition and quality of service.

THE GOVERNMENT'S NEW POLICY ON THE INFORMATION INDUSTRY

The Korean government has responded to the diversity and importance of the information industry by recently developing and implementing comprehensive policies. Most important, the Ministry of Communications was reorganized as the Ministry of Information and Communications (MIC) in 1994. It drafted its integrated information policy in February 1995. While retaining many of the old policies drafted by other ministries, it has accounted for the latest trends in technologies and underlying conditions.

The MIC is developing policies with six key objectives: create an information society, promote strategic development of the information industry, strengthen competitiveness within the telecommunications industry, enhance relevant R&D, promote new media, and improve Korea's position within the global information infrastructure.

The new ministry is considering the extreme importance of both the demand and supply sides of the information industry. It recognizes the key demand-side imperative to be the informatization of both the public and private sectors. On the supply side, it identifies the need to support the growth of new for the information and telecommunications industries, as well as for the tele-communications industry as part of the Korean Information Infrastructure (KII).

Recognizing the future importance of multimedia technology, which supports both the computing services and broadcasting sectors of the industry, the MIC should promote free and fair competition to enhance creativity and vitality in the private sector.

The National Information Infrastructure Project (to promote KII) represents the major thrust of information policy as well as the primary building block of the information industry in the next twenty years. The project both deploys epoch-making physical facilities and supports the development of the required technologies and software products. The project is estimated to cost the government 45 trillion won (U.S.$57 billion) through the year 2015, and it is estimated that it will result in an annual economic output of 100 trillion won (U.S.$128 billion). The project is expected to add 560,000 jobs to the economy. The goal of the KII is to establish optical fiber communications connections to every home by the year 2015. KII used to be the responsibility of a task force, led by an assistant minister and composed of government officials. However, MIC is now taking sole responsibility for the KII project, and the ministry is inviting more and more private investment in projects. Four ministries—the Ministry of Trade, Industry, and Energy (MOTIE), the Ministry of Finance and the Economy (MOFE), the Electronics and Telecommunications Research Institute (ETRI), and KETI—are represented, but the private sector is not. Computer network services connecting ministers are already installed. There is a plan to connect the government agencies, with funding and advice from the National Computerization Agency. MIC hosted the Asia-Pacific Economic Cooperation forum (APEC) ministerial meeting on information technology in April 1995. This meeting initiated the idea of the Asia Pacific Information Infrastructure (APII).

As a means of promoting the informatization of society, the MIC has recently enacted the Basic Law of Informatization Promotion. One of Korea's most comprehensive laws, it aims at the following:

1. Expansion of private investment and fair competition
2. Establishment of an institution in response to changing conditions
3. Promotion of free and easy access to the information infrastructure
4. Promotion of popular information services irrespective of regions and economic conditions
5. Protection of privacy, intellectual property rights, and security of information
6. Promotion of international cooperation

It enables local governments to carry out their own programs of informatization without resorting to direction from the central government, leading to improved local development. In addition to creating the Information Promotion Fund, this law provides the government with an indisputable basis for promoting informatization in Korean society over the long term.

The MIC's new information policy also pledges continued support for further extension of the Government Administration Information System. Specifically, the policy promises support for informatization of the military and of education as high-priority areas. In addition, sectors of special interest such as telelearning and telemedicine are earmarked for assistance. Simultaneously, the government is improving laws protecting security of information and privacy by amending its Act for Utilization of Information Systems.

While supporting the informatization of Korea, new government policies are aimed at directly improving the condition of the information industry, emphasizing full support for small- and medium-size software-development companies. To reinforce this support, the new policy pledges to protect intellectual property and copyrights of software products. To ensure orderly distribution of software products, the policy will assist software product distributors, promote the use of original software products in place of pirated copies, and encourage making government-supported software available to the general public.

MIC support for the software industry ranges from development to the marketing and distribution of the software products. To implement this program, it has been given an annual budget of 100 billion won (U.S.$128 million).

The government's support for strategic development of the information industry includes a full commitment to expanding multimedia computing services. The ministerial program plans to introduce a multimedia computing service in the Government Administration Service Network to trigger demand for multimedia computing services in the private sector.

Other new government policies are intended to improve competitiveness within the telecommunications industry. To spur the evolving market, the government is making a transition from tight regulation to deregulation of the market. The first stage of this policy is in place, and additional licenses will be granted to applicants in such areas as the international telephone business, the personal communication server sector, and paging. Foreign operators will be permitted to enter the market.

Owing to the rigid regulation and great bureaucratization found in management in this industry, large organizations lack agility, flexibility, and motivation for enhancing productivity. To progress in a competitive environment, management has to work hard to stay lean and respond more to the market, rather than dwell on existing practices. To further improve the competitive capacities of domestic companies, autonomy of management will be granted to Korea Telecom.

Recognizing the necessity of R&D for core technology development, new government programs pledge R&D support of technologies for high-speed exchange switches, digital mobile phones, computers, and other telecommunications equipment. The R&D budget of MIC in 1996 is 176 billion won (about

U.S.$220 million). The government's new R&D policy is very extensive, covering information, communication, and broadcasting. It will direct the development of indigenous technologies, while promoting joint ventures with foreign R&D partners. New policies for CATV and satellite communications have been introduced. Since this new area offers enormous opportunity for new business, it is desirable to encourage as many business entries as possible. In terms of Korea's place within the global information infrastructure, the government shows readiness to negotiate issues such as standards and types of approval with trading countries.

Major hardware projects identified in the Strategic Plan have been merged into the New Plan with specific description and implementation dates. The semiconductor project was dropped from the New Plan, but three new equipment projects were included. The New Plan also calls for better coordination of information projects through changes in the ministry's research institutes.

MIC operates several such institutes. ETRI is a large R&D laboratory, one of the best of Korea's government-funded research institutes. The new digital wireless products, Code Division Multiple Access (CDMA), were developed at ETRI; there is hope that these products will have a substantial export market. ETRI is entirely project funded, primarily from Korea Telecom, but also performs projects for industry.

The Korea Information Society Development Institute (KISDI) is devoted to social science research; it looks at social effects of KII, supporting KII by providing advice on policy to MIC. KISDI has made valuable contributions in trade negotiations in the telecommunications market with foreign counterparts.

In the larger economic picture, the information industry stands to benefit from several aspects of the New Five-Year Economic Plan of 1993 to 1997. The Information Industry Sector Plan, made public in July 1993, and much of the Strategic Plan for the Development of the Information Industry (unpublished document in 1992) were carried forward into the New Economic Plan. The New Economic Plan places particular emphasis on the reformation of finance, government administration, and the fostering of a cooperative spirit in implementing the plan. The promotion of informatization for economic community has correctly been designated in the plan as an area of high priority.

FUTURE STRATEGIES FOR THE KOREAN INFORMATION INDUSTRY

The Federation of Korean Information Industries (FKII) has been designated to run the Information Subcommittee of the Civil Committee for Enhancement of National Competitiveness, an ad hoc organization created by leading business associations. A research team has been formed for the subcommittee to undertake an in-depth study of the Korean Information Industry. The following material summarizes the core findings and recommendations of the research team.

Many leading countries are dedicating an unprecedented amount of resources and efforts for the information industry in anticipation of the accelerating information age. Although core national strategies are usually focused on the completion of national information superhighways, each country's project has its own unique plan and procedures. By "information superhighway," we understand a system of interoperable digital networks supporting the full range of emerging information applications. The Internet is today's realization of the superhighway. Similarly, the Korean "highway" must be tailored specifically for Korean users. Systematic efforts should be made to create demand by consumers and industries for information. An additional infrastructure must be formed to support the information industry. The evolution of the networked citizen ("netizen"), networked business, information technology, and the information superhighway are the four components of this infrastructure.

The concept of the netizen signifies that we can reach a highly efficient and productive society only when citizens are fully networked by computers. We need to advance rapidly in this direction, despite our great progress in the past few years. In 1948, Charles Helmick, Deputy of the Military Government of U.S. Occupation Forces in South Korea, reported to Washington:

Korea can never attain a high standard of living. There are virtually no Koreans with the technical training and experience required to take advantage of Korea's resources and make improvements over its rice economy status. When U.S. occupation forces withdraw and stop sending in supplies that South Korea needs, its full economy will be reduced to a bull cart economy, and some nine million nonfood producers will not be able to survive.

The Korean War broke out two years after his report, destroying the existing, meager Korean industry. However, the Korean economy has skyrocketed during the past twenty-five years and achieved the "Miracle of the Han River."

Several different reasons can be mentioned as key factors for this success, but education was the core factor. Parents willingly put everything they had to provide better education opportunities for their children, and this effort continues to this day. The desire for higher education among the Korean people is extremely strong.

Our information industry must take advantage of the overwhelmingly education-oriented social environment for enhancement of the information infrastructure. When every school at every level can provide computer courses as a mandatory subject, we will witness some unimaginable gains. The demand for information will rapidly increase, and the use of human resources as a part of industry infrastructure will be abundant. With this change, we can expect that our country will be able to have numerous creative and well-trained personnel for the information industry in the near future.

The adoption of computers as a subject in the regular curriculum of high schools is an extremely effective means of grassroots informatization. The policy of urging students to become "memory machines" just to pass the entrance examinations for colleges inhibits effective mass computer education. This distortion does not lead to creative human resources, and it deprives young students of proper computer education. Some manufacturers are trying to encourage computer education. Several leading PC manufacturers and Korean Telecom have donation programs for computer education. We hope that all these efforts will succeed in turning Korean citizens into netizens.

In addition to fostering netizens, Korea must create information that will enhance the information industry. With the growing concern for multimedia, creative and useful multimedia data can enormously increase demand and new markets in fields such as medical care, education, defense, government administration, and industry.

Most important, digitalization of all the necessary economic activities in industries is indispensable. Various kinds of automation projects have been implemented in innumerable companies, industries, and countries, usually on a trial-and-error basis. Computerization efforts in small businesses in Korea have not been successful. A company that has business relations with multiple large companies must install as much interface software as needed to correspond to their different partners. Most of the business-related public and private networks are operated independently and are unable to adequately serve the growing needs of industry users.

An important tool for improving automation, efficiency, and overall business process reengineering can be found in Electronic Commerce (EC) and Commerce at Light Speed (CALS).[1] The concept of EC/CALS concerns the whole life cycle of products and business processes such as planning, design, manufacturing, distribution, maintenance, banking, payment, and disposal. It is thus one of the more sophisticated ways of leading industries into an advanced, information-based environment. The useful data created by and utilized on a CALS system will enormously enhance the efficiency and the productivity of all the involved companies, which will eventually be diffused throughout Korea. The new system will certainly be a most valuable asset to acquire for international trade as well as international collaboration.

The diffusion of EC/CALS is expected to take place in advanced industries in which computer usage is relatively high, such as the aerospace and automobile industries. As the beneficial effects of the new system become visible, greater diffusion should occur. Until then, business associations, such as the FKII, are urged to undertake promotional programs for accelerated diffusion.

As stated earlier, information technology is another cornerstone of KII. Unfortunately, Korea is weak in the foundations of technology. Although the nation has improved its competitive capabilities in the production of devices, the level is grossly insufficient to meet the growing need for information technology.

It would be nearly impossible to compete in the international marketplace without the development and support of indigenous technology. Furthermore, the National Information Infrastructure project would run aground if indigenous technology fails to support it. In order to improve Korea's information technology, two policies should be pursued: (1) to focus development in the areas where Korea sees a clear prospect of an indispensable core technology, and (2) to set up strategic plans to attract advanced foreign companies to Korea.

Partial reliance on foreign sources of solutions is unavoidable. With the collaboration of foreign technology, Korea has to firmly establish its own capabilities in areas such as multimedia software. There are various ways to pursue foreign collaboration: software publishing, mergers and acquisitions, joint ventures, negotiation, and joint R&D ventures, among others. Individual companies in Korea are trying these strategies in their own ways.

It is critically important to find creative ideas and plans that foster foreign collaboration along with the enrichment of indigenous human resources. The special research and planning team of FKII has made a suggestion to the government to build "Media Valley." Media Valley will be a new town where multimedia industry constitutes the leading industry, residing with related support industries. In the valley, foreign companies will be attracted to relocate based on the favorable factors. Ultimately, it should attract a sufficient number of foreign businesses to serve them as an Asian business center.

Another suggestion is that in this valley, the government should sponsor a "Media Academy." The Media Academy will enroll 10,000 graduate students specializing in software technology. To attract qualified and capable students, merits of full scholarship, exemption from military service, rich field experience, and other benefits should be offered. The academy would not only offer a fertile training ground for software engineers. It would attract a large number of domestic and foreign companies because it could claim a large concentration of low-cost media talent.

Media Valley would also have a multimedia theme park, a large studio for motion pictures, a distribution center, banks, accommodations, business centers, a multimedia information center, hospitals, schools, and government offices. This community would be a perfect testing place for new products. The government is showing positive interest in this project, and Korea Telecom has agreed to install the best B-ISDN if and when the project progresses.

Media Valley can be deployed as a comprehensive plan for advancement of information technology, especially multimedia software, and can work as a springboard for our economy.

In summary, the government has taken the initiative in establishing policy and setting goals for every phase of industrial activity. The administrative and political process is deeply embedded in the national information programs. Success will depend heavily on the strong will and efficiency of the government in carrying out these programs.

The sheer dominance of the role of the government in the policy may overshadow the role of the private sector. Nevertheless, the private sector is indispensable, and it will reap the benefits of the government's efforts. The private sector must respond positively and participate actively in the implementation of all related policy. It should also establish its own strategy in harmony with the macroeconomic needs of the entire industry.

We recommend that the president of Korea declare the information industry as the key strategic, national industry for the new century. Korea cannot afford to exempt itself from the trends in international information technology and the evolution of information societies. Government and business must take the long view, cooperate on a more highly integrated basis, and refrain from negative competition practices, such as dumping and cutthroat marketing. They must expend earnest and genuine efforts toward advancing the information industry and the information society. Given these intentions and commitments, Korea will surely enjoy all the successes and benefits of the new information age.

NOTE

1. The original acronym, CALS, reflects its origin in the U.S. Defense Department—Computer-aided Acquisition and Logistics System. CALS is now a worldwide, commercially oriented computer environment for interenterprise collaboration.

Part Five

CONCLUSION

Chapter Fifteen

THE NEXT STAGE
The Road to an Innovation-Led Korea

Lewis M. Branscomb and Young-Hwan Choi

The technocratic idea that all socioeconomic problems could be solved by a "scientific and technological fix" is both unrealistic and inappropriate. Korean society and the economy that supports it enjoy many strengths and face many challenges that lie outside the sphere of innovation and science. However, it is generally accepted in industrialized societies that science-based technology and technology-induced innovation will drive tomorrow's industrial competitiveness. In the process, they improve the quality of people's lives and make a nation more secure. The effectiveness with which the national system of innovation supports industrial productivity and growth is now accepted by economists and scholars in other disciplines.[1]

Needless to say, science and technology (S&T) are never ends in themselves, except in a purely cultural context. Scientific and technological capabilities, however, strongly determine a nation's capacity for socioeconomic development, particularly in highly educated but natural resource–poor countries. The capacity for technological innovation is a manifestation of a society's culture and values. But to be effective instruments of development, scientific and technological activities must have the capacity to induce or enable innovations in a broad sense, including sociocultural innovations. Accordingly, S&T

policy should focus not only on the promotions of S&T, per se, but on how they can induce, generate, adapt, and diffuse innovations. Furthermore, S&T policy must be integrated into a comprehensive structural policy.

For the past three decades, Korea has undertaken a modernization process, which can be depicted as the first stage in its industrialization. Together with the emergence of civilian-led democracy in the political arena, Korea's current level of industrial and sociopolitical development offers the base from which the next stage of development can be launched. However, internally, there are still many structural problems in socioeconomic areas—inadequately competitive industries, excessive concentration of economic power, regional imbalances, environmental degradation, and a still immature democratic political system.

Externally, Korea faces fierce international competition, the proliferation of regional economic blocs, intensified protection of intellectual property rights by advanced countries, and international regulation of environmental pollution. Korea's security situation is still perilous, despite the prospect of rapprochement with North Korea. And should that rapprochement be realized, there remain serious economic costs of reunification.

The emergence of a new, global economic and technological order offers special challenges as well as opportunities for the newly industrializing economies. They are expected to adhere to the policies of the leading economies even before they have become fully competitive. Challenged by domestic problems and surrounded by rapidly changing global environments, Korea faces a serious test in its transition toward the next stage in its development.

In order to enter that next stage, Korea needs a new science, technology, and innovation policy. Having mastered the ability to import and absorb advanced technology and to address world markets, the task is to internalize the ability to generate its own technology and create its own product, process, and market innovations. By incorporating science, technology, and innovation policies into a total system of economic, social, environmental, and national security–related policies, "a wave of innovation" could spread into all national sectors. For the industrial sector, an innovation-driven strategy is required. At the national level, an innovation-driven industrial policy must be accompanied by investments in the scientific and technological infrastructure of both public and private sectors.

Both public and private investments in science, technology, and innovation are driven by important national goals—economic growth, quality of life, environmental protection, and national security. Without national goals and a shared vision of the future, there is no basis for choosing policies for science, technology, and innovation that will be appropriate for the years ahead. How should those goals be reflected in the level and priority of investments in research and development (R&D) and in organizational arrangements?

The government has been, and still is, largely responsible for setting national goals, including those to be pursued through science, technology, and innovation policy. As the private economy strengthens and democratic political processes take hold, the government must evolve to express a national consensus on goals rather than directing them. To be sure, progress in science and engineering is critically dependent on creative individuals and even on serendipity. Discoveries cannot be produced on demand, and the system of relationships between technical creativity and successful commercialization and translation of innovations into public and private goods requires artful and careful management. Even in this circumstance, however, the vision and leadership of government is essential.

The Kim Young-Sam government's national goal, symbolized by striving to reach G-7 (Group of Seven) levels in certain fields by the year 2000, entails the construction of a "New Korea." The strategy is to develop fourteen strategic technologies to the level of the most advanced countries. Technologies in agriculture, environment, health, energy, and construction are to be raised to world levels. In fields of basic science, the strategy calls for Koreans to produce 30,000 research papers that meet international standards each year. These goals are impressive, indeed, audacious in the extreme. However, having such goals is not enough to assure their realization. Nor does reaching them assure the realization of the benefits that they are intended to bring. In this G-7 policy, the relationship between achieving such goals and the construction of a "New Korea" has not been fully explicated.

The organized deployment of talented people in effective public and private institutions, utilizing the enormous body of world knowledge to which Koreans have access, can yield a resilient, sustainable, and competitive economy, a higher quality of life, and personal and national security. But how should Korean investments be deployed to create new knowledge through advanced research and education? A consensus-based framework relating societal goals and research resource allocation is needed.

We propose establishing a National Forum on scientific and technological goals, uniting representatives of the scientific and technological community with others from many fields who are interested in aspects of society that depend on S&T activities. These goals should not be trivialized by numerical targets such as 30,000 published papers in science. They should address the core technical capabilities, the incentives for innovation, and the aspirations for scientific knowledge and trained people that Korea will require. By establishing a national consensus on goals for research and innovation, available resources and national energies could be mobilized to secure the foundation for building a New Korea. The precursor to this forum might be the creation, as recommended by the Organization for Economic Cooperation and Development (OECD) examiners of Korean S&T policy in December 1995, of a high-level Science and Engineering Advisory Committee. Subordinated to the highest authorities in charge of S&T policy formulation, it should evaluate Korea's science and engineering research capabilities and opportunities and guide the allocation of resources to the research universities.[2]

Many nations are debating the best method for achieving growth through scientific and technological innovation. In Japan, the United Kingdom, and Germany, panels of experts and Delphi surveys of the scientific community are being used to identify the most promising research directions for achieving economic goals of high priority.[3] In the United States, the suggestion has been made that a forum of the kind we suggest should be organized.[4] It would have to make explicit not only the kinds of research that might contribute to important goals but also the mechanisms for using research to accomplish these goals. Its greatest benefit might be the sense of shared commitment from all sectors of the S&T community.

Which of the national technology strategies identified by Henry Ergas and discussed in Chapter 12 would be most appropriate for Korea?[5] It appears that neither the mission-oriented policies of the United States, the United Kingdom, and France nor the diffusion-based strategies of Germany, Switzerland, and Sweden are fully appropriate. Korea's unique situation requires a hybrid strategy, because its scientific and technological capabilities exhibit a dualistic structure. Some technological sectors, such as the chaebols, have reached an advanced level, while still being dependent on imported technology. In 1992, the top twenty companies spent 1.8 trillion won on R&D, fully 50 percent of the industrial R&D and 36 percent of all the R&D in Korea. Small and medium enterprises (SMEs), by contrast, lag far behind. As noted in Chapter 10, Taiwan enjoys a much more robust small- to medium-size entrepreneurial industry sector than does Korea. As a result of the Korean policy of concentrating capital in the chaebols, impressively high levels of technological performance have been realized at the high cost of using imported technology and equipment. Licenses for imported technology in 1991 still consumed some 12 percent of sales in the electronics industry, up from 3 percent in the 1970s.[6]

In order to deepen an otherwise shallow technological economy, Korea must adopt an enabling or capability-enhancing policy—one that does not direct or control entrepreneurship but creates conditions within which firms, especially the smaller, independent ones, can flower on their own initiatives. Human resource investments are a particularly important part of such a strategy. In addition, Korean research organizations, both in public and private sectors, must become more self-sufficient. They need to generate indigenous discoveries and inventions to increase the value added in the Korean economy and gradually wean industry away from its past excessive dependence on imported technology. Spin-offs of high-technology firms from the government-funded research institutes, already demonstrated by the Electronics and Telecommunications Research Institute (ETRI), should be encouraged.

In other words, Korea should first follow a "diffusion-oriented" policy that places priority on developing human resources, building the basic research capacity, and forming linkages among academic laboratories, government-funded institutes, and firms of all sizes. At the same time, Korea should harmonize this diffusion-oriented policy with an emphasis on rapid technological evolution toward chosen strategic goals. Some areas of technology, such as information infrastructure, still require concerted national investment (see Chapter 14). Korea should continue to minimize risk and uncertainty by following the leading performers in the world market, seeking to add unique value and establish Korean brand names for products in established world markets.

We thus recommend a reactive, diffusion-based strategy. In areas where proactive strategy is appropriate, such as defense of Korea's strong dynamic random access memory (DRAM) exports, Korea should invest in base technology to protect its leading role in the world market. Another example is Korea's entry into the regional air transport industry, where an opportunity exists for a major market in China. Through this selective specialization strategy, Korea's limited resources would be directed toward certain areas in which Korea has the potential to gain a comparative advantage. This part of Korea's technology strategy is more mission oriented.

To implement such a hybrid strategy successfully, Korea must have a continuing, objective, and accurate assessment of its competitive strengths in S&T. Given the political significance of such assessments, the required objectivity may be hard to achieve. It is, however, absolutely essential. To this end, government-funded policy analysis institutes such as the Science and Technology Policy Institute (STEPI) are a major asset, especially if the independence of their analyses and judgments is respected. Balancing their access to senior levels of government with their need for independence will be very important. Korea does not have a long tradition of tolerance for bearers of unwelcome news, even when it rests on rigorous analysis.

The globalization of both economic and technological activities offers important opportunities to Korea. External resources such as labor, goods and services, capital, information, and technologies move more freely across national boundaries than previously. This trend is fueled by accelerated evolution of information and transportation technologies and by the global diffusion of both economic and intellectual assets in increasingly open markets. Perhaps the most striking trend in the leading industrial nations today is the expansion of outsourcing of innovations. Firms are accelerating product cycles, gaining access to unique skills and tacit knowledge, and narrowing the scope of their internal investments in R&D in order to ensure a high level of technical competitiveness in their core competencies.[7]

Korea is in a good position to utilize external resources for its own science, technology, and innovation. As Denis Fred Simon and Changrok Soh point out (see Chapter 13), Korea can broaden its external relations beyond its previously subordinate position to Japanese and U.S. multinationals. However, the ability to capture scientific and technological assets in world markets requires a command of sufficiently unique technologies domestically to be able to make mutually beneficial exchanges. As Korea's economic competitiveness approaches that of its G-7 rivals, firms in those countries will be increasingly reluctant to sell technology for money; they will look for equivalent value in Korean technology.

With this premise, Korea should leverage its limited domestic resources by seeking the following:[8]

- Strategic alliances, joint R&D programs, and participation in multilateral projects with both large and small firms in other nations
- Establishment of Korean subsidiaries and joint ventures in offshore markets
- R&D investments into overseas firms and research institutes
- Employment of foreign scientists and engineers, while continuing overseas training of Korean experts
- Gaining the trust of firms and governments in other nations concerning the openness of the Korean market and the security of their intellectual property in Korea.

In order to support this global approach, the Korean government should conduct a comprehensive review of all relevant laws, regulations, and policies and overhaul them as needed.

Thus, Korea must adopt a "multichannel knowledge acquisition" approach, through which Korea can obtain as much technological information from external sources as possible. To do so, it will need a very strong domestic capability in S&T to identify and assess the value of the technologies to be acquired, to be able to absorb them, and to generate the Korean innovations through which world knowledge can be leveraged.

Korea's most important asset is the quality of its workforce and the dedication of its people to education. According to STEPI's forecast, by the year 2001 the total demand for scientific and technological personnel—university graduates and above—will reach 438,000 people, whereas the current supply capacity can produce 387,000 scientists and engineers, leaving an estimate shortage of 51,000. Although no forecast exists for the technicians and skilled workers, they are also expected to be in short supply. It is noteworthy that Japan already faces critical shortages of technically trained people, despite its very extensive network of universities and its particularly strong capacity for training engineers. The anticipated worsening of the human resource gap can be ascribed to two main factors: insufficient and inappropriate investments by successive governments during the last three decades and to a university system that, while excellent in many ways, pays inadequate attention to engineering, technology, and the more practical and experimental disciplines.

Looking at the human resources for conducting research, there are currently 132,000 scientists and engineers in Korea, a small number compared to other advanced countries. Furthermore, the ratio of researchers to every 10,000 of the general population was only 17.6 people as of 1991, less than half the ratio found in the United States and Japan, and less than that in Germany and France.[9] Accordingly, the Korean government has set a target of 32 researchers to every 10,000 of the general population and has been undertaking several measures to reach this target:

- Increasing the universities' and graduate schools' student quotas for the fields of S&T.
- Actively promoting the Korea Advanced Institute of Science and Technology (KAIST) and establishing an additional KAIST in Kwangjoo City.
- Expanding the involvement of government-funded research institutes in graduate education and research.
- Repatriating additional Korean scientists and engineers from abroad and inviting leading foreign scientists and engineers to Korea.
- Supporting science research centers and engineering research centers in universities, and promoting "within-firm" graduate programs in areas such as industrial technology.
- Creating a government structure that provides full ministerial accountability for the contribution higher education can make to Korea's innovation-based development strategy. As suggested earlier in this chapter, Korea could broaden the responsibility of the Ministry of Science and Technology (MOST) to include higher education.

Korea has a robust numerical output of scientists and engineers with advanced degrees (Table 15.1). The number of doctoral degrees awarded to Koreans is quite competitive with the numbers in Japan (Table 15.2). However, as discussed in Chapter 10, the quality education of research people is highly concentrated in two institutions—KAIST and Seoul National University. Some 38.4 percent of articles published by Korean authors in international journals originate in these two universities.[10] Korea particularly needs to upgrade the quality and creativity of the scientists who are responsible for the upstream of the innovation cycle; its field engineers, technicians, and its skilled workers, who will be in charge of the downstream phases; and finally,

Table 15.1
Ph.D.'s in Science and Technology in Korea, 1995

Institution	Science	Engineering	Total	Subtotal
KAIST	56	252	308	
Seoul National University	119	202	321	
Other	472	671	1143	1,772
In U.S. Universities			490	
In Europe or Japan			100	2,362

Data presented by Duk-Yong Yoon, President of KAIST, Third United States–Korea Science and Technology Forum, Washington, D.C., December 12–13, 1995 (Arlington, Va.: Center for Science, Trade, and Technology Policy, 1996),57–59.

Table 15.2
Ph.D. Degrees Awarded in Science and Technology, 1994

Nation	Science	Engineering	Total
U.S.	8,800	6,000	14,800
Japan	730	1,140	1,844
Korea (1995)	647	1,125	1,772

Data presented by Duk Yong Yoon, President of KAIST, Third United States–Korea Science and Technology Forum, Washington, D.C., December 12–13, 1995 (Arlington, Va.: Center for Science, Trade, and Technology Policy, 1996),57–59.

its innovation-oriented entrepreneurs, who will manage and integrate each phase of the innovation cycle (see Chapter 10).

We have noted that government underinvests in university research. Breaking down the R&D expenditures by institutional sectors, universities accounted for only 6.9 percent, while research institutes received 29.8 percent and industry accepted 71.3 percent. These figures clearly indicate that R&D in Korean universities receives only one-fourth of the support given to Korean research institutes, while in the United States, their R&D expenditures are about equal. This demonstrates the modest role universities play in Korean R&D, both in relationship to national research institutes and as a fraction of the total R&D effort.[11] Since universities have an effective means of transferring new technical knowledge to industry (through the industrial employment of the university's graduates), serious consideration should be given to shifting more of the government research investment from institutes to universities.

The underutilization of universities is aggravated by the fact that the Ministry of Education (MOE), which has vast responsibilities for universal education at all levels, does not give sufficient attention to developing postgraduate education in science and engineering and stimulating research in universities. The impressive capabilities of KAIST, which is operated by MOST, is an indication of what could be accomplished by shifting responsibilities in the ministries and devoting additional resources to higher education in science and engineering. The present government should endeavor, to its utmost, to remedy this deteriorating situation.

As another reform measure, government control and intervention in the administration of universities should be minimized; an objective accreditation system should be employed in its place. By using a performance-based accreditation system, universities with better track records will be granted more intensive support from the government. A core number of research universities should be identified, and competition between them should be encouraged.

To expand the supply of skilled workers, the government has been supporting both public and on-the-job vocational training, increasing the number of vocational training instructors, and running national skill-test and qualification systems. Despite these efforts, it is doubtful that the quantitative and qualitative requirements will be met. At primary and secondary schools, the number and quality of teachers, equipment, facilities, and curricula are very poor.

The most important factor in the human resource structure is brainpower. Special measures should be devised to ensure that a certain percentage of Korean students will be able to compete against the best students in the world. One possible measure is to promote intensively the Special English Science and Technology Educational System, in which talented students will go through Science High Schools, the Korea Institute of Technology (a university), and KAIST (a graduate school).

The emphasis in vocational training should be shifted from public to intra-industry training. Several nations have found effective incentives to induce employers to provide skill-enhancing training to their employees. In France, for example, there is a payroll tax which is forgiven if the firm spends the equivalent amount on employee training. The tax revenues are then used to provide training for workers of firms that do not provide such training.

Science education at primary and secondary school levels should be drastically improved because it is the foundation for the development of all scientists and engineers. Special emphasis should be given to helping students develop their creativity and interest in S&T at an early stage in their education. Young Korean women should especially be encouraged to study mathematics and science. Korea, which has a much smaller number of women in the technical workforce than most of its competitor nations, could almost double the number of highly intelligent specialists by including as many young women as young men.

To remedy this situation, the Korean government should create a comprehensive and workable blueprint for national S&T human resource development, including an overall forecast for projected demand in all categories of S&T.

The Korean government currently levies a special tax for education. It has not fulfilled its intended function because the revenue generated from this tax has been incorporated into the general education budget. This special tax for education should be restructured to meet its original purpose, or a new special tax for S&T should be established, and a substantial percentage of its total revenue should be allocated to the development and strategic deployment of scientific and technical personnel.

EXPANDING R&D INVESTMENTS AND MAXIMIZING THEIR EFFECTIVENESS

As noted in Chapter 1, Korea's national S&T investment (by both government and the private sector) has been increasing rapidly since 1980. By 1991, total R&D investment amounted to U.S.$5.45 billion, which is 2.02 percent of the gross national product (GNP). This amount is a tenfold increase from U.S.$0.54 billion in 1981. The Korean government anticipates that Korean expenditures on R&D, public and private, will grow at an astonishing 25 to 30 percent per year, at least until the year 2000.[12]

Let us look at 1991 as an example of Korea's characteristic pattern of investments. Only 20 percent of total R&D investment in Korea came from the government, compared to 17 percent for Japan. The private sector thus accounts for the great majority of total R&D expenditures, unlike the cases of other countries such as the United States (43%), West Germany (34%), France (69%), and Taiwan (46%).[13] From an economic perspective, this private-sector commitment is healthy, but it is far too concentrated in the largest firms. The five largest firms accounted for 33.2 percent of total R&D investment, the top ten firms provided 41.7 percent, and the top 20 firms accounted for 51.2 percent. These figures indicate that R&D investments in Korea are concentrated in the large conglomerates, while small- and medium-size firms have very weak R&D activities (see Chapters 3 and 4).

While Korea's R&D/GDP (gross domestic product) ratios are close to those of the advanced nations, this is deceptive because of the unusually high fraction of the Korean economy devoted to manufacturing. Looking at R&D expenditures as a percentage of sales by manufacturing industries, Korea was 2.02 percent, while the United States was 4.6 percent (1990), Japan was 3.47 percent (1990), and West Germany was 4.5 percent (1988). This shows that Korean manufacturing industries, on average, are underinvesting in R&D compared to the same industries in the other advanced countries. It is unlikely that Korea can expand its capacity for indigenous innovation without substantially higher investments.

Government also underinvests in university research. Looking at R&D expenditures by category, basic research received 14.9 percent of the funding, applied research received 30.7 percent, and development research accounted 54.44 percent of spending. Breaking down the R&D expenditures by institutional sectors, universities accounted for 6.9 percent; research institutes, 29.8 percent; and industry, 71.3 percent. These figures clearly indicate the modest role that universities play in Korean R&D, both in relationship to national research institutes and as a fraction of the total R&D effort.[14] Since universities have an effective means of transferring new technical knowledge to industry (through the industrial employment of the university's graduates), serious consideration should be given to shifting more of the government research investment from institutes to universities.

Finally, it should be noted that Korea's dramatic growth in R&D is relatively recent, dating back to the 1980s. As Dieter Ernst points out, "In 1985 . . . there were 5,249 persons engaged in R&D in the electronics industry, and this accounted for 32 percent of the researchers in all Korean industry. By 1990 this number had risen to 12,865 and accounted for 37 percent of total R&D personnel in Korean industry. A year later there were 15,923 . . ., 41 percent of total R&D personnel in industry."[15]

Thus, substantial R&D investments are very recent and have increasingly been concentrated among the chaebols and in a few industry sectors. Ernst points out that this R&D has led to only a limited growth of domestic sourcing of parts and components. This means that the takeoff in the sector that should be the most innovative—the high-technology and science-based SMEs—has not yet started.

The Kim Young-Sam government has set an objective to increase S&T investment to 3 to 4 percent of the GNP by 1998, which implies reaching 5 percent of the GNP by the year 2001. It has been making considerable efforts to meet these goals, which had been set by the preceding government. Some observers have expressed doubt and skepticism about the feasibility of this ambitious target. Even if Korea reaches its 5 percent target by 2001, this would only equal West Germany's absolute R&D investment level of 1985 and the Japanese investment level of 1983. An enormous gap in cumulated R&D investments exists between Korea and other advanced countries. In fact, the 5 percent of the GNP target is exceptionally ambitious. No other country has set such high objectives.

How could Korea's target level of R&D investment be reached? There could be shifts of R&D expenditures out of the national defense budget; that budget could be increasingly directed at dual-use technologies. Increased investments in R&D could also come from financial investment and loan special accounts. The current government has been undertaking such measures. However, these steps will not be sufficient. The most difficult part of achieving the 5 percent objective will, of course, be the growth required in private investment in R&D (and balancing the supply of technical human resources). Because of the current concentration of R&D in the chaebols, vigorous and effective policies must be implemented to encourage new firm creation. To help develop start-ups, the government should work to lower the risks of venture capital investments and make those risks more tolerable. It should also provide the large conglomerates with incentives to encourage innovation in smaller firms and offer these firms protection from predatory business practices. In any case, progress toward this goal must be gradual, since firms must create enough of their own technology to reduce expenditures on foreign licenses and important tools and instruments. Only at this point will companies have the funds to dramatically increase their R&D.

Encouraging Innovation and Risk Taking

Technological-innovation activities involve high risks and constant uncertainty; innovation policy should thus foster an environment conducive to risk taking, while minimizing uncertainty. The Korean government has been examining a number of supportive and incentive systems. Of particular importance in motivating industry for technological innovation are the following:

- Making the rate of return from technological innovation much more favorable than return from other investments (such as real estate)
- Improving the prospects for marketing the results of technological innovation, especially when offered by SMEs
- Providing more favorable financing from a restructured banking sector and from equity markets that can gain the public's confidence

A joint task force of government, industry, and academia should prepare for the National Innovation Council an evaluation of policies in areas such as taxation, banking, government procurement, standardization, the fair trade and antimonopoly system, safety and pollution regulation, and other matters related to enhanced technological innovation.

If the risk/reward equation is right, competition creates the conditions most conducive to technological innovation. When entrepreneurship can be displayed in freely competitive environments, intensive technological innovation takes place.

The Kim Young-Sam government has been working toward deregulation for creating competition among industry. However, many complaints are heard from the private sector. The government, therefore, should continue to eliminate all unnecessary regulatory activities so that effective competition conducive to technological innovation can be diffused under the fair "rule of games."

Externally, under the new World Trade Organization system and rapid globalization process, Korea should not only open its domestic market legally but make Korea "FDI friendly." This should result in a high influx of foreign competition into the domestic market. Using this influx as an opportunity, Korea could build momentum for strengthening of industrial competitiveness by concentrating its energies on technological-innovation activities. Since Korea has limited resources, fostering cooperation is equally important as competition. Korea should not overlook the fact that many other advanced countries, including the United States, have recently promoted "Cooperative R&D Programs," such as R&D consortia, more actively through legislation.[16]

Competition and cooperation should be harmonized to expedite the technological innovation. In the precompetitive stage, and for the basic, generic, or public technologies, the principle of cooperation should be applied. In the competition stage, and for the proprietary technologies, the principle of competition under fair rules should be used.

Up to the present, the importance of cooperation between industry and academia has been much emphasized by all sectors of Korean society. Despite the existence of an "Industrial Technology Cooperative R&D Consortium System," industry–academia and interfirm cooperation have been less active than expected. Many reasons could explain this, but mutual distrust seems to be a significant impediment. Government should provide incentives for major institutional actors like firms, universities, and research institutes to cooperate—vertically or horizontally—in risk sharing, resource complementarity, and mutual creativity.

To profit from technological innovation, high rates of productivity must be achieved. This requires enhancing institutional flexibility to expedite the flow of information and the exchange of ideas and to allow personal initiative to take root in a decentralized environment. Thus, government should maximize autonomy through deregulation, while establishing the physical and information service infrastructure to support efficiency.

The "information revolution" is like a new industrial revolution for this and the next century. If Korea fails to ride this "information wave," it will lag behind other countries, as other countries suffered during the first Industrial Revolution in the eighteenth and nineteenth centuries. Therefore, Korea must give top priority to promoting the information infrastructure and boosting the information industries as the leading sector in the economy.

The realization of high innovation rates depends on effective and rapid diffusion of technical knowledge between firms, institutes, and university laboratories. In every advanced country, information infrastructure is seen as a way to lower transaction costs, allow more decentralization of decision making, and to put more decisions into the hands of individuals. Its importance has been clearly seen by the Kim Young-Sam government (described in Chapter 14), which has integrated activities from a number of ministries to create a Ministry of Information and Communications (MIC) as the driver of the national information infrastructure.

To exploit the advantages of decentralized decision making, however, requires that decision makers be free to take the necessary risks while remaining accountable for their decisions. The tendency in bureaucracies to second-guess subordinates after risk taking has failed can nullify the advantages offered by decentralization and local empowerment. Korea has only recently begun to move politically in that direction, while still faced with a highly centralized industrial structure. The nation must pay especially close attention to this bureaucratic danger.

Technological innovation flourishes on fertile social "soil." National energies can be fully directed into science, technology, and innovation when the entire society understands, appreciates, and respects these activities. Results will follow when entrepreneurs are innovation oriented, scientists and engineers are enthusiastic, and creative young students flock to science-related careers.

Sweden's extensive involvement with the Nobel Prizes illustrates how a country can foster interest in S&T. The king and queen gather annually with cabinet members and representatives from industry, academia, and research institutes to review the previous year's science-, technology-, and innovation-related activities. After examining the prospects of these achievements for contributing to future welfare, the king recognizes the most outstanding achievements by awarding the coveted Nobel medals during ceremonies that convey deep interest and appreciation for the laureates. The media in Sweden generally treat science-, technology-, and innovation-related stories as high-priority items. Such events make Sweden's social atmosphere very conducive to science, technology, and innovation.

Korea's social atmosphere at present is excessively focused on politics; it should focus on innovation and creativity. Government leaders and political circles can redirect national attention, as can the media and opinion makers. Occasions must be created for leaders from all sectors of society to appreciate Korean scientific and technical achievements and encourage greater efforts (see Chapter 6).

Many stories exist about foreign firms that have pursued business alliances with Korean firms or have sought to establish businesses in Korea, often with difficult and unrewarding results. Such perceptions are to be expected whenever there are great cultural differences; and Korean firms, no doubt, experience similar difficulties when conducting business in North America or Europe. Regardless of whether such perceptions are justified, Korean firms will find it difficult to implement their globalization strategy until these perceptions are dispelled.

Western businesspeople working with Korea (as well as Japan) often complain that when the formal public policy treats local and foreign-owned firms equally, the administrative bureaucracy interprets regulations to favor locally owned firms. Foreign firms also express concern about the security of their intellectual property. In addition, they complain that Korean business negotiators have difficulty accepting terms that do not give the Korean partner an evident advantage, fearing future criticism by higher levels of management for making too weak a bargain.

Such concerns by foreign businesses have been addressed by Marion Paul Pina, Jr., who finds evidence that these conditions are rapidly improving, particularly in the protection of intellectual property.[17] Pina also cautions foreigners to understand Korean customs, such as the way that legal obligations in contracts are understood. He concludes that "Korea is a very difficult place to do business. However, the areas of difficulty can be reduced by rethinking misperceptions and out-of-date perceptions and by working around unchangeable characteristics."

Because of these perceptions, Koreans should take seriously the importance of developing the "social capital" that, according to independent scholars, has enabled the smaller nations of Europe that compete with Korea to succeed (see Chapter 11). To quote Hyung-Sup Choi, "Our efforts must be bent toward achieving that 'small but advanced' type of development which is exemplified by such European countries as Switzerland, Belgium, the Netherlands, Denmark, and Sweden."[18] The long-accumulated social capital of Europe has defined the ability of these nations to create and reproduce human and physical capital. The concept of social capital covers not only institutional arrangements but also tacit norms of obligation, conduct, and reciprocity that guide the myriad transactions. Social capital is reflected in low transaction costs and in efficient utilization of both physical and human capital. The development of these practices, policies, and institutional arrangements may well be the rate-limiting factor in Korean development.

How can Koreans ensure that "political power" gives proper attention to science, technology, and innovation, while allowing market forces and technical creativity to flourish with the necessary autonomy? The role of the president in Korea is absolutely crucial for science-, technology-, and innovation-based policy. The president wields pervasive influence over all policy agendas. The long history of hierarchical "top-down" political culture led to the adoption of a strong presidential system of government that can now be used to encourage science, technology, and innovation. The office can (1) promote innovation policy vigorously in both public and private settings; (2) give high financial priority to science, technology, and innovation; (3) appoint extremely qualified and influential technical experts and entrepreneurial managers to key government posts; and (4) keep them in their jobs long enough to be accountable for concrete results. A revolving door of Ministers of Science and Technology, with average terms of service of a little over one year, is a major barrier to the execution of policies for change. In this connection, the slogan of the current government should be changed from "reform," which implies corrective actions regarding past practices and structures, to "innovation," which has a future orientation and focuses on creation of new practices and structures.

The national assembly and the political parties should contribute more to science, technology, and innovation. Compared to other advanced countries, their contributions are still meager, although they recently have begun to express their concerns. Korean political parties should adopt comprehensive platforms on these issues. As the awareness level of the electorate increases, political parties that have sound platforms regarding science, technology, and innovation will surely receive greater support from the public. At the same time, they can serve the nation by mobilizing public awareness about the importance of the nation's technical and innovative capacities.

The national assembly has a Standing Committee on Communication, Science, and Technology that concerns itself exclusively with the functions of MIC and MOST. This committee is hardly sufficient for the promotion of science-, technology-, and innovation-priority policy as it affects the entire nation. A Special Committee on Science, Technology, and Innovation should enhance the nation's capacity to develop and diffuse S&T-based innovation quite broadly. The function of this new committee should not be defined by ministerial jurisdiction. Instead, it should deliberate, assess, and support all activities related to science, technology, and innovation of the administration, as the Special Committee on Budget functions regarding all fiscal issues.

Since the national assembly has few members with technical backgrounds, a specialized organization that can assist the national assembly on science, technology, and innovation issues may be needed. Despite its recent demise at the hands of radical conservatives in the U.S. Congress, the Congressional Office of Technology Assessment offers an attractive model.

A nation's administrative structure for science, technology, and innovation is determined by its political, cultural, and socioeconomic environment, national goals, and scales of available resources. According to the OECD's analyses, there are four types of administrative structures related to science, technology, and innovation:

1. "Pluralist System." Each ministry or agency performs its respective S&T activities according to their individual institutional missions and priorities, with relatively weak central coordination.

2. "Centralist System." A central ministry or agency is responsible for all important functions involved in science, technology, and innovation.

3. "Coordination System." Each ministry or agency performs its individual technical functions under the direction of a central administrative body that is responsible for overall coordination of activities of all ministries and agencies.

4. "Concerted Action System." Every ministry or agency performs its individual functions related to science, technology, and innovation. One ministry serves as the "lead agency," specializing in common, interdisciplinary, and strategic areas, and maintains responsibility for overall coordination of all other ministries and agencies.

The Korean government structure belongs to this concerted action system. One specialized organization (MOST) serves as the focal point, while many other ministries have substantial S&T responsibilities and resources. Its dual role—carrying out its own operations and policies while coordinating programs—has its origin in MOST's original position in the Economic Planning Board. It is difficult for MOST to coordinate the policies and activities of other ministries and agencies because of the lack of workable institutional mechanisms and its relatively weak position. This problem is not unique to Korea; the U.S. Congress established the National Science Foundation as the lead agency in a concerted action system, but political realities have brought the U.S. system to the coordination system. Additional large-scale administrative problems in Korea include interministerial competition over scope of authority and the failure of some ministries to attend to their necessary S&T activities.

The optimal administrative system for science, technology, and innovation has been strongly debated. Among the various alternatives are the following:

1. The position of Minister of Science and Technology could be elevated to the level of Senior Minister and chair of the National Council for Science and Technology, if he or she could be given sufficient authority to make this body truly effective.

2. MOST could be regrouped into a policy and planning activity board within the Ministry of Finance and the Economy (MOFE), perhaps called the "Economy, Science, and Technology Planning Board." This approach might help integrate technology policy with economic policy.

3. MOST could be combined with the Ministry of Trade, Industry, and Energy (MOTIE) to create a powerful Ministry of Commerce, Industry, and Technology, which might be sufficiently strong to effectively exercise its policy-making and program-coordination functions.

4. The policy functions of MOST could be split from its operational functions and either elevated to Deputy Prime Minister status (as stated in point #1) or combined into a policy-planning function within MOFE (as in point #2). The operational functions of MOST would then remain where they are. Alternatively, they could be combined with MOTIE or perhaps with MOE to form a Ministry of Education and Science.

5. The presidential office could include a Special Science Advisor or a Senior Secretary of Science and Technology. (At present, the Senior Secretary of the Economy is in charge of S&T, in addition to his regular responsibilities for overall economic affairs. He has a staff officer for S&T, but that officer occupies one of about forty such positions in the Blue House.)

All these proposed alternatives are based on their own theoretical grounds. Similar proposals are offered in the report of the expert examiners from the OECD. Alternative #5 is the most effective mechanism to couple the power of the presidency to the bureaucracy. However, it is not surprising that the bureaucracy's defenses against this level of centralization of authority over government S&T policy is strong. On April 22, 1993, the press carried a story of President Kim Young-Sam's announcement, one day after meeting with top scientists and engineers, that the government was "studying the formation of a new Special Science Advisor in the President's Office."[19] As a result of opposition from MOST and the Ministry of Finance and Economy, both of which would lose some freedom of action under the proposal, the idea lapsed.

Alternative #4, which is compatible with any of the other four proposals, might be the most politically workable way to get additional presidential attention to S&T coordination, although it would probably be less effective than the appointment of a Secretariat for S&T in the Blue House. However, even this more modest amalgamation of existing organizations is politically difficult and potentially disruptive to the very activities we seek to energize and promote. Each organization has its own idiosyncrasies and a vested interest in maintaining an independent existence.

The government should, therefore, devise interim, achievable steps. For example, it could establish a "National Innovation Council" under the chairmanship of the president, as is the case with the National Security Council. This council would be based on the premise that science, technology, and innovation must be considered equal in strategic importance to national security. The Vice Chairman of the National Innovation Council could be the current

Chairman of the National Science and Technology Council, which would continue to coordinate ministerial activities in S&T while attracting much closer attention from the president.

The other members could include the Senior Secretary of the Economy and Ministers with major S&T portfolios—Science and Technology, Industry, Technology and Energy, Information and Communications, Finance and the Economy, Transportation, Agriculture, and Defense—together with the Chair of the President's Council on Science and Technology and a smaller number of top representatives from industry, academia, and research institutes. The current Senior Secretary of the Economy to the President could serve as the general secretary of the National Innovation Council.

It should be noted that Japan has had such a structure for many years (see Chapter 9) and the United States created such a body in 1993. This group, the National Science and Technology Council, is chaired by President Bill Clinton. Vice President Al Gore, who has the responsibility for coordinating S&T policy in the White House, serves as vice chairman. This body is designed to compensate for the highly decentralized management of scientific and technological activities in the U.S. federal government.

The functions of a Korean National Innovation Council could be (1) making metapolicy on science, technology, and innovation, such as setting national goals for S&T, creating basic policy directions and strategies, mobilizing and prioritizing financial resources, renovating S&T education, and the like; (2) providing overall coordination of important policies and programs of related ministries and other organizations; (3) encouraging less active ministries and organizations; and (4) carrying out other important policy measures. A strong staff function is needed to support the council's work; this staff should report to the general secretary of the council.

The National Innovation Council could be convened by the president at least two times a year and whenever necessary. The decisions made by the National Innovation Council would be fully respected by all relevant organizations and officials because the president himself would have endorsed all the decisions. The National Innovation Council system would thus embody, both symbolically and practically, all policy on priorities in science, technology, and innovation in Korea.

How might the ministerial structure be modernized? Table 15.3 indicates the R&D expenditures and funds devoted to total government investments in R&D in each ministry.

MOTIE is shifting from prescriptive policies of regulation and subsidy for targeted industries to enabling investments in base technology—an area that MOST has been active in for more than twenty years. MOST is moving toward setting a high standard for both scientific research and higher education in S&T, thus entering an area over which MOE has cognizance. MOE, in contrast, is heavily engaged in reforming the system of public education,

Table 15.3
Korean Government R&D Budgets

Ministry	1993 Budget	1993 Percentage	1994 Budget	1994 Percentage	1995 Budget	1995 Percentage
MOST	575.7	40.0	677.2	34.5	835.1	34.4
MOTIE	156.9	10.9	242.2	12.4	364.7	15.0
MIC[a]	12.9	0.9	14.9	0.8	14.6	0.6
MOE	64.7	4.5	224.7	11.5	290.1	11.9
Defense	339.9	23.6	412.8	21.1	446.7	17.1
Others[b]	290.9	20.1	388.9	19.7	509.7	21.0
Total	1,441.0	100.0	1,960.7	100.0	2,430.9	100.0

Source: Organization for Economic Cooperation and Development (OECD), *Review of National Science and Technology Policy* (Paris: OECD, 1995), Table 6, p. 49.
Note: Exchange rates, U.S.$/Korean won; 1993 = $1/808.1 won; 1994 = $1/778 won; September 1995 = $1/770 won.
[a] MIC's budget is mostly supported through Korean Telecom and appears mainly in national R&D programs.
[b] "Other" includes Environment, Health, Construction, and Agriculture.

seeking a cultural shift from rote learning to logical thinking and problem solving. While each ministry is moving swiftly to address new priorities, there are gaps and problems that better guidance from the center would have addressed. The Environment and Transportation Ministries need attention as key S&T ministries. Meanwhile, the Ministry of Defense is examining the merits of a "dual-use" technology strategy for defense acquisition, which would couple these R&D resources to the civilian industrial base. MIC is struggling to find how to meet its responsibilities of creating the nation's information infrastructure.

MOTIE is the right agency to invest in technological research to support the economy, especially as it affects SMEs. However, MOST's institutes have much of the technical talent that could manage such activities. Perhaps some of this technical talent should be transferred to MOTIE. MOST has done an excellent job in setting high standards for advanced research and education with its creation of KAIST, the Korea Science and Engineering Foundation, and the centers of excellence projects in universities. Neither MOST nor MOE, however, has taken financial responsibility for upgrading the quality and the resources of the top dozen research universities. MOST should be asked to accept broader responsibility than KAIST for building research quality in research universities, and it should then receive the full cooperation of MOE and resources from MOFE. This is one of the solutions suggested by the OECD examiners.[20] Alternatively, a Ministry of Higher Education could be created, as suggested in Chapter 7, combining some functions of both MOE and MOST.

In conclusion, we agree with the observation of Dieter Ernst, who notes that "the very same features of government policies and firm strategies and of the resulting industry structure that until the late 1980s were conducive for the rapid expansion of Korea's electronics exports now have become important constraints for attempts to sustain Korea's export performance through an upgrading of its technological capabilities. . . . In order to keep up with the new challenges of global competition, a shift is required to a process of technological deepening that involves strong product innovation capabilities, closer attention to client needs and the development of new markets. Strengthening the financial and technological capabilities of domestic small- to medium-sized enterprises (SMEs) is a second essential element of such a paradigm shift. Third, a selective liberalization of imports and inward FDI [Foreign Direct Investment] is essential for improving access to generic technologies and core components through closer participation in international networks."[21]

Thus, the diagnosis is easy. The OECD experts came to very similar conclusions. The real test will come with the nation's response. Korea continues to pursue a high-risk, high-growth strategy. The extent to which the chaebols are leveraged financially allows little room for failure at that level, which in some ways makes the government hostage to the chaebols' success. Yet, the changes required for Korea's future are rapid in pace, deep in scope, and broad in scale. They reach deep into the nation's culture and traditions. Such changes will not be as easy as the shifts that created many extraordinary achievements over the past three decades. On the other hand, the Korean people have astonished the world with their ability to dedicate themselves to a common purpose, especially in economic terms. The next generation of changes will be driven primarily by the science, technology, and innovation factor. Given the strong response that Koreans have always provided when called to rise to a new challenge, a New Korea will indeed emerge in the twenty-first century.

NOTES

1. Richard R. Nelson, *National Systems of Innovation: A Comparative Analysis* (New York: Oxford University Press, 1993). It should be noted that today no industrial innovation system is strictly national, since each nation is heavily dependent on the exchange of goods, technology, talent, and capital with other nations. The national system is intended to denote the combination of government and private institutions, enterprises, and policies that largely determine the capacity of the nation to compete in world markets and satisfy its economic needs.

2. Organization for Economic Cooperation and Development (OECD), *Reviews of National Science and Technology Policy: Korea* (Paris: OECD, December 1995).

3. In Japan, the Ministry of International Trade and Industry conducts a national Delphi study to determine the consensus views of the technical community on the most promising technologies that can contribute to economic and social goals. The United Kingdom initiated such a review in 1994, as did Germany. Setting research priorities, however, is only one link in the chain of innovation policy. More important are the processes that link technical creativity with successful commercialization.

4. Carnegie Commission on Science, Technology, and Government, *Enabling the Future: Linking S&T to Societal Goals* (New York: Carnegie Commission, 1992).

5. Henry Ergas, "Does Technology Policy Matter?" in *Technology and Global Industry: Companies and Nations in the World Economy*, ed. Bruce Guile and Harvey Brooks (Washington, D.C.: National Academy Press, 1987), 191–245.

6. Dieter Ernst, *What Are the Limits to the Korean Model? The Korean Electronics Industry under Pressure* (Berkeley, Calif.: Berkeley Roundtable on International Economics, June 1994), 60. Quote from Jin-Joo Lee in "The Status and Issue of Management Dynamism and Four Case Studies in the Republic of Korea," in *Management Dynamism: A Study of Selected Companies in Asia* (Tokyo: Asian Productivity Organization, 1991), 132, 139.

7. C. K. Prahalad and G. Hamel, "The Core Competencies of the Corporation," *Harvard Business Review* (May–June 1990).

8. See Chapter 6, which reports concerns, particularly among Japanese business leaders, about the ability of Korean partners to secure their proprietary technical knowledge.

9. In comparison, the United States had 38.4/10,000 (1991); Japan had 40.9/10,000 (1991); Germany had 28.5/10,000 (1989); and France had 20.5/10,000 (1990).

10. OECD, *Reviews of National Science and Technology.*

11. In the United States, which is famous for its government's generous support of its research universities, university R&D is about $20 billion out of a national R&D expenditure of $150 billion. At 13.3 percent, this is twice the Korean percentage. This U.S. investment, however, is heavily distorted by massive investments in health-related academic research.

12. The Honorable Kyong-Shik Kang, Member of the National Assembly of Korea, addressing the Third United States–Korea Science and Technology Forum, Washington, D.C., December 12–13, 1995. Remark repeated by the Honorable Bohn-Young Koo, Vice Minister of Science and Technology. To be published in conference proceedings.

13. However, if military R&D is deleted from the U.S. figures, only $40 billion out of some $150 billion comes from the government—a modest 27 percent.

14. See note 11.

15. Ernst, *What Are the Limits?*, 96.

16. The Cooperative R&D Act of 1984 in the United States provided immunity to triple damages in civil antitrust suits for groups of firms that register their plans for cooperative R&D with the Department of Justice. Many hundreds of such registrations have taken place in the United States, although they still represent a tiny fraction of all industrial R&D.

17. Marion Paul Pina, Jr., "The Changing Business Climate in Korea: Implications for American Firms," *Korea's Economy 1995*, vol. 11, ed. Korea Economic Institute Editorial Board (Seoul: Korea Economic Institute of America, 1995), 29–35.

18. Hyung-Sup Choi, "Industrial Development and Use of Technology," Keynote address at the POSCO Research Institute–RAND Corp. Conference on Technology Transfer under the WTO Regime, POSRI, Pohang, Korea, August 17, 1995.

19. *Daily Economic Newspaper*, Pohang, Korea, April 22, 1993.

20. OECD, *Review of National Science and Technology*, 17.

21. Ernst, *What Are the Limits?*, 5, 8–9.

GLOSSARY

APEC   Asia-Pacific Economic Cooperation forum; a regional economic consultative body

APII   Asia-Pacific Information Infrastructure; an organization providing regional cooperation for the development and transnational harmonization of a national information infrastructure in the Pacific region

Blue House   the executive offices of the President of the Republic of Korea

CALS   a U.S. defense department acronym for Computer-Aided Acquisition and Logistics System. CALS standards and processes allow OEMs and their supplier chains to share design, development, and production processes electronically. Used in civil commerce for enterprise integration, the acronym is nicknamed "commerce at light speed."

chaebol   industrial conglomerate, typically owned by one family, but usually highly leveraged with debt borrowed from the domestic banking sector. Because domestic banks, although nominally privatized, remain under the de facto control of the government, the chaebols are subject to government policy discretion. The formal government definition of a chaebol is any company group with more than 400 billion won in earnings ($50 million at 800 won to the dollar). In 1992, seventy-two chaebols met this definition.

Confucianism   a cultural and religious tradition that exerts profound influence in Korean life, even though only a minority of Koreans are active in its formal practice. Confucianism celebrates learning and the political participation of learned individuals, while disdaining technical, scientific, and merchant activities. Koreans widely debate the influence that Confucianism has on economic life.

DACOM   a privatized, value-added telecommunications carrier formed in 1984

Daeduk Science Town   a "technopolis" completed in 1992

EC   electronic commerce; also European Community, now usually referred to as European Union

EPB Economic Planning Board; now merged into the Ministry of Finance and the Economy. Before 1969, the science-and-technology policy responsibilities of MOST were imbedded in EPB as the Bureau of Technological Management.

ERCs engineering research centers; like SRCs, funded by MOST in selected universities to ensure access to first-class facilities

ETRI Electronics and Telecommunications Research Institute; a large government research institute operated by the Ministry of Information and Communications

FDI foreign direct investment in a national economy; it plays an important role in many countries in the introduction of advanced technology

FKII Federation of Korean Information Industries; a business association concerned with computing and telecommunications

FL foreign licensing of technology; an alternative to foreign direct investment and strategic alliances for acquiring foreign technology

GDP gross domestic product

GERD gross expenditures on research and development; the total of national R&D, public and private

GFL government-funded laboratory; the Korean "national" laboratories are set up as quasi-government institutions. They are exempt from civil service staffing requirements and have their own boards of directors, but most are largely or entirely dependent on government funding, usually from a single ministry. Thus, government control is quite strong. KIST, ETRI, and KSRI are three prominent examples. (Often referred to as GRIs, government-supported research institutes.)

GNP gross national product

government corporations enterprises directly operated by government ministries, such as the Korea Railroad Corporation, Korea Postal Service, and Office of Government Supply

G-7 the seven market-economy nations with the largest gross national products whose heads of state and finance ministers meet annually to discuss the global economy and related matters

HAN Project Highly Advanced National Project; initiated in 1992. Often informally referred to as "G-7," it reflects the ambitious goal of elevating the technological capacity of Korean industry to parity with the leading nations in strategically selected areas.

innovation the successful market introduction of products, processes, or services that are newly created in a firm

IPRs intellectual property rights; typically covered by patent and copyright law

KAIS, KAIST Korea Advanced Institute of Science; a graduate school for science and technology formed in 1971 by the MOST. KAIS was renamed KAIST in 1988.

KAITECH Korea Academy of Industrial Technology; the principal government-funded laboratory of the MOTIE

KERI Korea Economic Research Institute; a think tank serving the needs of the Ministry of Finance

KETI Korea Electronic Technology Institute, supported by MOTIE

KIEP Korea Institute for International Economic Policy

KIET Korea Institute for Industrial Economics and Trade; supporting MOTIE

KII Korean Information Infrastructure; its development is the responsibility of the MIC.

KISDI Korea Information Society Development Institute; a think tank of MIC concerned primarily about education and social issues associated with the development of the KII. It has also contributed to trade negotiations in the telecommunications market.

KIST   Korea Institute of Science and Technology; Korea's first major government-funded laboratory, it was created in 1966 with U.S. help to modernize the economy.

KITA   Korea Industrial Technology Association

KMT   Kuomintang; the mainland China political party led by Chiang Kai-shek. The ruling party in Taiwan.

KOSEF   Korea Science and Engineering Foundation; modeled on the U.S. National Science Foundation, KOSEF awards competitive grants to university researchers

KRISS   Korea Research Institute of Standards and Science; a government-funded laboratory roughly comparable in mission to the U.S. National Institute for Standards and Technology

KSF   Korea Science Foundation; a nonprofit institution founded in 1967 to encourage public interest in science, especially among young people. It is funded primarily by MOST.

KTDC   Korean Technology Development Corporation; financed initially (1981) by the International Bank for Reconstruction and Development

MIC   Ministry of Information and Ccommunications; formed in 1994 by adding functions in MOST and MOTIE to the prior Ministry of Communications. MIC represents a government commitment to Korean information infrastructure (KII) development.

MITI   Japan's Ministry of International Trade and Industry; Korea's MOTIE, after a recent reorganization, is also sometimes referred to as MITI

MOE   Ministry of Education; responsible for all higher education (except for KAIST) as well as primary and secondary education

MOFE   Ministry of Finance and the Economy

MOST   Ministry of Science and Technology

MOTIE   Ministry of Trade, Industry, and Energy (reorganized from the former Ministry of Commerce and Industry and the Ministry of Energy and Resources)

NAFTA   North American Free Trade Agreement

NCST   National Council for Science and Technology; a coordinating body chaired by the Prime Minister and comprised of the ministers of the more technically intensive ministries. The minister of finance serves as vice chairman.

OECD   Organization for Economic Cooperation and Development; an intergovernment institution of twenty-five nations. Korea is a candidate for membership.

OEM   original equipment manufacturer; it usually refers to a firm that integrates components from a supplier network along with its own production to create finished products, which it markets

PC   personal computer

PCST   President's Council on Science and Technology; an advisory committee to the president of Korea, it is comprised of well established scientists. It has little involvement in government structure or operations. Instead, it provides a high-level mechanism for expressing the president's policies as well as providing scientific perspectives on broad policy issues.

POSTECH   Pohang University of Science and Technology; established in 1985 by the Pohang Iron and Steel Company (POSCO), the second-largest steel maker in the world. The Korean government owns a 25 percent equity share in POSCO. POSCO's central Research Institute (RIST) is co-located with POSTECH.

R&D   research and development

science-based development   an economy in which firms derive their competitiveness substantially from creativity, in contrast to labor, capital, or raw materials

SEMATECH   a semiconductor industry consortium in the United States. It shares R&D to revitalize the manufacturing tool supplier industry and produce common standards for integration of production tooling. Funded jointly by participating firms and, for ten years, by the U.S. Department of Defense.

Seoul National University   Korea's most prestigious university. Its graduates constitute a network of individuals who can expect preferential access to coveted government appointments.

SMEs   small- and medium-size enterprises; in Korea the size is defined by employment, with different metrics for manufacturing, services, and levels of labor intensity. For capital-intensive manufacturing firms, "small" firms must have no more than 20 employees, and "medium" firms must have no more than 300.

social capital   the combination of cultural, social, political, and institutional traditions that determines the efficiency with which traditional factors of production produce economic wealth

SRCs   science research centers; they are cross-disciplinary research centers sponsored by MOST in selected universities to ensure access to first-class research facilities

STEPI   Science and Technology Policy Institute; the think tank for MOST. STEPI not only performs policy research but supports the coordination of national projects for MOST. STEPI is formally attached to KIST but reports functionally to MOST headquarters.

Taejon Expo   a major international exposition in 1993; the first internationally sanctioned in a developing country. It was used by the Korean government as a kick-off for policies to encourage innovation.

TBI   technology-based innovation; the use of new or established science and technology-based ideas, methods, or concepts to create new products, processes, or services that improve cost, performance, or efficiency. It is essentially equivalent to science-based innovation.

technology transfer   the process through which one party acquires technology from another, with the second party's agreement. Technology transfer is distinguished from technology diffusion, which concerns all the paths through which technology finds its way from creators to users.

Three Lows   low oil prices, low interest rates, and low exchange rates combined to support the economic boom in 1986 to 1988

TRIMs and TRIPs   trade-related investment measures and trade-related intellectual property (rights); two sets of WTO rules, requiring significant modification of many national practices

TSI   technology support institution; an acronym used by the World Bank to refer to institutions that provide technology-related (industrial extension) services to small and medium firms

WTO   World Trade Organization; the multinational institution established to administer and enforce the trade agreements completed in the last round of the General Agreement on Tariffs and Trade

SELECTED
BIBLIOGRAPHY

Amsden, Alice. *Asia's Next Giant—South Korea and Late Industrialization*. New York: Oxford University Press, 1989.

Choi, Hyung-Sup. "Industrial Development and Use of Technology." Keynote address at the POSCO Research Institute RAND–Corp. Conference on Technology Transfer under the WTO Regime, POSRI, Pohang, Korea, August 17, 1995.

Chu, Yuan-Han. *Authoritarian Regimes under Stress: The Political Economy of Adjustment in the East Asian Newly Industrialized Countries*. Ph.D. diss., University of Minnesota, 1987 (Minneapolis: University Microfilms International No. 8727407, 1990).

Eckert, Carter, J. Ki-Baik Lee, Young-Ick Lew, Michael Robinson, and Edward W. Wagner. *Korea Old and New: A History*. Seoul: Ilchokak Publishers for Harvard University's Korea Institute, 1990.

Ergas, Henry. "Does Technology Policy Matter?" In *Technology and Global Industry: Companies and Nations in the World Economy*, edited by Bruce Guile and Harvey Brooks, 191–245. Washington, D.C.: National Academy Press, 1987.

Ernst, Dieter, *What Are the Limits to the Korean Model? The Korean Electronics Industry under Pressure*. Berkeley, Calif.: Berkeley Roundtable on International Economics, June 1994.

Freeman, Christopher, and Bengt-Ake Lundvall, eds. *Small Countries Facing the Technological Revolution*. London: Pinter Publishers, 1988.

Johnson, Jean M. *Human Resources for Science and Technology: The Asian Region*, NSF 93-303. Washington, D.C.: National Science Foundation, 1993.

Kim, Linsu. "The Evolution of Public Policies and Private Sector Responses in Science and Technology." In *Korea: Changing Technological Environment and Policy Responses*. Seoul: Science and Technology Policy Institute, 1991.

Kim, Linsu. "Technology Policy for Industrialization: An Integrative Framework and Korea's Experience." *Research Policy* 21 (1992): 437–452.

Koo, B. "Role of Government in Korea's Industrial Development." In *Industrial Development Policies and Issues*, edited by K. Lee. Seoul: Korea Development Institute, 1986.

Korea Industrial Technology Association (KITA). *Major Indicators of Industrial Technology 1994*. Seoul: KITA, 1995.

Korea Industrial Technology Association (KITA). *1993 White Paper on Industrial Technology* (in Korean). Seoul: KITA, 1993.

Korea Science and Engineering Foundation (KSEF). *1995 Data Book and S&T Indicators*. Seoul: KSEF, 1995.

Ministry of Science and Technology (MOST). *Science and Technology Annual Report* (in Korean). Seoul: MOST, 1993.

Mody, Ashoka, and Hirofumi Uzawa, eds. *East Asian Infrastructure Strategies*. Washington, D.C.: World Bank, 1995.

Nelson, Richard R., ed. *National Systems of Innovation: A Comparative Analysis*. New York: Oxford University Press, 1993.

Niwa, Fujio, and Toshiya Nanahara. *Systemic Comparison of Science and Technology Activities across Countries*, NISTEP Report 7. Tokyo: Science and Technology Agency of Japan, June 1989.

Organization for Economic Cooperation and Development (OECD). *Economic Surveys: Korea*. Paris: OECD, 1994.

Organization for Economic Cooperation and Development (OECD). *Reviews of National Science and Technology Policy: Republic of Korea*. Paris: OECD, 1996.

Rich, Robert G., Jr. *Korea's Economy 1995*, vol. 11. Washington, D.C.: Korea Economic Institute of America, 1995.

Rich, Robert G., Jr., ed. *Economy and Regional Cooperation in NE Asia*. Vol. 6 of *Joint U.S.–Korean Academic Studies*. Washington, D.C.: Korea Economic Institute of America, 1996.

Simon, Denis Fred, ed. *The Emerging Technology Trajectory of the Pacific Rim*. Armonk, New York: M. E. Sharpe, 1995.

Simon, Denis Fred, and Changrok Soh. "Korea's Technological Development." *Pacific Review* 7, no. 1 (1994).

Simon, Denis Fred, and Changrok Soh. "Orbital Mechanics of South Korea's Technological Development: An Examination of the 'Gravitational' Pushes and Pulls." *Technology Analysis and Strategic Management* 6, no. 4 (1994): 437–455.

Simon, Denis Fred, and Changrok Soh. "U.S.–Korean Industrial and Technological Cooperation in the Context of Globalization and Regionalization." October 15, 1995, unpublished paper for the sixth U.S.–Korea Academic Symposium on Economic and Regional Cooperation in Northeast Asia, Chicago, September 6–8, 1995.

Skolnikoff, Eugene B. *The Elusive Transformation: Science Technology and the Evolution of International Politics*. Princeton: Princeton University Press, 1993.

Song, D.-H. *Public Enterprise Management Policies in Korea*, Research Volume 91–26 (in Korean). Seoul: Korea Development Institute, 1991.

Wade, Robert. *Governing the Market: Economic Theory and the Role of Government in East Asian Industrialization*. Princeton: Princeton University Press, 1990.

World Bank. *The East Asian Miracle*. New York: Oxford University Press, 1993.

World Bank. *East Asia's Trade and Investment*. Washington, D.C.: World Bank, 1994.

INDEX

ABOUT THE CONTRIBUTORS

LEWIS M. BRANSCOMB is the Aetna Professor of Public Policy and Corporate Management, emeritus, and former director of the Science, Technology, and Public Policy Program, Center for Science and International Affairs, at Harvard University's John F. Kennedy School of Government. A physicist and prolific author on science and technology policy and a science advisor to Presidents Johnson and Carter, Branscomb has served as vice president and chief scientist at IBM and director of the U.S. National Bureau of Standards (now the National Institute for Standards and Technology).

YOUNG-HWAN CHOI served as president of the Science and Technology Policy Institute and prior to that as vice minister of the Ministry of Science and Technology in the Republic of Korea. Choi has been a visiting fellow at the John F. Kennedy School of Government at Harvard University, where he collaborated with Branscomb. He is currently president of the National Railroad College in Korea.

SUNG-CHUL CHUNG is director of International Science and Technology Cooperation at the Science and Technology Policy Institute (STEPI) in Korea. He previously served as director for Science and Technology at STEPI and was a professional associate for the Presidential Council on Science and Technology.

HENRY ERGAS is an economist specializing in telecommunications regulatory policy and the role of innovation in economic growth. A consultant to the Trade Practices Commission of the government of Australia and a former professor in the School of Management of Monash University, Ergas has also served as a senior policy analyst at the Organization for Economic Cooperation and Development in Paris. In 1994 and 1995, he was a visiting professor at Harvard University's John F. Kennedy School of Government.

BYOUNG-JOO KIM is a senior analyst for the Korea Foreign Trade Association, where he specializes in U.S.–Korean trade politics. A doctoral candidate in International Political Economy at Massachusetts Institute of Technology, he has worked at the World Bank Economic Development Institute as a research analyst. He also holds a Ph.D. in communications from the University of Washington.

HAK-SOO KIM is professor and chairman of the Department of Mass Communications and director of the Research Institute of Media and Culture at Sogang University in Korea. Kim is also vice president of the Korea Science Writers Association.

HYUNG-KI KIM was an advisor in the office of the director at the World Bank's Economic Development Institute. He previously held a variety of positions at the World Bank in education, industry, and projects policy. He has served as vice minister of education in the Korean government. He held additional positions in both the President's Economic and Scientific Council and the Ministry of Science and Technology.

KEE-YOUNG KIM is a professor of operations management at Yonsei University in Seoul, Korea. He has been a visiting faculty member at Massachusetts Institute of Technology and has recently edited a special issue on global quality management for *Decision Sciences Journal*. Dr. Kim holds a Ph.D. and an M.B.A. from Washington University.

KWANG-DOO KIM is professor of economics at Sogang University in Korea. He is a member of the Monetary Board of the Bank of Korea and a Korean Broadcasting System radio columnist. Kim holds a Ph.D. in Economics from the University of Hawaii.

YOUNG-GUL KIM is professor and head of the chemical engineering department and dean of the Graduate School at Pohang University of Science and Technology in Korea. He also serves as president of the Korean Institute of Chemical Engineers. Kim is former professor, dean of faculty, and vice president for Research and Planning at the Korea Advanced Institute of Science and Technology.

BOONG-KYU LEE is a doctoral candidate in the Sloan School of Management at Massachusetts Institute of Technology. He has worked in the corporate planning and strategy division of the Daewoo Group and the international marketing division of Samsung Electronics. Lee holds an M.B.A. from the Wharton School of the University of Pennsylvania.

YONG-TEH LEE is chairman of TriGem Computer, Inc., and of ThruNet Company, Ltd., in Korea and chairman of the Federation of Korean Information Industries. He also serves as president of the Asian–Oceanian Computing Industry Organization; chairman of the Council for the Policy of Information and Communication; and chairman of the Special Committee on Informatization, Committee for the National Competitive Industries in Korea.

SEONG-RAE PARK is professor of history and dean of the College of Arts at Hankuk University of Foreign Studies in Korea. Park has held visiting professorships at Kyoto University in Japan and Pohang Institute of Science and Technology in Korea.

ISBN 0-275-95147-2

EAN

9 780275 951474

90000>

HARDCOVER BAR CODE